JOHNNY BALL

MY PREVIOUS LIFE IN COMEDY

MY PREVIOUS LIFE IN COMEDY

PART ONE OF MY AUTOBIOGRAPHY

JOHNNY BALL

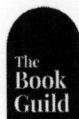

The Book Guild

First published in Great Britain in 2025 by
The Book Guild Ltd
Unit E2 Airfield Business Park,
Harrison Road, Market Harborough,
Leicestershire. LE16 7UL
Tel: 0116 2792299
www.bookguild.co.uk
Email: info@bookguild.co.uk
X: @bookguild

The manufacturer's authorised representative in the EU for
product safety is Authorised Rep Compliance Ltd,
71 Lower Baggot Street, Dublin D02 P593 Ireland (www.arccompliance.com)

Typeset in 11pt Minion Pro

Printed and bound in Great Britain by 4edge Limited

ISBN 978 1835741 665

British Library Cataloguing in Publication Data.
A catalogue record for this book is available from the British Library.

To my dear wife Dianne, who, as you will see,
gives this book a very happy ending.

CONTENTS

INTRODUCTION

At eighty-six years old, I have left it rather late to publish my autobiography. But so far, my memory has not diminished one iota as regards the detail of all the stories I am about to tell. To keep the narrative tight, I have given every story its own title, which enables me to cut to the chase as quickly as possible. Furthermore, in line with the title, it is invariably the comedy of the situation that warrants its inclusion, even if the humour comes from an unfortunate mishap.

As with my TV scripts and my comedy performances, there are very few wasted words. Mark my word. (Oops – I could have cut 'mark my word'?) In fact, I have so many experiences that I feel are worth relating that this book ends over forty years ago, around 1981, when I had passed through my joyous stand-up comedy stage and was now established as a writer/presenter of maths and science TV shows, and my far more commercial but still comedy-filled career was just beginning.

The second reason for ending this book at the chosen point is because the influence of my wife Di had now changed everything for the better. The second volume, when it comes, will still cover the ups and downs of our lives, but they will be confined simply to *Stories That Must Be Told!*

But I do hope you enjoy this lot – first!

Johnny Ball, March 2025.

CHAPTER 1

WHAT DO YOU GET FROM YOUR PARENTS?

WARTIME ANTICS

I was born on 23rd May 1938. The Second World War started fifteen months later on 3rd September 1939, but Dad always said, "We didn't cause that!" However, it did have a great bearing on my early life and that of my parents.

My mum, Martha Anne Edwards, had run away to Bristol to marry Danny Ball when, after years on the dole, he finally secured a job in Bristol, moulding parts for shunting locomotives. When war was declared, he moved into aircraft production, much of which was focused around Bristol.

Dad was a born comedian, but the cards never fell in his favour in his entire life. However, that didn't stop him saying something funny almost every time he opened his mouth.

Clay sewage pipes were just lying around everywhere at Dad's factory. But they made ideal umbrella stands. They were a yard long with a collar at one end and finished in a shiny brown ceramic. But how would you get one through the factory gates? Dad thought, *Why not wear it?* Throughout the war, Dad worked nights, making aluminium parts for aircraft as fast as was possible. Throughout the conflict, he got up to all kinds of antics, mostly for laughs. So, at the end of one shift, Dad squeezed into a pipe, which was lifted and tucked under his arms. Long wires passed over his shoulders, inside the pipe, and were bent up at the ends to support it. It was a very tight squeeze, and the pipe came down to below Dad's knees. He was around five foot seven. So, in a huge, borrowed, gabardine coat, with mates all around him, he walked past the security guards and out of the gate with his little feet going nineteen to the dozen. The stunt was more daft than theft?

BULLET DODGING AND BUS CATCHING

Mum always insisted she was once machine-gunned in Kingswood High Street, and it was true that a German aircraft, after attacking Bristol, would head that way home.

With me in the pram, Mum tried to get into Woolworths' doorway for safety, but a chap said, "Sorry, Mrs, we're all full up here!" so Mum and I were left to find shelter elsewhere.

But Bristol people could often be far more friendly than that. Once, Mum, with me in tow, got a cup of tea from a café which was too hot to drink. Then suddenly her bus appeared, and she had to hurry.

Sitting on the next table was a knight of the road in terribly dirty clothes he had probably slept in for days. He had already decanted his tea into the saucer to cool it down, and, seeing Mum's predicament, said, "'Ere you are, Mrs. Have this one m'dear. It's already puffed and blown!"

WHY IS THIS BOOK ABOUT COMEDY AND NOT MATHS?

Most people who know me would say that the most important aspect of my life and career has been my love of maths and science, which resulted in my writing TV series like *Think of a Number* and several books, five musical shows, and many maths and science lectures. But, in truth, the driving force throughout my life has always been to follow Dad's example and see the finny side of things and make a joke about almost everything and everyone around me. My whole life has been driven by comedy.

I was a stand-up comedian for seventeen years, turning pro in 1964. But after that, through my informative and educational TV career, it was my comedy training that helped me write factual info scripts that were never boring, but always had a joke or a fun idea at every turn.

Mum and Dad were always singing and that influenced me greatly as well. Mum's choir held a musical concert evening with a cast of twenty-eight girls and one solitary boy, aged around four – me! So, dressed as a farmer with straw in my hair, I sang the very old traditional song, "To plough and sow and reap and mow, to be a Farmer's Boy-ahoy, oh to be a farmer's boy!" As the only lad, naturally, I stopped the show! Or perhaps it came to a shuddering halt?

PUB GOINGS ON

My dad was always a happy man in a pub, and at weekends we would often walk miles to meet some of his workmates at a distant pub. A favourite was The Queen's Head in Hanham. As everyone worked very long hours, visiting pubs to relax was encouraged and most had children's rooms, so there was always someone for me to play with. Grown-ups would pop in to check we were OK for lemonade and crisps and often show us some trick to keep us happy. One chap popped in on one occasion and showed me Russian multiplication, and that story forms the introduction to my book *Wonders Beyond Numbers*. But clearly that moment was to have a bearing on my future career, stronger than I could ever imagine, for further research led me to discover its origins in four-thousand-year-old Egyptian maths and its direct link to binary numbers, which today power all our modern digital technology.

One of Dad's mates was a very tall ex-policeman who, as a sideline, charmed warts. He would tell wart sufferers to go home, count their warts and write the number on a piece of paper. When they came back, he would look at the number and throw the paper on the fire. If the warts weren't gone in days, he made them go and count them again – everyone swore it worked! Amazingly, he had a large shiny bump on his forehead and Dad always reckoned that was where all other people's warts ended up.

One evening the genial wart charmer came into the children's room with a huge garden snail. He then opened his mouth wide and placed the snail on his tongue, where it started to crawl inwards. Slowly but surely, as half a dozen kids gaped in astonishment, the snail crawled further and further down his throat, until suddenly he just crunched it with his tongue and swallowed it, shell and all. I can still hear that crunch.

A WALK ON THE DARK SIDE

The problem with visiting pubs often miles away was getting home in the dark in wartime Britain, where the blackout was total. On a cloudy night, with no street lighting, you couldn't see more than a few yards ahead.

So, one night, aged around four or five and already asleep, I was perched on Dad's shoulders holding on to his hands or his ears as he walked steadily and solidly home, not on the pavement, but in the gutter – a neat trick. In the dark, one foot could always brush the curb to keep him on track.

On this night, however, they agreed to pop to a friend's home for a night cap. Dad, as usual, was walking five yards ahead of everyone else; a trait I inherited and have maintained all my life. When they came to the turn for our friend's house, Dad walked straight past. They shouted, "Dan, it's down here," but got no answer, and through the darkness, they could hear he was still walking on. So Mum ran after him, shouting, but to no avail. When she caught him, she saw that he was completely asleep and, up on his shoulders, so was I. Though he had passed several roads off to the left, somehow his second sense had managed to find the gutter again and keep going at his steady and reliable yet unconscious rate on the right road for home, in total darkness.

MY FIRST DAY AT SCHOOL

The toughness and resilience of kids in those days, compared with now, seems quite staggering.

On my first day at school, Mum showed me to the door and simply said, "Go on, walk along with the others," and off I toddled for perhaps half a mile to High Street Primary School, Kingswood. There, I remember, after a good first hour or so, learning to write 'a', 'b', and 'c'. We reached playtime but were first offered a small bottle of milk. That was the start of my problems. The milk was warm with a distinctly sour smell. As it touched my lips, I cockled. The others drank up quickly and went out to play, but I sat there with my untouched milk, refusing to drink a drop. So the horrible teacher with a whiskered wart on her chin, like the witch in Disney's *Snow White*, kept me at my desk at playtime on my very first day at school. I don't recall hating another person in my entire life, except perhaps for that day.

TAIL END CHARLIE

Being wartime, all our shoes had hobnails hammered into the soles so they lasted longer. They would slide fabulously on pavements, which made for a great schoolyard game. Around six to eight kids would hold hands tightly to form a chain and start to run round our large playground. The last kid in the chain would hold on with both hands and crouch like a water skier. Sparks flew from his hobnailed shoes as the slide started, slowly but going ever faster until the chain swung in a tight loop and slammed the skier into a wall – good game, eh?

Of course, the idea was to let go at the last minute and avoid hitting the wall or, better still, slam into some other kids to cushion your arrival. I don't remember any shortage of risk-takers and I could never get enough goes as Tail End Charlie. Amazingly I still had my own teeth.

Today, kids are kept well clear of building sites for reasons of health and safety. Haha! For us, an empty building site was our 'adventure playground' as post-war building began apace. In the very harsh winter of 1947, the snow completely filled foundation trenches. So we copied the Laurel and Hardy gag of walking along nonchalantly and then suddenly disappearing completely down an unseen snow-filled hole.

OUR OWN WAR EFFORT

One of the most enjoyable moments of my young life was just at the end of the war when factory life became less frantic. Dad, Mum and I went into the aircraft production business. I had a small Fort, but the lead soldiers were always delicate and easily broken, so Dad decided to put them to good use. One at a time we would pop them into a ladle held over the open fire and watch them melt, adding more till the ladle was pretty full. Then we would carefully pour the molten lead into small moulds held in a calliper – Dad did that. After a few moments, cooled in water, out would come a small Spitfire or a Hurricane aircraft. I would file the burrs off the lead models and Mum and I would paint them in green and brown camouflage colours and stick the round RAF symbols on them. Eventually, we had half a dozen for me and two for half a dozen of my friends in the street.

Did we ever wash our hands during these lead-ladling sessions? Never. How much lead did I ingest? I don't know, but playing football, I did seem to have a low centre of gravity.

A MAN OF MANY PARTS

Dad suddenly had the toy-making bug as the war ended and he had time on his hands. First of all, he made a roundabout, with horses that went up and down, just like the real thing.

Then he had a more ambitious idea. Buying a Meccano set at that time was just about impossible. So why not make one? Dad guillotined strips of aluminium and locked ten of them into dies. He then drilled holes half an inch apart and rounded off the ends. Slowly, he completed sets of every part that Meccano offered and some extra ones besides. He bought brass bolts, or, more likely, 'borrowed' them from work, but he disliked the square brass nuts that Meccano provided and so made hundreds of hexagonal aluminium nuts himself.

So, for Christmas around 1945, I got a Meccano set larger than any on the market, in the wooden box he had also made – three foot long, fifteen inches wide and four inches deep, with compartments for all the various parts. It was unique and all mine – at least, when Dad wasn't playing with it himself.

Aged seven, I made a lift which sat on the dining room table and lowered or raised my old but very precious Dinky cars to or from the floor. But Dad had bigger ambitions and started work on a project inspired by our favourite place on earth – the Pleasure Beach at Blackpool.

DESTINATION BLACKPOOL

Every year from the war ending, in the summer holidays, we would travel north by train to Bolton and West Houghton for a week with Mum's family, which was pretty dull, as they all seemed so very old-fashioned.

But soon the Bolton week was over, and we headed for a magical second week in Blackpool. Dad always had a standard gag for when we passed through a station. Mum would say, "Where are we?" Dad would look out of the window and shout, "Cheltenham!" Now, you cannot pass Cheltenham between Bolton and Blackpool! But the one name you were guaranteed to see on any railway station was 'Gentlemen' in large letters at the end of the platform. A terrible joke? Not when accompanied by my dad's simpleton grin so reminiscent of Stan Laurel.

As we neared Blackpool, we would get the first glimpse of the Tower, in the far distance on the left of the train. Then it was gone and, five minutes later, there it was again, but this time out of the right window.

Dad would say, "I know the fella who drives the lorry!"

"What lorry?" I would ask.

"The lorry that carries the Tower up and down the prom – how else do you think you can see it out of this window one minute and that window the next?"

You have to understand that Blackpool and jokes are inseparable. Even today, people spend ages reading the saucy postcards on their revolving stands. Mum and Dad would laugh and enjoy them but never stoop so low as to buy something quite so 'mucky'. It was more a case of spotting the new ones that weren't around last year.

What was always certain was that we would buy candy floss and get our picture taken. As we never owned a camera, these annual pictures are more or less the only visual evidence of my childhood years.

ALBERT AND 'AROLD AND OTHERS!

Undoubtedly, my greatest comedy influence during our early Blackpool trips was when Dad bought a copy of Marriot Edgar's poems, featuring 'Albert and the Lion' and the tale of a Lancashire lad eaten by a lion at Blackpool Zoo.

Edgar's poems were made famous by the London-born Stanley Holloway on BBC Radio, but to be honest, Dad always hated Holloway's childish pseudo-Lancashire delivery. His terrible over-the-top accent made Lancastrians sound like idiots – "There's a fame-us sea-side place called Black-poool, that's note-ed for fresh air and fuun."

I agreed with Dad; as the poems stand up so well, no comedy delivery is required at all – the laughs are in the writing. Actually, 'Albert and the Lion' wasn't one of Marriot Edgar's favourites, which is why he wrote the sequel, 'The Return of Albert!', which I much prefer.

Marriot Edgar is a huge comic hero of mine, as he found ways of achieving comic effect with the lightest of comedy ideas. There is wit in every line. Take the moment Albert is regurgitated:

'Wallace [the lion] felt better directly,

'And his figure once more became lean,

'But the only difference with Albert was,

'his hands, knees and face were quite clean.'

In fact, in bringing up our own three kids, time and again in moments of crisis, I have quoted the Edgar line just a few verses later – 'Let's look on the bright side,' said Father. 'What can't be helped must be endured!' I don't continue with, 'Every cloud has a silver lining and we did have our Albert insured!'

When we got home to Bristol, I devoured Edgar's poems and amazed my parents and myself. I soon found that if I set my mind to it, I could learn and recite a poem of around seventeen verses, in just three readings, which also meant committing to memory the rhymes and the jokes forever.

I still have total recall of around ten of them and can recite them at the drop of a hat.

CLIMBING INTO CRIME

It was in Blackpool that I first experienced crime, of sorts. Dad took me to watch Blackpool versus Arsenal at Bloomfield Road, where we entered a side terrace. It soon got so crowded that I was locked in a dark valley of people, with a small patch of sky right above me. Suddenly, to escape the crush, someone climbed up into the seated stand behind us. Dad's face lit up. In a jiff, he had lifted me high, and I hoisted myself into the stands. Dad then got a foothold so that he too scrambled over to join me. Trying not to look anyone in the eye, we guiltily made our way up a good few rows and along to some vacant seats.

By now the police were stopping others from following us and the mad scramble had ended. But we weren't safe yet. Police officers were circulating, asking people to show their tickets and turfing out the interlopers. Slowly but surely, a huge ruddy-faced police officer came closer and closer to Dad, who had his arm around me. We held our breath. Eventually, he looked us both over, suspiciously, and then gave us an exaggerated wink and, without a word, moved away. I don't remember the score or even Stanley Matthews. But I still remember that policeman's smiling face.

DAD, AND WHAT MIGHT HAVE BEEN?

My parents would sing around the house every day and cover everything from hymns to popular songs. But I never heard Dad actually perform until, on one occasion as guests at a large wedding, Dad totally surprised Mum and I by suddenly appearing onstage and singing 'Shake Hands with a Millionaire', a song which had originated in America's Great Depression and told of a down-and-out whose only treasured possession was the little lad who called him "Dad!". We were amazed at how professional his performance was, but Mum and I didn't really hear much after the first verse, as we both dissolved with tears streaming down our faces.

CHARABANC ANTICS

With the war finally over, soon petrol was available, and Charabanc, or bus tours, were new ways for people to start to relax in those days before domestic cars. Enjoyment was the watchword as, with adults and kids on board, each trip would leave a pub with reserve crates of beer in the aisles and head for destinations like Cheddar Gorge or Weston-super-Mare or mystery tours that found some far distant pub in the wilder parts of Gloucestershire or Somerset.

But there was never a dull moment, as the singing started within the first five minutes. All the old wartime songs were sung but many slightly or very rude songs soon crept in and became very popular, with Dad in the aisle leading the singing. The words became at first a revelation to us kids, but soon, perhaps, even part of our education?

However bawdy it got, it was all just pure fun and people still exhausted from the war effort were at last letting off steam. But Dad was always the first one up in the aisle leading us all through the songs and especially the funny naughty bits.

DAD'S RECORDS AND MY INTRODUCTION TO COMEDY

It was my dad who led me to appreciate comedy. I have always said that had he had the chance, he would have been a wonderful comic. He honestly couldn't utter a straight line. Dad had a very old wind-up gramophone with a handful of records, all so old they did not have a 'run on' and 'run off' track. You pushed the needle until it caught a groove.

All these old records were comedy. 'Slippery Sam the Stoker' was backed by a male choir. In the song, Sam explains he was once wrecked with a stewardess, and he flew his shirt to show their distress. But when it blew away, he suggested it was now her turn and he would close his eyes while she was taking them off. As a young lad, I found it very saucy.

One featured a chap on his honeymoon who somehow got locked overnight totally on his own in the waxworks Chamber of Horrors with Crippen, who stood covered in blood. But the last and favourite record Dad bought was the LP of 'Max Miller at The Met', which was the Metropolitan Theatre in the Edgware Road, London, where Max played many times. Every joke was cheeky but, by today's standards, not at all offensive or over the top. Max would show a white book and a blue book and ask which one he should take his jokes from tonight. Always, it was the audience who called for the blue book, giving him the excuse to be rude, because that was what the audiences wanted. I was to follow a similar tack with very young club audiences many years later. Max's innuendo was often very mild and hardly ever offensive, and he definitely never ever swore. But at his peak, he was Britain's most successful comic. When he overran in the Royal Command Performance, because an American star had been given three times as long a spot, the producer said, "You'll never work for me again!"

To which Max replied, "You're £40,000 too late!"

That was a huge fortune in those days, before TV.

SEEING GEORGE FORMBY

I was still under ten when I was taken to see the greatest Blackpool Star of all – George Formby. At Blackpool Opera House, George would reach some 40,000 people a week with hit songs like 'My Little Stick of Blackpool Rock'! He would tell of a little Scottish lad walking up and down the Blackpool beach following a donkey, over and over. When he asked why, the Scottish lad said, "It swallowed my tanner!"

He would ask if folks had had a donkey ride and say, "Oh, you can hire the donkeys, you know? Oh yes. They have a little screw under the saddle. You can have them as high as you like!"

Then, as a surprise, a donkey would come onstage, and George would tickle its ear and chat about it. Then, as he talked, at the other end, the donkey would deliver a 'pile'! The audience tried to tell George, without being too rude. But he would remain oblivious, until his nose finally twitched, wrinkled and twitched again, and at last he said, "Ooh? What an effluvia!"

A stagehand would rush on with pan and brush, and while they swept, he would say, "See if you can find a tanner!" Then, as they left the stage, he would say, "Where are you going to put that?" and get the reply, "I'll put in on my rhubarb!" And George would end the sequence with, "Ooh heck? We usually put custard on ours!"

The routine was perfect, more so as everyone talked about the donkey and how it had misbehaved when they saw the show. Then they all realised that it happened every time, as in tickling the donkey's ear, George pulled a lever and the false stomach released the stage poo, mixed with a little dry ice for the steamy effect.

It was all such a success that when George toured Great Britain, the donkey went with him!

WHO WANTS HOMEWORK? WE WANT HOMEWORK!

The week in Blackpool was soon over and we were back in Bristol. I was very happy there and just loved school.

I recall, when we were only seven years old, we asked for maths homework. Our teacher, who must have been doing something right, came back with, "Oh no – you don't get maths homework until you are nine."

I'm not sure he was ready for the response. One or two of us immediately started banging on our desks and soon all the others followed, with the chant, "We want homework – we want homework!"

Soon, with the primitive 1945 technology, he was making awful, smelly, oily copies of a hundred sums, starting with simple addition and then, over the next few weeks, progressing through subtraction, multiplication and division.

As he handed them out, he said, "If you do ten sums tonight, I'll be happy. OK?"

Well, that is what most kids did, but for four or five of us, it was different. We did the entire one hundred that night while listening to the radio with our parents. It was such a different atmosphere in a home before television. With the radio 'always on!', all the family carried on doing other things.

Eventually, I was eleven and it was time for my Eleven-Plus. I took the exam and found it very comfortable indeed, though no one could be sure whether we had passed or not. However, around that time, suddenly everything changed.

THE END OF OUR TIME IN BLISSFUL BRISTOL

Suddenly, one day in Bristol, there was talk of my parents moving 'back up North'. I don't recall this as an idea that built up. It was suddenly there.

Dad went up to Lancashire for a few days and came back declaring that he had found a house, or, rather, a shop. This was to be a new start. They would open a greengrocer business and become self-reliant. It was settled. No more iron founding for Dad or stitching army boots, which Mum had done throughout the war. We were leaving Bristol for Bolton, where they had grown up and where they now were seeking a new happiness.

Sadly, Mum and Dad were in no way aware that they would never again match the happiness they knew being young parents through those glorious, precious and so-called 'terrible' war years in Bristol.

CHAPTER 2

BOLTON BLUES AND A BOLTON SCHOOL

A MOVING EXPERIENCE

It was March 1949 when we moved to Bolton, where Dad had originated. They had decided to open a greengrocer's shop which had been closed for years. It seemed like a perfect new beginning, taking them both away from factory life for ever.

Sadly, it wasn't to work out that way. The shop had failed before because a railway cut the area in half and it had a tiny catchment area of no more than a couple of dozen houses. A couple of huge cotton mills gave work to hundreds of mill girls, but they never passed the shop.

So after a year we moved, and moved again a year later, until Mum and Dad at last found themselves back in the jobs they had had before they met: Dad as an iron founder and Mum as a mill girl. So throughout my secondary school years, we were to be really very poor.

But my wonderful primary school in Bristol had started my education off well, so I was very confident when I took my eleven-plus before the fateful move up north that I would pass.

THE CORRIDOR OF FEAR!

In Bolton, we soon learnt from Bristol that I had indeed passed. So with just one term in the local primary school, where it seemed I had a better grasp of the subjects across the board than my new Bolton mates, I was set to start next term at Bolton County Grammar School. Previously being called 'The Bolton Municipal', it still carried the nickname 'The Loony Simple'!

But for me it was great news because the school badge was the Bolton coat of arms – an elephant and castle in gold on blue. However, I soon learnt that the County Grammar had a reputation as rather a tough school, and the first-day initiation ceremony was renowned. Its approaching horrors gave me nightmares.

The day arrived and I got dressed in my new school uniform for the very first time. It was clear that I would stand out from the other boys. Instead of being navy-blue, my jacket was grey.

With the shop driving us ever more in debt, Mum just didn't have the money and had got my jacket from the Co-op, who sold things on an 'interest-free, shilling in the pound per week' basis. Either the Co-op didn't sell navy-blue blazers, or, more likely, Mum found a grey one that was cheaper. For the first two years, I was to be the only grey-jacketed lad in the entire school.

However, on the very first day, I knew that I had more to worry about than the wrong colour jacket. I had to endure the notorious and dreaded Corridor of Fear!

The building is still there today in Great Moor Street, Bolton – a handsome four-storey red-brick building with a narrow school yard at each side, one for boys and the other for girls, with boarding behind the iron bars shielding the girls who played netball from prying eyes.

Outside the boy's gate that morning, there was a small crowd and a few very anxious mothers. I had forbidden my mum to come, as I had been warned that special treatment was reserved for lads who had brought their mummy for protection. On getting close, the reasons for the small crowd and for the weeks of trepidation were confirmed.

Inside the gate there was an animated corridor of braying, scowling, threatening lads, each carrying some weapon, be it simply a school ruler, bike pump, pair of football boots swung on long laces or, more ominous still, a loaded satchel. Old boys were allowed in through the side of the line, but for new lads, there was only one way in – down the Corridor of Fear.

Each new arrival could see those before them being beaten unmercifully by lads often four years older. If anyone tried to turn back, the blows came thicker and faster until they gave the idea up as futile – once in, nobody came out. An older lad advised, "Don't wait – they can see which ones are most scared!" And so, without pausing for an instant, I bent low and pushed my way in.

I didn't seem to feel much at all, as the fear alone dulled my senses and made everything seem to happen in slow motion. After three yards, the lad in front lost his cap and turned back to pick it up. As he did so, some lout started hitting him directly on the head. I grabbed the cap, shoved it in his hand and shouted, "Leave him alone," into the face of the lout. Suddenly, I was no longer in the corridor of fear. The lout, seeing a sign of bravery, simply grabbed my jacket and hauled me out.

"Hey! You're alright," he said. "You stick behind me, and you'll be safe."

We both backed away from the mad flailing corridor and, against a wall, I got my breath. Then I began to observe the scene around me, which was straight out of Dante – the devil's disciples were taunting and torturing lads in every square yard of playground. Some kids were frantically chasing their caps, satchels or shoes as groups of lads threw or kicked them from one to the other. Some kids were wet through and crying, having been ducked in sinks or toilet bowls, while others were scaling walls to retrieve clothing thrown onto the low roof of the toilet block. This was surely hell on earth.

But then, in retrospect, it all became clear. No one was really hurt. For every bully, there were others coming to the rescue of kids who had suffered enough. The roughing-up was intended to be memorable, but momentary. Only those who collapsed with fear suffered longer, but even then, large lads would come to their rescue. As the bell went and everyone started to file in for assembly, items of clothing were retrieved and returned to their owners and kids visibly shaken and still scared were consoled by older lads and led into school.

That event was witnessed from a window by the new deputy headmaster, his first taste of Bolton County Grammar, and the result was that I and my year group were to be denied their turn next year, as had been our right for many, many years. The new master announced that the ceremony would never happen again. As far as every boy was concerned, he had missed the whole point. Experiencing and surviving this event was a rite of passage and one that everyone proudly talked about, especially to those kids not privileged enough to go to the County Grammar.

The following year at assembly, the first years knelt on all fours whilst the second years (us) sat on their backs. These were the new young elephants, as seen on our blazer badges, who had to repeat some awful doggerel and bray like elephants. It happened once and was scrapped as a total disaster, but sadly, the Corridor of Fear was never allowed again.

T'WANDERERS

A definite plus as regards moving to Bolton was, of course, going to watch Bolton Wanderers. Their ground at Burnden Park was no more than ten minutes' walk away, and they were just coming to their greatest post-war period of success, with the rampaging Nat Lofthouse doing what centre forwards were supposed to do.

At first Dad took me, but soon I was going on my own. I would take up my place on the open Kop which had been the scene of one of football's greatest tragedies just three years earlier. On 9th March 1946, with an estimated 85,000 watching a cup tie against Stoke, some barriers collapsed. Hundreds of people were crushed and injured and thirty-three people lost their lives. By now, the strength of the crush barriers had been improved, making it safe. But I do remember nearly passing out on almost every visit.

Now the danger came from Victory V Lozenges, which were made in Nelson and contained liquorice as well as both ether and chloroform! To say they were moreish was an understatement. I chain-scoffed the lot with probably twenty in a small packet. Then, offering Bolton a bit of encouragement, I would call out at the top of my voice a long drawn-out, "Come on the whites." I then *passed out!*

Well, almost, as having evacuated my lungs completely of oxygen, the ether and chloroform induced a high and almost oblivion. How close each of these experiences brought me to death or at least brain damage, I'll never know. On checking, I wasn't surprised to see that modern day Victory Vs carry no ether or chloroform – no wonder sales have slumped.

ON THE MOVE AGAIN

It was very soon clear that the shop was not going to work, and after almost exactly a year, we moved to a house in Mornington Road, off the very smart Chorley New Road.

I would catch the bus to school each day right across the road from the private Bolton School, which stretched out wide with three magnificent entrances and expertly maintained lawns. The playing fields were so well kept that Bolton Wanderers practised there before their 1953 Cup Final appearance.

What I didn't then know was that I would visit that school once a year for the next five years and savour magnificent triumph, not on their playing fields but on the chequered field of black and white as we slaughtered them at chess.

On starting at t'County Grammar, I latched onto chess immediately, though never having played before. Soon I was climbing the Junior Chess Ladder by challenging and beating the boys in any of the three places above me, till, by Christmas, I was in seventh place, earning me a place on the Junior Chess Team. It was the happiest school option I ever took and in the next five years, playing other grammar schools across East Lancashire, though as individuals we lost from time to time, no team that I played for ever lost a single match.

So, at the end of my first year, I took the Chess Prize and the Maths Prize from our teacher, Mr Meredith, who was brilliant, introduced us to hiking across the Lancashire moors, and later became head.

So I was quite miffed when, for Year Two, instead of joining class 3A, they put me in 3C. I later realised that parent pressure had probably swayed the decisions and favoured other students.

However, a greater problem occurred in that year that further effected my education quite badly. I had a painful accident.

A NEAR-DEATH INCIDENT

Just across the road from our new house was The Raikes Parade Hotel, which was surrounded by mature gardens but had seen better days. It was a huge, rambling, stone-built place, and the walls were very easy to climb in rubber-soled shoes, so, as a gang, we would spend hours using the valleys between slate rooves as our den.

Getting down again was no problem till we arrived on top of a five-foot-high stone wall. From a sitting position, it was easy to push ourselves off the wall and land on an old patch of garden, until someone had a bright idea. There was a small shrub around eighteen inches high and we would push off with our hands to land on the other side of the bush, which was fine until some bright spark carved the top into a point.

So, having done it many times before, one day I pushed off and landed safely over the bush, except that, by now, the landing ground was soft and slightly damp. So, as I landed, my feet slid forwards just an inch but dramatically altered my centre of balance.

I fell backwards, and the sharpened point of the bush would surely have made a hole in me had it not found the hole that was already there. I was impaled on the bush, and I screamed in agony as the others scrambled around to lift me off and get help as blood just gushed from my rear end.

In minutes, an ambulance had arrived, and I was in hospital less than a mile away, where Mum and Dad soon arrived, having learnt the news on returning from shopping. The doctor was smiling when he told us that I was just a fraction from being mortally wounded.

The healing and convalescence lasted a couple of months, and I missed almost the entire autumn term at school, meaning I fell behind in all subjects and was never given any help whatsoever to repair the damage to my education. So, for the next year, I was dropped to 4D and languages. It was disastrous.

ANOTHER MOVING EXPERIENCE

Meanwhile, our second house in Bolton's Mornington Road was not good for us. Mum had to go back to work and the only job she could get was back at the cotton mill that she had left some fifteen years earlier to marry Dad. Also, Dad was now back in the iron foundry. So for transport reasons we relocated again, but this time, like a homing pigeon, to the area where Dad had grown up.

In his teenage years, Dad had lived at number 6 and number 12 Peveril Street and was born in Sloane Street, the next one along. Rather than a terrible step backwards in time, Peveril Street (this time at number 7) actually worked well for us all.

We had a good-sized front room with room for the snooker table, with just a couple of places where the butt end of the cue had to be raised up the wall in order to take a shot. I was just under thirteen when we arrived and over the next few years, the snooker table was sadly to become a vital part of my education.

A BIT OF A BALLS-UP

Also, it was around this time that I had an operation and learnt what the word embarrassment really means. When a lad is born, after a short while his testicles drop – not onto the floor; they drop from just inside the torso into the scrotum sack. With me, it was only a partial success. One dropped; the other, on my right side, didn't. As Peter Cook might have said, "I have nothing against your left testicle, but then again, neither have you!"

Mum and Dad were concerned, but the doctors advised that when I was four years old, the simple process was to locate it and press with the thumb, to push it down. So when I was four, they went back to the doctor, who said, "These days, it is considered best to do it at seven." So, they came back at seven and the doctor said, "In most cases these days, we don't sort this out until they are eleven." Now my becoming eleven coincided with our traumatic move to Bolton, so it didn't get done then. Which is why, when I was fourteen, the Bolton doctor said with alarm, "Why wasn't this sorted out when he was four?"

Now, sorting this problem with a fourteen-year-old is a different proposition. At four years of age, any rupture is minor and has a long time before puberty to repair itself. To do this at fourteen would cause a serious rupture which might debilitate the patient – me, for gawd's sake – for life. So the gallant Bolton doctor decided to try the method that he had just looked up in a textbook – I assume. Under anaesthetic, they cut my lower torso just above the groin and removed the offending testicle and, I presume, held it up to view. They then cut the scrotum and inserted the testicle in its rightful place. What additional plumbing had to be done to make this a complete success, I don't know and I'm sure the more squeamish of you won't want to know either.

Suffice it to say that the Ball ball-op was not a balls-up, but a complete success. However, any embarrassment suffered so far was nothing compared with what was to come.

Over the next few days, my scrotum swelled to the size of a large grapefruit, only instead of being yellow, it was a painfully, bright, vivid red, with blue veins clearly visible and all stretched to its absolute limit – perhaps inspiration for alien monsters in major feature films?

As the operation is a rarity, every few hours in the days that followed a gaggle of student doctors and nurses would appear. Unceremoniously, my hospital nightie would be lifted and my 'strange exotic fruit', as the doctor called it, would be stared at and even felt, prodded and otherwise examined. If that wasn't bad enough, from the moment they covered me up again, every single female nurse had the temerity to look me straight in the eye.

If I can be a little bit personal for a moment, I have to admit that during the week or so that my scrotum was in full bloom, being a fourteen-year-old, an orgasm did take place. All I can say about this one was that it was unique, as every part of the bulbous area tingled so extremely that my whole body shivered and trembled and then, thankfully, it subsided without actually exploding – but I bet it was a close run thing.

The result of the operation was another extended period off school – missing over half of the autumn term again, with never a chance to recover. A long convalescence was advised to give the operation time to heal, but also to keep me away from the rough and tumble of teenage school life – ha ha! I went out and got a job!

For the next two months, this poorly convalescent lad would work at Bolton Lad's Club, often setting or stacking two hundred chairs on my own and keeping the place clean before the kids arrived in the early evening.

THE BIRTH OF 'JOHNNY BALL'

In 1953, Bolton Wanderers were flying high and reached the FA Cup Final against Blackpool in what was to become the Matthews Final.

I have always thought Stanley was very lucky on that day, as in those days there were no substitutes and if you were injured, you either limped on or your team was down to ten men. Early in the game, both Bolton's left-back Banks and left-half Bell were severely injured and became mere passengers. So, late in the game, Stanley Matthews twice got the ball and faced no opposition. So his two crosses produced the winning goals.

One fit player on that day was the Bolton right-back, Johnny Ball, and that was the name given to me by my schoolmates. But I instantly liked it more than my given name, Graham and I have been known as Johnny ever since. The only downside was they also made me play right-back, when the only position I ever fancied was centre forward.

WHAT ARE FRIENDS FOR?

As a teen, most of my friends were two years older than me and already working. I was popular with them because I had a billiard table, and the advantage soon became apparent.

In 1952, the lads chose Butlin's Holiday Camp, Filey for their holidays. As they were working, the cost was not a particular problem. But to me, on 8/– a week (40p today) pocket money, I saw that I could only make the holiday if I saved the whole 8/– every week for twenty weeks. Surely that was impossible? Well, not necessarily!

I became 'the Hustler'. I had been playing snooker for six years now and was clearly quite good. But my mates were happy to play a simpler game, called 31, but for money! In 31, on potting their first ball, each player secretly took a number from one to eleven which they deducted from thirty-one to set their secret target. With just the colours, yellow, green, brown, blue, pink and black, on their spots, to start, someone played the black. After that, each player could play for and pot any ball, which was then re-spotted. Play would continue until someone reached their secret score which, with the number they had drawn, made thirty-one. Had they drawn number six, then their secret target was twenty-five.

Like pool, this simple game is more about safety than anything else. We would play for 2d per person per game. The dubious art of hustling is winning whilst always giving your opponent the impression that they had nearly won. So for twenty long weeks, I managed to win every penny I spent and saved my entire 8/– pocket money at least – and I did it without losing their friendship. Now, whether that is to my credit or to my eternal shame, I'm still not sure.

A TRICK SHOT

It was around this time that I started playing on full-sized snooker tables. It took some time before I was as good on the larger table, but Dad's snooker education gave me an appreciation of possibilities and mathematical angles perhaps wider than most other players. This showed itself one very memorable but acutely embarrassing night.

I was fourteen and it was raining and cold. The local nine-table billiard hall was a huge wooden shack that had been there twenty years earlier when Dad was a lad. On this night, I arrived very wet in my gabardine mac to find eight tables dark and empty while some twenty people watched a grudge match reach its climax on the immaculate match table.

The protagonists were both first-team players. One, in his RAF uniform, was clean-cut and confident and a perfect role model for a lad my age. The other was a good player but a loutish, grumpy sod, now in trouble as he had to hit the yellow ball, but the pink ball was in the way.

The reds had all been potted and just the colours remained, all on their spots except for the pink. The white was just above the left side pocket and the pink was close and between the white and the yellow. He was snookered, but badly. He could not play off the top cushion as the black, on its spot, was in the way. He could not play down to the bottom cushion as the green and brown, on their spots, were in the way. He could not play off the side cushions, as the blue was in the way crossing the table and the nearby middle pocket stopped him going the other way. What could he do? For a minute or two there was silence. Then someone spoke. Sadly, it was me!

"Why don't you play it off the angle of the middle pocket?" I said, and at once wished I hadn't.

The lout looked round with a sneer. "Play it off the angle? Don't talk bloody stupid."

There were laughs all round until his opponent said, "Why not? It is possible."

The lout looked at all the possibilities again and still found no solution.

"Do like he says," said his opponent, which received a grunt of disgust.

Then someone said, "Let the lad play it!"

I was horrified. Now an argument started as to whether we were playing a serious game or just messing about. Sadly, the chorus of 'let the lad play it' got stronger.

All the balls were on their spots except the pink and white, so the RAF lad raised each and put a small spot of chalk to mark their position and replaced them. Then he turned to me and said, "Go on, lad – have a go!"

The lout was grumbling about wasting time; the crowd were laughing and joking; I was still in my wet belted gabardine mac, and uncomfortably close to a coke-fired heater. I was flustered and red as a turkey cock. But there was no option – the RAF lad handed me his cue.

I needed to hit the white across the table to strike the sharply curved angle of the pocket so that it bounced off at roughly a right angle, to hit the yellow on its spot. Also, there had been much discussion about the position the balls would end up in if the shot was missed.

I bent down and aimed the strange cue, feeling rain on my forehead. I held my breath and played. The white hit the angle and bounced perfectly towards the yellow, striking it full ball and pushing it gently so it came to rest touching the bottom cushion. The applause was deafening.

The balls were re-spotted, and the lout played the shot another way and missed anyway. I think I left almost immediately in total embarrassment.

LEANING TOWARDS THE FUTURE

We really settled well in Peveril Street and at last the family home became a happy place to be. When we moved in, the four-metre square front garden was full of stones as though someone had thought about making a rockery and then given up. Dad always did all our decorating and was soon repapering the front-bedroom ceiling. He stood on planks crossing the room so he could reach the ceiling easily. However, in a moment of lapsed concentration, Dad smoothed out a bubble in the ceiling paper and walked sideways across the planks, rather than along them! In a perfect back tuck without twist, he smashed through the lower half of the bedroom sash window beautifully, without beating his brains out on the cross bar. He also had the presence of mind to raise one hand and halt his fall by grabbing this cross bar. Had he missed, he would most certainly have landed headfirst in the rockery. Glass had ripped through his decorator's coat, his jumper and shirt, but it didn't even puncture his skin.

Dad was always very handy with all kinds of jobs around the house, something that I inherited and passed on to my sons. One day, Mum complained about not having a whisk to mix pancake batter. Dad set out instantly to fix that. He got an old fork, cut the handle short and twisted the prongs at right angles. He then got his electric drill, which was mounted on a sliding device which would bring the drill straight down to drill a hole exactly where you wanted it. Mother passed him the bowl full of pancake mix just as I arrived with Dave, my mate from across the road.

"Watch this!" said Dad. The broken fork was set in the jaws of the drill, which he lowered into the mixture. He then pressed the switch. The drill gave a high-pitched sound that immediately tailed off again as Dad immediately removed his thumb – too late. No one had flinched – there wasn't time.

The batter and been whisked up and thrown out in every direction in a perfect circular spray. There was a stripe of batter across all our chests, but also, where it had missed us, on the walls, fireplace and doors across the room. As it started to drip, we started to laugh – for ages.

When we at last got a television, for the late queen's coronation in 1953, it was set next to the fireplace in our kitchen dining room. To save space, we had a table with legs quite close together and flaps that folded down each side, when not in use. Dad had extended the flaps to make it open out larger than normal and we always had a cloth over it so no one could see. I ate my dinner with my back to the fireplace and when I had finished eating, I would turn my chair round and watch the TV from there. So, one night, I turned my chair around and sat down on it. Something was wrong. Mum and Dad, in their chairs by the fireplace, looked behind me in horror!

What had I done? I had inadvertently set my chair back to rest against the table, with its back legs slightly off the floor. In sitting down, my chair levered the table to rock back onto two legs. I spun round to see the table tilted in perfect balance. For an endless couple of seconds, it was in perfect equilibrium, until something on the table slid. Then the whole table continued on its backward journey and crashed to the floor.

In those days, people were always breaking the spout off the teapot. It was clearly an everyday occurrence because you could buy extension spouts with a piece of rubber tubing, which stuck onto a broken spout. I know because we had one. So of the three sets of cups, saucers and plates, the milk jug and sugar bowl, every one was smashed. The only thing that didn't break was the broken-spouted teapot.

SIGNS OF THINGS TO COME

I began to realise that I seemed to be more energetic than most other kids. One evening, coming home from school, I found that I only had a single penny in my pocket, while the fare home was 1½d. No problem – I would get off two stops before my usual stop. So, as the bus came to this stop, I let its speed catapult me forward and started to sprint. I beat the bus to the next stop and turned the corner to run, now uphill, to my usual stop. I made it with about three yards to spare.

It was so exhilarating that it became my daily ritual and had nothing to do with saving the halfpenny. Soon, regular travellers and bus crews got to know my antics and I gained certain notoriety, though for me, the run was the thing, not the exhibition. But exhibiting myself or showing off a bit was becoming more apparent.

Lying in bed at night, I would remember the jokes I had heard on *Take It from Here* or *Life with the Lyons* or *Ray's a Laugh* with Ted Ray. Mum had taken me to see Blackpool Pier shows and I was using facial expressions and comedy movements to get laughs from my mates.

As we were much too young to use pubs, we would gather at a coffee bar in Morris Green Lane. The place was popular because of the couple that had taken it over. He was a chap with a smiling character and his blonde wife had a chest that turned each of us into a tongue-tied quivering mass as we ordered a *ho-ot V-v-v-imto*. They became even more glamourous in our eyes when she told us her husband had played drums with The Squadronaires, which had originated in the RAF and become one of the most popular big bands in the UK.

So, one day, I plucked up courage to tell him that I fancied being a drummer and straight away he offered to teach me – and he did, showing me how to hold the sticks and the very basics of reading drum music – and that was it. Just one session. I never ever had another lesson, but I was suddenly drumming mad. But surely I couldn't become a drummer, even without a pair of sticks? Well, I did have my fingers.

MY FIRST BUTLIN'S HOLIDAY

At last, Bolton Wakes Week came around and we boarded a coach for Butlin's Filey. I was two years younger than all my friends and looked it. In the pub each night, the teenage crowd would all focus their eyes on me – aged fourteen but looking no older than twelve!

As I sat there with my first pint, a commissionaire came up and said, "How old are you?"

Well, I wasn't going to get away with eighteen, so I thought I'd meet him halfway and replied, "Sixteen!"

He laughed at my sheer nerve and walked away. The next thing, people were sending pints over just because I looked so young. My mates, themselves still under eighteen, were overjoyed as I needed them to help consume my free beer.

The holiday held many similar embarrassments. In the dance hall, asking anyone for a dance was beyond my wildest imaginings. So I stood for hours watching the big band drummer. Then, on the last night, back in the chalet lines, there was an impromptu party. One chalet with an open door had the radio tuned to the American Forces Network, Europe. The station had a habit of fading away and so I went into the chalet to tune it in properly. The DJ said, "And now, from the 1938 Jazz Concert at Carnegie Hall, we have the full recording of Benny Goodman's 'Sing Sing Sing'."

Wow. When they played the concert, they were aware of recording possibilities and had paused for a couple of beats halfway through so the performance would just fit two sides of a

12 inch 78rpm record. I had a copy at home which I had played it until you could see daylight through the grooves. Here it was again, and I was fourteen and drunk.

So I began rapping out the famous drum rhythm with my fingers on the perfect-height four-drawer chest, which gave a totally acceptable tom-tom sound. I was away, in more ways than one, copying Gene Krupa beat by beat. As I recall, the entire record lasted about seven minutes and finished with fast triplets for sixteen bars. My fingers were a blur as I drummed along to the final finish! Then came the shock. A round of applause burst out. While I had been playing, I had been oblivious to everything else so had no idea that a small crowd had gathered at the door of the chalet. They had loved it. Then, as they dispersed, the pain hit me. The alcohol had made me oblivious to the fact that I had worn the skin completely off the inside surface of my two forefingers. They were raw and swollen for a week.

There was one other influential happening which occurred on that holiday's very first day. The Butlin's programme said, *Your house captain will take you on a tour of the camp.* So we went along, and a very cheerful Redcoat gave us all kinds of incites like, "Over there is the Pig and Whistle. That's where the pigs go to whistle. And across the road is the Palm Court Café, so called because the door has a strong spring and if you're not careful, you'll get your palm caught, ha ha ha." Corny? Not to a fourteen-year-old – he was hilarious.

A couple of days later, we were passing the exit of one of the theatres and the outer door was open, as the show was about to finish. In the corridor was the same Redcoat with the comedy mayor, Gordon Mitchell, who did the craziest things in different costumes and mostly ended up in the pool or covered in custard. The two of them both suddenly burst out laughing with such complete and utter joy that it influenced me greatly. These were professional laughter-makers, and they were laughing harder and stronger than their audiences ever did.

I vowed there and then that I would follow our house captain, and I never wavered from that goal for one moment. Eight years later, I too became a Butlin's Redcoat. Oh, the Redcoat's name? It was Des O'Connor.

CHAPTER 3

GOODBYE, SCHOOL – HELLO, REAL WORLD

WHAT DO YOU MEAN? NO SEX EDUCATION?

My last days in formal education, aged sixteen, were pretty uneventful, though sex was playing an ever more important part in all our minds.

We had a Californian exchange teacher with a wonderful nature and an amazingly sun-cracked and craggy face for someone still only in his forties. He was very popular because he was so ready to listen, so open-minded and so easily sidetracked. Ask any question remotely connected to his subject, biology, and you could guarantee we never got back to the actual theme of the lesson, which was probably the life cycle of a daffodil.

One day, the most precocious of the girls asked if he thought couples of mixed race should be allowed to date. We all knew that she was going out with an older, athletic Afro-Caribbean lad with great looks and I am sure everyone, boys and girls alike, rated it as 'exotic'. She was the envy of all the other girls. Happily, the quiet American teacher came back with his views that there was nothing wrong in this at all, which was the answer she was looking for. So immediately she followed up with, "Is it true that black men have larger, er, um…" She couldn't find the right words to end the sentence, which didn't matter because the laughs and sniggers would have drowned it anyway. Once again, our guest was wonderful.

"Well, I don't have a lot of experience in that area," he said. He was a total hero and heads and shoulders above our regular staff.

The girls were clearly maturing faster than us boys and they would turn conversations to sexual matters just to see us blush in confusion. I had a cousin in our class called Lucille Ball who had been 'clubbing' for several years already. This was the age of jazz dance crazes like The Creep. The Creep needed no partner contact apart from hands, as in jive, but you did it slowly and each new foot position was never completely off the previous footprint. Also, the girl craze was flat black shoes, which they changed into at every break time and danced as they sang together, cutting everything and everybody else out of their own little groovy world.

Suddenly, the upper fifth's Christmas dance was looming just a few weeks away. Unlike many of the girls, we lads had not started going to dance halls. So, horror of horror, the school decreed we would all attend basic dancing classes. I don't really recall fancying any of the girls in my class, but I was horrified when just about the one I fancied least, a very frail girl with frizzy hair, made a beeline for me as a partner. Worse was to come as she moved in much closer than was necessary and made every effort to get one leg so far between mine and up into my crotch that I thought she was trying to kick the couple behind.

The dance went well, with us all dressed as maturely as we could manage. It was also great to find that the more mature girls, including my cousin Lucille, made the greatest effort to relax and coax some kind of performance out of me. By the end of the night, I was Creeping and Smooching with the best.

THE EXAM RESULTS

The O'level results came through and I had got Geography and Maths, but had failed English Language, English Lit and History. For two years I had done little homework and hated the set books, so perhaps that was inevitable. Maths was never in question and I was pretty sure I had scored very close to 100% – just one question required a geometric construction and final measurement to two decimal places.

I was right. I had found no problem with the paper even though I had hardly taken a note in the previous two years. Things mathematical were just about the only things in my life that I faced with total confidence. I recall teaching myself trigonometry when I had missed it through sickness.

So with just two O Levels I was now a confirmed failure, not good enough for sixth form. But then a startling thing happened. The Senior Mistress and Head of Maths, a stately galleon of a woman called Miss Boyle, was examining our work books while we read quietly. Suddenly she enquired, "Which one is Ball?" I had been there for five years and invisible to her. She had definitely never taught me, as her efforts were reserved for the A and B groups.

She called me out and to quietly explain how I had arrived at a particular answer in my book? I explained with a finger, that if that equals that and and those two equal that one, then it is clear that this must be equal to that? "But you've never been taught to do it that way?" she said.

I shrugged and said, "Well, it's obvious, isn't it?" and went and sat down. She thumbed through my book for a few minutes and then said, "Ball! You have a brilliant mathematical brain!" That was that.

Now it didn't matter whether I had or hadn't got such a brain. It didn't matter anymore that she had never taught me and that those who had had spotted nothing unusual. What did matter was that someone with some clout had confirmed what I believed, but didn't have the confidence to proclaim! Looking back, that was the first step of my educational recovery.

Today, having been involved in education for the past 40 years, one thing I tell young people is, "Never worry about the level you are at right now. Because it doesn't matter. What matters is your gaining confidence and maturing , however slowly.

Whatever damage modern education does to our kids, there is relief in knowing that in almost all cases, the damage is repairable.

NO JOBS FOR FAILURES?

I don't recall one jot of advice on careers while at school. But as luck would have it, as I ran daily from the bus stop and round a few alleys for the shortest route to school, I passed, on a corner, The Youth Employment Bureau? So one day, completely off my own bat, I popped in to see them. There were two smart and energetic blokes there who gave me a two man interview. Why wouldn't they? There wasn't another sole in the place. Their advice was "Aim High!"

During my convalescences I had been able to roam the streets in school hours and knew the feeling of freedom that induced and I really didn't fancy being locked up in a building from nine to five. I also loved maps, hiking and the great outdoors and with my maths, I declared "I'd like to be a surveyor."

As 5 O Levels seemed to be the minimum requirement to even be accepted, I immediately volunteered to re-sit Eng Lang, Eng Lit and History, which were the very three required for Surveying along with the Maths and Geography I already had.. Now it was their turn.

They started to ring every company who handled surveyors

and coax them into at least seeing me and giving me an interview. Soon I was on strange buses heading for companies far and wide, but all simply had no jobs available, irrespective of my lack of O levels. For a good few months, into September and October, this continued without success.

Then they produced a different possibility. Would I write to De Havilland Aircraft Corporation at Lostock near Horwich. Of course I would and did and eventually I was summoned for an interview.

I remember walking down the road to the factory and passing the executive offices with the large cars parked outside and the lawns trimmed so neatly. It was petrifying. Surprisingly the chap interviewing me seemed no older than about 21. He was the son of the De Havilland family, had just come down from Cambridge and was simply wonderful as he chatted with and about me! "This is a bit disappointing - only two O levels. Your friends at the Youth Employment Bureau said you would sit three more? You've already booked in? Great. Also, your letter was very good indeed, and you scored 100% in our Maths and English tests. I think what you need is a chance. Don't you agree? Right!

We have a five year business course at De Havillands, which most future management people follow until they gain their qualifications. From your Maths, I'd say you would make a good Cost and Works Accountant. What's that? It's an Industrial Accountant. Our Main Cost Accountant does all the maths to make this place work. He calculates how much we spend on things we buy from other people. He works out how much our staff and workforce costs us. He even works out how much tax we have to pay and finally what profit we are likely to make. Does that sound important enough for you?

OK. By far the largest amount of time in your apprenticeship will be in the Cost Office. You would have at least eighteen months of the five years, in there. So if we start you in there, while you get your other O levels, then later, when you are on the course proper, we can move you through all the other departments!"

Wow. This was a truly great moment and memory in my life. I had been talking to someone who didn't doubt for a moment that I could handle everything he was suggesting and that was a vital first for me. So after nearly three months of searching, I finally started work.

MY FIRST JOB

I loved it from day one. It was probably day two, when one of the older women who was so welcoming and friendly, decided I needed some advice and said, "Why don't you do something about your hair? I've seen better hair on a side of bacon!"

I worked in a room with around 30 people. Two of the lads were on the business course, and wasted no time in telling me that they had around 7 O's and 5 A levels each. There were also three young girls who had immense amounts of filing to do, and basically nothing else, and I was put with them, to help with the filing and learn what went on.

Within a few days, I realised that there were a few problems for the girls. Three of the four walls of the office were covered in narrow shelves which held Punch Cards. These cards contained all the work effort of every machinist in the factory, and they were all grouped in job order. There were also a couple of huge filing rooms with shelves of ring binders full of Job Sheets. But the system was collapsing.

The factory had been making aircraft parts and mostly propellers since well before the war. Now the propellers and 1940's aircraft stuff was obsolete. This was 1954 and the firm was moving into Guided Missiles and all the new electronic technology that would entail. As a result, there was plenty of space to file the stuff they no longer made, and nowhere at all to file the stuff that was going to make the firms future.

It was only after about two weeks in the job that I went to the boss and said, "Excuse me Sir, Your filing system doesn't work!" He looked at me and his jaw dropped. "Let me show you," I said and lead him to the filing rooms. It didn't take long to explain that the system needed an overhaul by getting rid of stuff that no longer mattered, shrinking the space for the stuff we were making less of, and enlarging the space for the new stuff, to which he replied, "Well who the hell is going to do all that? I haven't got time" To which I replied, "Well, I'll do it!"

So in my first few weeks, I was now re-organising the De Havilland Cost Office entire filing system. The three girls and I were shown a dismal storage space in a cellar reached by an antiquated lift and full of spiders, but we had filled the place in a week or so and labelled everything so it could be found again if it was needed. Then we shuffled the space in the filing rooms and then stripped the wall shelves of cards that were no longer required. In a couple of weeks and total effort, we had sorted the whole thing out.

THE BIG COST

The brightest fella in the office was a tall, curly fair haired rising star called Howard. From his desk at the back of the office, he never missed a trick and one day said, "I want that lad with me." He stuck me on the desk in front of him and started to show me how the costing system in a large factory works. No one asked him - he just did it and started to give me costing jobs to do, and whisper that none of the old codgers around the place were going to get the work done in a month of Sundays. He also chose me over the two lads on the Business Course. Little did I know where this was leading?

Suddenly one day, there was a meeting of the senior office staff. Our boss, the actual Cost Accountant, needed the cost of a new Propeller, but fast. We had over the previous few years, made the propellers for the Bristol Britannia, which was a very successful passenger aircraft.

Now they were producing the Blackburn Beverley - a huge military transport plane, but with exactly the same propellers apart from the length of the propeller blades.

The boss had demanded the full cost of the Beverley props a.s.a.p. even though the first batch was still being made on the factory floor. Everyone pleaded that they had important work that they couldn't drop to do this job. So Howard said, so the whole office could hear, "You won't take it on, because most of you wouldn't know how to go about it. But I'll show you how quickly it can be done. More than that - I'll give it the lad to do!" Then the shock hit me!

I dropped everything and pulled my chair up to his desk. He took out a sheaf of blank double page foolscap with narrow maths lines across it. He ruled several upright lines and columns for the first few pages and then explained - I was to get the parts list and copy it by hand onto the sheets. I was then to go and find the cost of everything that had been bought in and every operation that had been machined on every part on the Beverley Propeller - how many parts? Howard guessed at between 14 and 17 hundred. How many operations on each part? Perhaps 12 to 20 in most cases. The only preparation he gave me was a lesson in writing clear figures, as mine were a little scrappy and untidy. Oh, and no ink - all in pencil only.

The job was to take seven weeks. By the end of it, I had got to know the top machinists on the factory floor. I was so close to them that often I was waiting as they finished a job, to mark down the very minute they clocked it. Then I was back in the office working out the actual cost, based on the minutes taken.

Every machinist had a rate, which might be 63d an hour - just over 25p. Then from the time taken I would work out the actual cost of that single operation. So the task might be 63/60 x 84 minutes = 88.2 pence.

In those days factories had comptometer operators who would do these sums on their machines in seconds. The problem was, I was the junior of juniors and all the other cost office clerks would drop their calculations in the trays to be worked out. The girls simply left mine till last, because I was the kid. So, I had no alternative but to bypass them. I taught myself to do the calculations in my head.

Then I got another lucky break, as there was a chap in the office who had been in the Music Hall before the war, but his wartime experiences had left his nerves shattered.

The ex Music Hall chap had been half of a Mental Arithmetic act and once he knew of my love of figures, he was explaining the tricks he would get up to. I met most of these tricks in later life and must say that very little has changed as regards mental agility. Most theatre magic requires that you mislead the audience, rather than actually use your brain. So the tricks he showed me were really quite basic - but oh, the confidence I gained as I learnt them. A deeper love of maths was cemented forever.

Each day I would trace the minute and hourly rates for each and every operation as the propellers passed slowly down the production lines. Then I would get back to my desk and do the maths in my head, while the comptometer girls sat doing their nails.

Each day, we clocked out at 5.03, as the 3 minutes over five days added to a quarter of an hour in the week and made our working time balance with our employment contracts. At the end of the day, staff were allowed to get our coats at 4.55 and queue at the clock until the hooter went at 5.03 precisely. Then they would clock off in turn and be off for our buses. The Reebok

Stadium where Bolton Wanderers play today was built solely on the bus park where dozens of double deck buses stood ready to whisk us off in all directions.

When I was calculating, I was oblivious of time or movement around me. Only the 5.03 hooter would break the mood and I would look up and see 30 people queuing for the clock while I was the only one still at my desk. I would only now stop work, grab my coat and clock off last.

Then I would dash out of the side gate and sprint around the outer edge of the factory some 300 yards, to be almost first on my bus, nabbing my favourite back seat, to be first off at my stop.

The job continued for around seven weeks. Then on the very day the very first Blackburn Beverley propellers were being crated up, to be shipped by road to meet the rest of the aircraft, I called to Howard, "Finished!" The entire cost had been totalled. Howard gave it the once over and grinning from ear to ear, disappeared with it into the boss's office.

I thought I heard a loud snort and in just a couple of minutes, Howard emerged looking shocked. He threw the sheaf of papers more at me than at my desk. "He says it's rubbish!" said Howard and in front of some 30 people, I burst into violent uncontrollable tears.

A few minutes later I had calmed down and we started to go over the items, large costs first and then smaller costs. We found no errors at all. Back it went to the boss and this time it did not come back. Soon I realized the reason for the first rejection.

The previous Bristol Britannia Props had been made using a Peace Work system. Assuming the basic wage was £8 a week, a machinist was given a time for each job. If he completed the work in half that time, he got 100% bonus and if he kept that up, he ended the week with £12 wages.

However, just before I had arrived, some bright accountant, encouraged by the unions had suggested a new system. The workers didn't need to be driven by incentives. If we all worked together as part of a happy team, then everything would improve and get better year on year. So they scrapped "Peacetime Working" and gave the machinists their £12 a week. What was the result? Within 6 months, each job was taking at least twice as long to complete and often much longer and costs were out of control. The whole factory was in jeopardy.

My huge Blackburn Beverley costings, thanks to the new system, were over twice as much as the almost identical Bristol Britannia. In fact, my cost was definitely the quickest ever at DH and probably the most accurate as well - I was still only16.

THE JOB TURNS SOUR

Howard immediately asked for a rise for me. The bosses convened and said that I could have the 5 shillings a week rise (25p) which all new junior workers got at the end of the first year. Howard said, "Well, if that's all you think this lad is worth, then you can stick it!" So I never got the five shillings that everyone else got as a matter of course, till the error was spotted.

But I loved the job and felt so completely at home. It was clear that I was functioning as well as any of the Business Course chaps. Unlike school, I was being rewarded for my efforts and my confidence soured.

Howard and I became great friends and he introduced me to Rugby League and Leigh Rugby Ground. Leigh had an enormous hulking great prop forward called Charlie Pawsey who could just growl and wingers would run into touch.

For my first ever match, we arrived at the ground just after kick off. We climbed the cinder embankment and I saw the ground for the first time and the action. The opposition winger was steaming down the left touch line in front of us. Charlie Pawsey launched himself at the winger and as it happened, straight in my direction. With his beer belly, Charley was incapable of leaving the ground altogether, so with his toes trailing along the ground, his dive coincided with the winger's path. His left hand went to the back of the winger's head while his right arm swung in a wide arc and his fist crunched into the winger's nose. While the trainers tried to repair the hapless winger, I had chance to take in the wonderful Rugby League atmosphere.

In that same first match, I saw Jimmy Leggard kick 11 conversions and penalties out of 12. The last kick, almost on full time, was the most amazing of all. We were roughly on the halfway line and the wind was very strong blowing straight down the pitch. Jimmy spotted the ball almost on the touchline and considered the wind. He then kicked the ball almost exactly across the pitch. The wind caught it and swung it round almost 90 degrees and carried it over and through the posts. I never again saw a swerve like it.

From that first visit, I would go to watch Leigh every other Saturday and Bolton Wanderers the alternative weekends for the next two years.

Meanwhile things at De Havillands were changing, and not for the better. Not only did this new pay structure ruin worker relationships across British Industry. It made British Industry less competitive and strengthened the unions to an enormous degree, where confrontation between management and workers became an everyday occurrence. It also ruined my job.

Within weeks, instead of striving to clock the achieved minutes which drew the 100% bonus, machinists with no incentives, were taking twice and even three times as long. They gave every excuse imaginable and everyone's lives became a misery. In no time at all, the costs had gone through the roof, the company was losing money. The management hated the workforce, the workers hated them and us, the unions increased their confrontational activities and we hated the whole damn job.

Howard was given the job of tackling the problem. We suddenly all had clip boards and would go down onto the shop floor, tell machinists the time they should be able to do a job in and watched them while they failed to do it. This was the birth of Time and Motion Study.

Howard's empire blossomed. From having just two people under him, his Time and Motion brigade was soon some 30 strong, with me showing the newcomers the ropes, including the chap who had got me the interview when he was at the Youth Employment Bureau. Now he had come to De Havilland for the better money.

The new recruits were totally different from the often crabby old cost office crowd. Most had just come back from National Service and were around 4 years older than me and more mature.

I was still a kid and egged on by my new mates, I latched on to every office prank that was going. All our phones were black and so at lunch time, I rubbed the earpieces on the black ink pads. When they came back, I rang them from across the room and watched them slap the phone and the ink to their ear - haha. I would put elastic bands around the phones and when they reached to pick up the receiver, the whole phone came with it - haha. I carefully took out desk drawers, held the things inside and slotted them back in place, upside down - when they opened the drawer the contents showered onto the floor – Haha!

We all became experts at elastic band firing. The best way is to stretch the band between the ends of your middle finger and thumb, but make sure the band has a half twist. This evens out the tension and it flies in a much straighter line. I could fire them into tea cups or knock the ash off a cigarette a couple of desks away. By stretching a band along the edge of a ruler, they could reach perhaps 8 yards, with some accuracy.

A TEENAGER AT LARGE

In social terms, aged sixteen, while clearly failing at school, I also changed my attitude to life several times.

I found a local Methodist youth club where I could play table tennis without having to go into town. They welcomed me and then hauled me into the YPPT – the Young People's Preaching Team – would you believe?

Each Sunday evening, the team would go to Methodist churches in Leigh, Atherton or Wigan where, as people arrived, we would hand them slips of paper. Then, instead of a sermon, the YPPT would answer the questions the adults put to us. Mostly it showed that we understood old people and what reasonable behaviour was all about. We also expressed our feelings about the world of the fifties, including Teddy Boys, juvenile delinquency and the generation gap.

I loved it, and the experience proved to me that kids often have more sense and decency than their actions and manners suggest – not only in those days, but also today. I finally left the group, as, apart from the YPPT events, they were all pretty stodgy.

At the same time, I had another group of friends who were not that commendable at all. I followed my schoolyard football crowd and became 'almost a Teddy Boy'. I bought a diagonal-striped, brown, double-breasted suit and brown, suede, crepe-wedge-heeled shoes and a crocheted tie and was for a time a fashionable Ted. The shoes soon scuffed, but that was OK, as they became the best schoolyard football shoes I ever had. They had almost as much bounce as a modern trainer. We would see how many running steps we could take along a vertical wall before we had to get our feet back on the ground to stay upright.

But my schoolyard football days came to an end when things started to get out of hand. With sexual maturity came increased male aggression and suddenly, one day, from our local coffee bar, we saw another 'gang' outside, just waiting for us. We invited them in for a chat and when that failed, we ventured outside to meet them.

We eyed each other up. Then someone suggested that instead of an all-out gang fight, we should each choose one person to represent us – it was *West Side Story* on the South Side of Bolton. Jack Winyard, who was already a working coal miner, was the least co-ordinated lad I had ever met. He had a great personality and, with his long gangly legs, produced walks predating Monty Python but every bit as funny. He was a good six inches taller than the rest of us, and so Jack, in his light-green gabardine suit, was selected as our champion.

The two protagonists walked around to the back street. We and the other gang followed, all surprisingly close to each other, which made for a very nervous few minutes. Our two champions faced each other. The other lad lunged and Jack sort of tripped over a curb and grabbed the other fella, almost as a way of staying on his feet. Now the lad's head was under Jack's left arm. A few right-hand punches in the face and the fight was over and the issue settled.

But I dropped that crowd instantly. It wasn't cowardice, though I know every one of us was shit-scared as we walked into that back street. It was just mindless juvenile antics and was going to lead to trouble, and for what?

A MORE DRAMATIC LIFE

But my next action, for a time, put me in fear of the gang I had been a member of. I joined the amateur dramatic society that met in the school hall where we played our football. I came in from the cold because a couple of my jazz-loving mates had already joined and through the windows I had seen that they were surrounded by girls.

The St Bede's Amateur Dramatic Club was to be of great help for my future, once the previous crowd had stopped heckling me through the windows. The established members were older on average by some five years and were mostly in the church choir. The vicar, Reverend Craster Pringle, had a son, Bryan, at RADA on his way to an illustrious National Theatre career. Bryan sadly died in 2002, but I still remember his wonderful delivery, reading the lesson on Sundays when he came down from Cambridge.

I became a church sidesman, ushering people and taking the collection, which we counted in the vestry after the service. During the service, two or three of us would sit at the very back and try to match in volume, if not quality, the choir at the front. Great fun! We often even sang the right words, although, 'for those in peril on the seas' might become 'for those in peril with DTs'.

There was an ulterior motive in going to church. On an English Sunday in those days, absolutely nothing at all happened. Nothing at all.

But after the service, half the choir would walk a good mile to one of the girls' bachelor flats. While the girls went straight there, we lads – now too far away be recognised – ducked into a pub. I was now sixteen but looked more like fourteen. In winter, Threlfalls Brewery sold Four X winter ale which was so strong they only sold it by the nip or third of a pint. I remember the first time I had one of these on top of a couple of pints.

As we got to the flat to join the girls, the cold winter air had got to me, and I was incapable. I leant against the wall in the lounge to stop myself falling over. I didn't fall. I just slid down the wall as my feet slid on the linoleum. That night, when I got home, I rushed upstairs and fell on my knees in front of the toilet bowl and up it all came.

My mother shouted to Dad, "Help him, Dan," to which Dad shouted, with a grin, "Help him? He paid for it. He can do what he wants with it now." When I came downstairs looking whiter than a corpse in a fridge, he said knowingly, "Tha pays thee own fines, tha knows?"

Next day, when he came home from work, he said, "Tha wants to lay off that Four X." His workmate used the same pub and had recognised me.

MY BRUSHES WITH THE OPPOSITE SEX

It was around this time that I found an essential part of a young lad's life. My first girlfriend! She was the daughter of the St Bede's school caretaker with a waist that defied belief at just twenty-one inches around. I was so mesmerised by that waist – it wasn't waste, it was bloody useful – that I made a loop of string twenty-one inches around and, in idle moments at work, I would take out the loop and wonder how anyone could fit into that tiny space and breathe. She affected my own breathing quite often, but sadly the family moved away and after four separate bus expeditions, I packed it in as a waste of time.

Besides, love had now arrived at work. When I was doing my propeller costing, I had to chase all kinds of information, even before it reached any files. This involved me venturing into the Powers-Samas machine room, which was full of girls punching cards. The massive tabulating machines would be going, with their relentless *one, two three, bump, one, and-a-three, bump* rhythm. It was Samba time and as they moved around the room, in their flat black slip-on shoes, the girls would shuffle-dance all day every day.

This was shark-infested water for a sixteen-year-old lad. As soon as I appeared through the door, there would be wolf whistles and any girl dancing past would grab me to join in. This would continue amid rising laughter as I turned redder and twisted around to escape.

I would calm myself and ask, "Have you got any stuff on the Beverley Contract?"

"Ooh, I could make a contract with you, love!"

Or I'd say, "Where are the Beverley punch cards!" and get back, "Ooh, you can punch my card any time you like, chuck!"

After a few minutes, I would rush out and lean against a wall while I got my breath back.

Then Kit arrived. Kathleen came straight from school as a well-rounded girl and joined the filing group and filled her light-blue dust coat better than any of the others. They clearly never had her size, and her coat was so tight the whole office was in fear of losing an eye from a flying button. There was no health and safety in those days, thank goodness.

Kit was full of fun, and so was I, but suddenly whenever we were in the room together, we would both go very quiet. "You two getting on alright?" everyone would ask, with a knowing wink. But being in the office was not the problem. The problem was us both meeting in the filing room and being left alone. Brushing past each other became an ordeal as the slightest contact sent electric shivers through us both. We would utter single-syllable sentences to each other.

"OK?"

"Yep!"

We would work ever closer, and our eyes would meet, and then one of the double doors would flap open and we would jump like scared rabbits. Holding my clipboard low to hide my erection was a daily or even hourly requirement.

As Kit lived in Aspull, near Wigan, and I lived about five miles away in Bolton, I didn't ask her out until the Christmas party came around, and I walked her home. It was also the coldest night I ever remember and after dropping her at her house, I walked the five miles home as the frost actually gathered on my greasy hair. In the last mile, my head wore an icy crash helmet, and the cold gave me a headache like I had never known. Teenage love isn't easy, you know.

We did go out a few times together and I thought the world of her. But it was much too early for anything serious, as far as I was concerned.

HE'S A DRUMMIN' MAN!

In the Amateur Dramatics group was an ex-army drummer called Brian who had played bop in the forces. I had some bop records – including Charlie Parker's 'Night In Tunisia', with Dizzy Gillespie and George Shearing's 'Lullaby of Birdland', which I played endlessly.

After the pub on Sunday nights, Brian and I would play drums, but without drums, sticks or music. We would use tightly rolled newspapers as drum brushes on the seat of a leather dining chair while we knelt, facing each other. For music, we both scatted or hummed through the tunes and played four-bar breaks one after the other – sheer heaven, with rolled-up newspaper.

The big advantage of now working was being paid, and soon the inevitable happened. In the *Bolton Evening News*, I saw an ad: *Drum Kit for Sale £20*. Two bus rides away, I found the house and the kit. I remember their faces when I asked if I could pay in weekly instalments.

I paid twenty-five shillings down and agreed to pay twenty-five bob a week till it was paid off and they drove me home with the kit. After twelve weeks of four bus journeys and sixteen pounds five shillings paid, the lovely family let me off for the rest – it was a week before Christmas.

The drums were placed in our 'best' front room and the snooker table was gone for good. The kit was, frankly, awful. It had a large old-fashioned base drum, a hi-hat with terrible cymbals, an awful ride cymbal and a stool. The snare drum was the saving grace, with a wonderful crisp tone with very little ring. It was by a little-known maker but was to prove a godsend for me in a couple of years' time. It was a good year later when I lashed out and bought a fabulous pair of 15" Hi-Hat Cymbals and a 19" Ride Cymbal all by Avedis Zildjian – the best.

In those days, I could find just two drum tutor books. One by the already legendary Gene Krupa and one by the brash young upstart Buddy Rich. Buddy's book was the easiest by far and every drummer seemed to stick to that. However, Krupa's was far more complex. He used a set of accent signs indicating three different drum strokes using the wrist, the forearm or the whole arm. He advocated starting with your weaker left hand. The drum rudiments included flams, flam taps, roughs, ratamacues; five-, seven-, nine- and thirteen-stroke rolls; and single, double and triple paradiddles. Getting through the Krupa book was to be a long ride.

Every session followed a pattern. I would warm up with five minutes on the drums. Then I would move to a table tennis bat strapped with elastic bands to the arm of an easy chair and would work through the exercises in each book, page by page. Then, at the end, I would have just ten more minutes on the kit playing to records. This, Mum, Dad and I figured, would be all the neighbours could stand. In two years, we never had one complaint.

MORE AND MORE MUSIC

I suppose my drama-club friends could have been described as lightweight in many ways. They definitely didn't play snooker or football. Dave Gregory used an asthma inhaler, played the violin, and loved jazz and classics. His aunt had an expensive Black Box record player and at her house we would sit and listen to Beethoven, Tchaikovsky and Saint-Saëns' *Rondo Capriccioso*.

When we met, Dave had just lost his flute-playing pal who had declared himself a 'conscientious objector' at his forces medical. They banged him up in a jail cell, but they let him keep his flute. I kept trying to imagine the poor bloke, who wouldn't hurt a fly, sitting in a prison cell with his flute in his hand. I imagined they caught him chiselling bricks out of the wall with his cutlery.

"Aha, trying to escape, are you?"

"No, sir. My bed is against the wall; I'm removing a couple of bricks to make room for my flute when I play it in bed."

Through Dave, I met a trumpet player and another Dave (the one who was hit by the batter mix) who played saxophone, and with a pianist we had the makings of a group. Dad made professional-looking music stands and 'The Metronomes' were born. Each week, I would buy a Jimmy Lally orchestration for the band for four shillings. Being a four piece, we didn't need the violin parts. However, we always had to trawl through all the brass parts to make sure we had all the top lines of the orchestration. We were probably as pathetic as our name suggested. We never got one paid gig.

Through The Squadronaires' drummer, who ran a temperance bar, I did play two gigs with bands I had never seen before and never saw again. One was with a blind pianist and sax trio, which wasn't too bad. Next came a sighted pianist and sax. We played at Bolton Golf Club and the audience thought we were terrible, but only because we were. I was so young, sitting there at my antiquated drums, smiling apologetically, that suddenly the members called a halt, paid off the piano and sax, and bought me drinks and ran me home at the end, drum kit and all.

This was 1955/6 and skiffle was just arriving. But for me, the aim was always modern jazz as I started to absorb Charlie Parker, Gillespie, J.J. Johnson and Kai Winding, Stan Kenton,

Mel Tormé, Shorty Rogers and Shelly Manne. Then, suddenly, there was Dave Brubeck. Even today I can still 'sing' Brubeck's long piano solos from end to end.

Meanwhile, I was taking to amateur dramatics like a duck to water. It all began with a review, which gave everyone a chance to do something. I was saddled with a novelty comedy number. The routine had three of us, dressed as Egyptians, and we entered to eastern music, doing a sand dance. We looked like something left over from a giant nativity play.

Also new to amateur dramatics was Arthur Unsworth Tunstall. He had been in my class and wasn't a bad lad at all, but he had had a humour bypass. When he saw me playing the drums and keeping an even tempo, he said, "Why doesn't somebody design a machine to do that?" Perhaps it was funny after all?

Next came the senior member of the drama group, with his own dress suit, would you believe. He always seemed a little snobbish to me. He once heard me whistling and said, "Hang on. That's Saint-Saëns' *Rondo Capriccioso*. How the hell do you know that?"

Years later, when I had been in TV for some fifteen years, two kids who had brought their rare-breed dogs to *Blue Peter* saw me and came across.

"You know our mum and dad. They were in St Bede's Amateur Dramatics with you."

I immediately remembered them and their names. I then said, "Wow, I was awful in those days."

To which the kids replied, "Yes, they said you were!"

Anyway, the song was 'Cleo and Meo' from a recent American hit parade. This was the pop music we had in those days, kids. To make the absurd even funnier, we did a little dance at the end of each verse, and on the third go, I had to turn the wrong way and get it wrong.

It brought the house down, but only because everyone thought it was a genuine cock-up. No amount of pleading that we had rehearsed it that way convinced anyone.

After the review, the numbers were reduced to just those involved in the next play, so most of my mates left. But I stayed on – the smell of the greasepaint? I suppose it was. I got a part in *Rebecca* and *When We Are Married*, but I only had eight lines in both plays combined. But just being around the rehearsals meant so much to me. I found that after a few weeks' rehearsal, I could recite, in bed to myself, the entire first act of each play, character accents and all.

In *When We Are Married*, I was the reporter who appears very early in the first scene, has two lines and is never seen again. However, whatever part you play, it always leaves an unforgettable mark on your relations.

A year or so before my parents died in the 1990s, there was a revival of *When We Are Married* at London's Whitehall Theatre, with a great cast including Mollie Sugden. So we took my mum. Sadly, we got there late and, even more sad, we were in the second row of the stalls. They let us in, surprisingly, and about eight of us shuffled along the row. I was smiling apologetically in case I was recognised. We were interrupting the three major couples sitting for a photograph. While the drunken photographer is setting up, the reporter delivers his two lines.

My mum's mind flashed back to the St Bede's school hall all those years ago, and as we shuffled along the row, in her bright, clear, Lancashire voice, she said, so even the gods could hear, "There's our Johnny!"

After a few minutes, the cast recovered, and the laughs started flowing again in this funniest of plays. And at last I slowly lifted my head to show my face again.

AN AMBITION FOR THE FUTURE

By now, a life ambition had started to take shape. I told my mates that in five years I aimed to be as good as the excellent drummer at the Bolton Palais de Dance. But I clearly had more in mind than that. I would trot out routines of gags that I had picked up on the radio and somehow extended, and I recall Kit, who I saw more of now, saying that when I was a star, she would one day 'watch me from the wings'.

Then came my annual interview with the De Havilland bosses. They started by saying how well I had worked in the first year and a half under Howard and that I had impressed everyone very much. I said that of course that had all been ruined when they latched me on to the time and motion study group and the work had bored me rigid. What I had wanted was a transfer to another department to broaden my cost accountancy experience. However, they had noted that since I had got my extra three O Levels, I had done little or no work on my Intermediate Exams for Cost and Works Accountancy. How could I? With snooker, drums and amateur dramatics and drums and chess and girlfriends and drums, what time did I have to study?

They explained that I could apply for a deferment from National Service until I was twenty-five, but, well, I was such a 'live wire'. They'd all loved having me around but didn't I think I should take the opportunity of two years in the forces to calm down a little?

Calm down? Did they not understand? I was only just starting. I had already made my mind up. I was joining the forces for the sheer experience, thrill and adventure. I was off. They emphasised that they would keep a place for me and welcome me back any time, but in my heart I knew a return to De Havillands was never an option.

The older lads that I worked with came in two basic categories. Those who had hated the forces as two years of wasted time, who worked humourlessly from day to ever more gloomy day. Then there were the others who had taught me so much and regaled me with tales of their antics in the forces; who had cheerful and playful spirits and an attitude to life that I was dying to emulate. With broad grins, they had filled me with warnings about the harm that can come to a young lad in the forces. Beware, they said, of the dangers of catching crinkle crickets, roozles and the dreaded Phan Todd, the symptoms of which were an uncontrolled rising of the bed sheets first thing in the morning. Apparently, they told me, though unavoidable, it was against forces regulations but was easily cured by the application of a quarter master's stick.

The depressed and depressing ones told me to keep my head down and never volunteer for anything. The cheerful pranksters told me, "Get in there, get stuck in and volunteer for everything, and make sure you are first every time!" Their guidance was all I needed, and I knew just how I was going to treat the forces experience – if I passed my medical.

I can honestly say that after leaving school and finding success in the workplace, and learning to cope with aggression or snobbishness, I never felt inadequate again and I never doubted that I could take on any new challenge.

Failure was never a word that troubled me, until I got my 'call-up' papers and turned up in Manchester for my medical. For the whole week before, I couldn't sleep, I couldn't settle, and the nerves got worse and worse. My mind nagged at me day after day with one horrible thought – *What if I fail my medical?*

CHAPTER 4

MY FORCES UNIVERSITY

FIT TO BEAT THE BAND?

The day of my forces medical arrived and off I went to some school hall in Manchester, taking my nerves with me. Once inside, some eight or ten of us were grouped together and moved into another room, where we were told to strip off and wait to be called.

Suddenly we were being ushered past a line of examining 'doctors'. All the jokes from my ex-forces workmates were swimming around in my head:

"I want you to pee in that flask on the shelf."

"What? From here? I thought this was for the army, not the fire brigade?"

Then there is the tale of the lad who wore a borrowed truss in an attempt to fail his medical. At the end, the doctor stamped his papers with a large *M E.*

"Oh, is that medically exempt?" he asked.

The doctor replied, "No, it stands for Middle East. If you can wear a truss upside down and inside out, you can ride a bloody camel."

After the bending, balancing, ear-probing, scrotum-feeling, coughing, tongue sticking out and aah-ing, and eye testing (Doc: "Read the lowest line you can on that chart." Recruit: "Printed in Birmingham." Doc: "Next!"), we dressed and moved to a second room and waited.

My name was called, and I was declared A1. It was never in doubt, but the fear I had that I might fail was almost overwhelming. But that was the last of my self-doubts. I was fit; I was normal.

"Congratulations," said the chap, "you're in the Lancashire Fusiliers!"

"Oh no I'm not!" I said.

I had planned every detail for this moment. The first decision I had made was that I would 'sign on' as a regular for three years as opposed to the National Service demand for two. Why? Because from day one, you received exactly twice the National Service pay per week and for an eighteen-year-old lad, that means twice as much beer money. Secondly, as a regular you can choose your service and your trade.

"I want to join the RAF," I said, and the army chap's expression changed to one of disgust as he slowly handed me my papers and pointed to a door with the RAF insignia on it. In I went.

"Oh, hello!" said Flying Officer Kite as he spun round from idly gazing through the window to show his Terry-Thomas grin and moustache. "Welcome to the RAF."

Then, after studying my educational qualifications and work experience, he asked what I would like as my trade.

"I want to be a radar operator."

"Oh no," he said, "your qualifications are far better than that." He suggested radar technician, but that required eight months' training. Similarly, radar mechanic needed six months' training. Radar operator, on the other hand, required just six weeks' training and then the maximum chance of deep overseas posting; perhaps even Hong Kong or Singapore.

Very quickly it was all signed and sealed, and on 2nd January 1957, Mum and Dad accompanied me to the station. I could see Dad was looking for words of wisdom to convey as I left them for the big wide world. I think he put it simply but beautifully.

"Always do what's right!" he said and winked knowingly and grabbed my hand.

He didn't need to say any more. Coming from him, that said it all. Dad didn't really know how to not 'do what's right' to or for other people.

But now began three blissful years of RAF life. We were kitted out at Cardington, Bedfordshire and a couple of days later were on an overnight train to somewhere.

DRUM BREAKS

The somewhere turned out to be West Kirby on the Wirral Peninsula, which we reached around 6am on a freezing January morning. No one had slept and we were all shattered.

So was the brief silence. Suddenly nasty-looking drill instructors were screaming at us, "All out, with your kit, in three lines. Now! Move!"

Carrying kit and full kitbags proved almost impossible for the frailer ones, but somehow we were cattle herded onto the platform and prodded into line.

"No talking," said the one in charge. "You are going to be marched off to your barracks." Then, with a snide edge to his voice, "But we have a little weeding out to do first. All those who play a musical instrument and would like to audition for the Station Band, take one step forward. Go."

I was horrified. It seemed that about one in four of over a hundred of us wanted to be in the band.

"Jesus!" said the drill sergeant. "Right, now all those who *think* they can play the drums, take a further pace forward. Go."

Oh no! There must have been a dozen of us. My dream of getting into the band was looking decidedly shaky. But with musicians in one truck and potential drummers in the other, we were off. My heart was in my mouth.

From the word go, my main aim had been to get into the band at square bashing camp. It wasn't just a dream, and failure was not an option. So I had set my stall out to succeed in this aim.

In the months before, despite working forty-eight hours a week and my many other social activities, I managed twenty-four hours' drum practice each week. I would perform a drum roll against the clock until the sticks fell out of my aching hands. I would listen to the top drummers and work till I could copy them. My *Drum Suite* LP was perfect for this. It featured four drummers taking it in turn to impress with their distinctive style. I tried to master the lot. I practised copying Shelly Manne's ability to play a roll without a discernible starting or end beat. I copied hi-hat patterns till I could do them in my sleep. When I wasn't practising, in my head I would sing every tune and solo. Even today, lying in bed, I can play many of those solos with my hands on my chest.

But now was the moment of truth as I trudged into the West Kirby band room with eleven other would-be drummers. Would I be good enough? First name called into the office – 4191154 AC (aircraftsman) Ball GT. My name gave me an alphabetical advantage. The first thing that hit me was the temperature. The room was roasting, and an iron stove was actually glowing red-hot at the top end. Outside, it was still dark and below freezing. I was in my best uniform plus great coat and hat. I did take my gloves off. In a few moments, I was worried about leaving a puddle of sweat at my feet.

A short Scottish bandmaster was seated at the desk. Standing nearby was a sergeant drum major and the smartest man in uniform I ever saw. Also, there was a grumpy-looking corporal. How did I know the bandmaster was a Scot?

"Ha, ye ever played a side dddrum, sonny?"

Oh God – what a question! What should I say? If I lied, it would almost certainly show. If I said no, then that might disqualify me before I had even touched a stick.

"No, sir, but I'm sure I'll be able to," I said.

And the reply came, "Jimmy, gee'm a dddrum!"

'Jimmy' attached a strap to an old-fashioned rope-tensioned marching drum. He pushed the leather thongs down to tighten the drum skin but didn't do it with any force. I took the drum and placed the long strap around my neck. The drum hung low in front of me and the three of them slowly began to grin broadly.

"Nay, laddy. You put one arum through the strap. Yer left arum."

Jimmy handed me a pair of sticks, more like sawn-off brush handles. I had a pair of military sticks from my bop-drumming mate, but they were balsa wood toys compared with these.

"Right, laddy. You OK? Right. Gee us a rrroll."

Trying to steady my nerves and stop visibly shaking, I adjusted the sticks in my hands and applied them to the drum. The drum disappeared around the back of my left leg and suddenly I was playing fresh air. I tried again. So far, no roll, but I was getting laughs.

"Oh Jesus, no. Jimmy – hold it for him, will ye?"

So Jimmy stood to my side and held the drum to stop it swinging away.

"Now, laddy – just calm down. Now – gee'us a roll!"

I took a deep breath as a bead of sweat ran down my nose. My hands were wet and clammy. I had practised playing every kind of roll for literally hours. I had to get this right.

I started with an open mamma dadda roll just like a beginner. The drum was horribly flabby, and I hated it. But the heavy sticks helped, and I concentrated on keeping the roll smooth. I found the edge of the drum head gave the best response. I steadied it down and then started to raise the volume. Shelly Manne used a press roll perhaps more successfully than any drummer I knew, and I started towards the very tight press that he achieved. Then, at last, I cranked it up to an almighty *zzzzzzzzip* and finished.

"Jesus Christ, that's the best f—ing roll I've heard in years," burst out of the wee Scots bandmaster. "My God. Can ye read music?"

I nodded. *Yes!*

"Oh my God, he can read? Jimmy, some drum music quick."

The three of them rummaged around until the bandmaster chose a half-sheet of music and popped it on the trestle table in front of me.

"Can ye read that, laddy?"

I said I could!

"Well, go on then, play it, lad!"

"Where?" I asked.

"On the table here. Go on – have a go!"

Suddenly, the sticks were going *rat tat-a-tat, rat-atatle-tatle-tat* at a fastish march or quickstep speed.

Then the bandmaster stopped me and said, "Aye, son, that's fine – fine. But it goes…" and he played: *rat- – tat – a – tat, rat – a – tatle – tatle – tat.* His face was covered in a very broad grin. I had played it perfectly, but at precisely double the required speed!

"Aye, yer in the band, lad. Have ye a drum kit? Where do ye live?"

To which I replied, "Bolton."

"Jesus, that's within forty miles. Laddy, yer going home for the weekend."

We were all wreathed in smiles, and I left the furnace of a room to cool down and make way for the other auditionees. But I didn't stop grinning for hours. In the eight weeks' square bashing, you only got one single weekend leave after week five. I was going home on the very first Friday!

We didn't have a phone at home and so when I arrived on Friday afternoon, my mother nearly fainted. She thought I had been thrown out of the RAF for some crime. The truth was worth a pub celebration, after which Dad spent the weekend making cases for the drums out of hardboard and canvas and a wooden box for the stands and sticks. Then it was back to West Kirby on the Sunday to begin as beautiful a two-month period as any in my entire life.

The first week alone was exhausting, getting the new musicians and drummer into presentable shape. But that was essential, as the band had a major gig at Liverpool stadium on the Saturday.

We slowly went through the whole musical pad. Towards the end of the week, our wee Scottish bandmaster was saying, "Aye, well, it'll need to be better than that on Saturday, but let's get on to the next one." Success was not a foregone conclusion.

Luckily, my snare drum was crisp and perfect for the band and my press rolls and rim shots could be heard even when the entire brass section was in full flow.

That Saturday, we arrived at the Liverpool stadium for 'the Combined Forces Boxing Championships'. We couldn't believe the size of the place. But never mind the boxing – I was going to play my first ever drumming gig to four thousand people!

With the tournament ring at centre, another boxing ring in a corner was our bandstand. I was stuck in the back corner and every new row of musicians would push me further back. Eventually, I was standing upright on my pedals. My snare drum was now practically vertical in front of me. I had never played it in that position before, and definitely not with four thousand people watching.

We had a quick warm up and broke for a cup of tea before the start of the show. When we came back, the place was jammed.

The wee Scots bandmaster looked around and said, "OK, lads, let's give 'em Hell. 'Oklahoma'!"

My heart practically leapt out of my chest as we fumbled for the music – 'Oklahoma', more than any other tune on our pad, is driven by the drummer. It starts with a solo snare drum roll rising in volume for four bars. He raised his baton – and brought it down pointing straight at me. I hit the snare drum and wound up the biggest roll I had ever managed.

Zz zz zz zz, zz zz zz zz, zz zz zz zz, zz zz zz zz, o o o o zip.

Ta tata, tata ta ta, tata tata ta. Dap a dap dap.

We were off at breakneck speed, and it was fantastic. My snare drum was rapping out the off-beat and filling in everywhere. What an opener! The rest of the night was a wonderful, beautiful blur.

I was a real drummer, driving a forty-piece band in front of four thousand people and all the practice had been worthwhile. This was an incredible moment in my life – and my nerve had held. Wonderful! The next day, we were back to the reality of square bashing.

QUITE WONDERFUL SQUARE BASHING?

Square bashing camp is all about knocking everyone into some kind of shape so that you could march, stand, walk and even run smartly, with or without a bulky 303 rifle. More than that, it forged you into a totally unselfish supporter of the team of mates who went through it with you.

At each session, the drill team would focus on marching or handling a rifle or working as a team. They would seek out the slow, the nervous or shaky and the cheeky and they would come down on them at any moment.

"Don't stand there looking like a bloody seductive blonde! If you don't swing that arm, laddy, I'll rip it off and beat you about the body with the soggy end!"

For the lads who couldn't easily change their idle ways, it was tough. But slowly everyone began to get the hang of it. Suddenly we were enjoying it and the hatred for the drill corporal changed to respect as he got us jumping through hoops. On the last evening of our eight weeks, we carried our drill corporal around the NAAFI bar on our shoulders and he cried to be losing us.

I do wish the kids of today could have the experience we had, not just for the discipline but because it was a wonderful rite of passage. You started out as someone totally inept and after eight weeks, you were disciplined, smart, energetic, fit, supportive of your mates in ways you had not felt possible and probably happier with yourself than at any time previously in your short life.

TO JAB OR NOT TO JAB?

One morning in an early week, new recruits were all marched off for injections and inoculations. We were released from band practice but couldn't find our group, so we pushed off to the NAAFI (it stands for Navy, Army and Air Force Institute, or 'never 'ave any fags in'). We figured, *Why have the jabs? If everyone around is immunised, then surely there would be no one to catch it from?* Good logic? Of course! Besides, you can't play a drum with a sore arm.

However, our little ruse created another problem two weeks later. We were told to get to sickbay again, this time to get our medical documents to certify that we had been jabbed. Oh? So the same three of us sauntered off and sheepishly put our names and numbers on blank cards.

The orderly stood there with his copious lists of names and his ink pads and rubber stamps.

He looked us up and confirmed that we were on the list and started stamping, as he said, "You [*bang*] f—in' band-flight berks [*bang*]. I'm stamping these [*bang*] f—in' cards and I [*bang*] don't even know [*bang*] if you've had the [*bang*] f—in' jabs in the [*bang*] first place. [*Bang bang.*] That's it, now f— off." And that was that.

Soon square bashing was over and after one last booze-up, we were off home before moving on to trade training. I was not to know that I would never play with a concert brass band again. I had loved every minute of that exhilarating and totally memorable experience.

That weekend, my mum was coming home on the bus, and she saw a lad in RAF uniform walking along the road, looking incredibly smart. As the bus passed, she turned and her jaw dropped open. It was me and she hadn't recognised me from behind because I appeared a good four inches taller than just a few weeks ago. I had clearly changed in many ways, and all for the better.

RADAR TRAINING

Soon I was on the train again and arriving in Calne in Wiltshire.

Just outside the station was the tiny town hall, flanked by two factory buildings over twice as high with great *HARRIS* signs on them. Even the town football team was called Calne and Harris United. Harris was a leading mass-production butchers and I was to take very kindly to Harris over the next six weeks.

Our transport whisked us a couple of miles to Compton Bassett to be taught how to be a radar operator. My memories are very skimpy, but I remember feeling, as the recruitment officer had warned, that I was a little overqualified. Along with a large Scots lad, we were getting around a hundred per cent in every test, though a few were finding it difficult.

But my lasting memory is of the food I consumed, thanks to Harris. It was staggering. The appetite of the group of eighteen-year-old lads was immense and towards the end of the course, I totted up what I ate in one single three-meal day. Besides bacon and eggs and chops and steak and chicken and liver, over just three meals, going back for more a couple of times, I devoured twenty-four pork sausages – in one day! I don't remember much about eating anything green. I definitely had enormous puddings. There were also plenty of potatoes in Wiltshire, because they have Devizes for Chippenham!

We all made easy work of the six-week course, with the Scots lad and I coming out level top. However, he was a National Service lad and I was a regular, and that was to make the difference. With our results came our postings. This was crunch time because I was hoping to get myself as far across the world as the RAF stretched – ideally Singapore or Hong Kong.

The results were announced. My whole course was going to Germany, except for one person. Which one? 4191154 now LAC (leading aircraftsman) Ball GT. I was going to Aberporth. Where the hell was Aberporth? Well, it was abroad, if you call Wales abroad.

RAF ABERPORTH

The Aberporth trip was memorable in that I was extremely drunk from the end-of-course party the night before. My mates had to dress me and get me and my kit on a bus at around 7am which delivered me to the station, after which I changed at

Bristol for Carmarthen, where a Land Rover picked me up for the trip to Aberporth. That took another two hours, as the driver stopped halfway and disappeared inside a house with a rather attractive housewife.

At Aberporth camp, now ten hours later, I was dumped with my kit outside a billet hut. Once inside, I looked at myself in the mirror. My God, what a mess! My mates had half-dressed me in that they had secured my collar and studs but forgotten my tie. Someone had kindly dabbed Duraglit on my coat buttons and cap badge. However, they had no time to clean it off, and so I had seven white blobs hiding the shiny gold metal. I was sick for the umpteenth time that day and collapsed on a bed to come round more than a full day later. Unknown mates cared for me and reported nothing.

It was only then I began to take notice of the place that was to be my blissful home for around ten months. There were just four billets, each under half full with no more than forty of us, all told. There were no officers on the camp and just one orderly sergeant who looked after the place. There were no police and, indeed, no security at all, as they had recently resurfaced the entrance to the camp, with the gate open. The two gate bottoms were now encased in four inches of tarmac.

Soon I was venturing the five miles to Cardigan on Fridays and Saturdays. Only around seven of us did this, as most National Service lads went home for the weekend. Now when a forces camp has anything up to two thousand personnel on site, the locals hate them, as they dominate all pubs and dance halls in the area. Cardigan was different! They were not used to smartly dressed lads in jackets and ties frequenting their pubs. So they welcomed us with open arms. More than that, they practically presented their daughters to us. Very soon, we found girlfriends, though I assure you, in those days, heavy snogging was almost always all that went on.

However, the lure was too much for some and four of our small gang were to marry and spend the rest of their lives in the Cardigan area. That included my mate Mick from Dudley, who had a motorbike. I introduced him to a local girl and trips home ceased and he was always available to run me the five miles into Cardigan.

The road was straight and downhill all the way, and I would take the pillion position, with no protection other than to turn my smart jacket back to front. Mick told me that the bike could do one hundred miles per hour, but I didn't believe him. So one night, on the road into Cardigan, he shouted over his shoulder, "John – look, a ton."

I stood on my pedals and craned my neck over his shoulder to see the quivering dial hover around and then over the one hundred mark. No, I did not have crash helmet.

WORKING WITH THE 584S

Every morning we were bused a couple of miles to the Royal Aircraft Establishment, Aberporth. That did have police and was a very secure place indeed. In 1957, this is where they tested ground-to-air and air-to-air guided missiles and tracked them on radar screens, which was the job they had sent for me to do!

On a map, Cardigan Bay is like a backward letter 'C' with RAE Aberporth on a bump of land at the most southerly point, facing north. Missiles are fired directly north into Cardigan Bay and shipping maps show a fan shape, indicating the 'no-go area' range.

In our day, no shipping ever ventured into these waters, except for Russian trawlers, with large aerials and radio equipment, who decided this was the only place in European waters to catch fish. How could they possibly know what we were doing? Psychic, I suppose.

Being a radar operator, I was looking forward to seeing our modern radar gear. What I got was quite unbelievable. On the top edge of a high cliff there were three caravans. One was very modern, with a wide aerial spinning at three revs every four seconds, sweeping the area to give a clear picture of everything and anything in its sight to the north. The other two caravans were old Second World War US Anti-Aircraft Radars, called 584s. They were designed to not only detect German bombers but also to lock onto them so that anti-aircraft guns could locate them, aim and fire. Frankly, they didn't work very well and arrived too late, as German bombing had then almost ceased.

But twelve years later, an English technician realised he could quadruple the range and make them far more efficient. I had to learn not only how to operate them, but how to detect what, if anything, was making it not work. This was not going to be easy. There was a floor-to-ceiling bank of electrical boxes with dozens of dials and meters, showing how everything worked – if, that is, it was working. I counted 127 switches! On the top was a large, heavy, perforated radar dish about six foot in diameter.

In my radar operator training, I had been told how to read a radar screen and identify what was an aircraft and not a flock of birds or waves at sea. I was taught to relate what I saw to other people, like fighter pilots, to help them attack aircraft that weren't our friends.

I had never been taught how to 'operate' radar equipment, but this is what I had to do here. It was both utterly bonkers and wonderful – I was handling a computer game, before computer games had been invented, and I was using real aircraft. With one control, you could tilt the aerial to the required angle and with another scan left and right, trying to spot the plane. A circular radar trace had a jagged line of needle-shaped 'noise', as the radar beam cut through the atmosphere. When it spotted an aircraft, this trace developed a bump, like a worm going over an invisible stone, which told you the distance to the plane. Now by bringing two cursor lines over the bump and slightly adjusting a four-inch diameter wheel in each hand, with skill, you could hold the bump within the cursor lines and lock on. It was like something out of Dan Dare and the *Eagle* comic.

If the aircraft was flying at an angle to your aerial, both direction and range were always changing, as well as the elevation, as the aircraft flew nearer or further away. But holding the aircraft was possible – if you were good at the game. If a plane flew overhead, you had no chance of holding it, as the aerial spun around violently, and you lost your plane and had to start searching to find it again.

Good game, good game, as Brucie would have said, and it was. We especially loved beating the other 584. It was one long, game-playing holiday only ruined by the weather. As all firings had to be recorded on film using long-range film cameras, we didn't actually work if it was cloudy.

TWO RAF DISASTERS

After about six months on 584s, I was transferred to the main control room to join my motorcycle mate, Mick Williams, who kept various plotting machines in working order.

We had a very flashy modern horizontal plotter, which would 'not bloody well work'. One magical day, Mick was told to fix it by lunchtime, as the Duke of Edinburgh was coming that afternoon. So, Mick was seated on the floor with his hands inside the machine when he touched something he shouldn't have, and the shock skidded him, in a sitting position, five yards across the room and into a wall.

Mick said, "Oops! It shouldn't do that."

We had a flight lieutenant with bad nerves who smoked holding the cigarette so close to his mouth, that every drag produced an *fffft* intake of breath. So, Flt Lt Fffft rushed in, trying to tidy up. He grabbed Mick's soldering iron by the very hot end. He was to spend the rest of the day hiding his bandaged hand.

We had a very reliable vertical plotter which would plot the course of planes on its screen perfectly, fed by information from our radar scanners. So we were ready. However, the duke had another visit to make first.

This was National Geophysical Year 1957 and as the UK's contribution, Aberporth had built the UK's first ever intercontinental ballistic missile launcher and today was the very first test day. A suitable ICBM missile had been delivered, so the duke and a whole bevy of top brass came down to see the jolly old thing go bang, what?

The launcher was a sort of tube of metal rings sticking up in the air. The very bottom quarter of the thing was split in two, and half hinged up so the missile could be inserted. Then you would close it, light the blue touchpaper and retire. So the duke and entourage arrived and shortly after them, the missile arrived on a low loader. The bottom gate was hoisted, and the low loader was brought in close, until someone shouted, "Stop!"

A question was asked if the gate would open wider and the answer was, "No!"

The next question asked was, why was the missile on a five-foot-high low loader?

Apparently this was the lowest low loader. Next question was, "Could we lift the missile off the low loader manually and insert it up the tube?"

The answer was that no one had any idea whether dropping the missile would damage the missile or, indeed, damage Wales?

The whole thing was postponed. But all was not lost, because now it was our turn.

With the central control room totally in control, we were going to fire a missile at a drone aircraft so that the duke and party could see on the vertical plotter exactly how a missile is fired and how it misses the target but gets near enough to be called a 'hit'.

Drone aircraft are very expensive and not designed to be knocked out of the sky by test missiles being fired at them – we always had to aim to miss. It's quite logical.

The VIPs arrived, and the duke shook hands, wondering why Flt Lt Fffft didn't appear to have a right hand. Our rather rotund wing commander explained that we take control of the drone and fly it remotely from a small control desk. I was by the desk on headphones to Llanbedr Airfield who provided the drone. They were very excited and had apparently worked every hour God sent for two weeks to get this drone ready for today!

On the very reliable vertical plotter, Wing Commander Cuddles had drawn a racetrack which ended in the middle of the screen and the middle of Cardigan Bay. This is where the drone had to be when we fired a missile at it. This is not to say that we couldn't hit targets at different points or at different ranges! We always aimed to hit – sorry, miss – the target at this particular spot, so that all our observers could film the hit – sorry, miss – for close analysis later.

Cuddles marked off five one-minute intervals from the central zero point, back along the track to minus five. He took control of the drone aircraft from me, while I remained on the headset to keep Llanbedr informed.

With a deft twiddle from Cuddles, the plotter began drawing a line, showing the drone as it reached the five-minute mark, and Cuddles said, "Five minutes to firing. Five minutes to firing." Now the whole site, drone team, launch team, missile team, radar team, camera team, management team and VIP team synchronised their clocks and we were on countdown. However, after just thirty seconds, the drone had reached the minus four-minute mark. That wasn't right. The duke wanted to know why that was, but nobody told him, because nobody was listening. Cuddles, now a reddish colour, said, both too early and too late, as the plane had passed the appointed mark, "Er, um – four minutes to firing. Four minutes."

The duke wasn't convinced by this, and neither was anyone else, because according to the vertical plotter, the drone was fast approaching Dublin. It had been going just one minute since the five-minute time but had gone far enough to reach the three-minute mark had it turned, but it hadn't turned because Cuddles hadn't turned it.

Cuddles snapped into action. "Abort. Abort," he said and turned the drone around.

The duke was crestfallen.

"Don't worry, sir, we'll go around and start again," said Cuddles. But the same thing happened all over again and after another abort and another, with the gallant duke on his knees with his fingers crossed, which got a laugh from both top brass and press, Cuddles admitted defeat and asked Llanbedr to take the uncontrollable drone home.

You could have cut the atmosphere with my coffee spoon, as the duke and entourage slunk out. As soon as they had gone, I was free to talk to Llanbedr in anything other than a whisper and I told them we hadn't been able to control the drone at all.

"But we've worked around the clock for two weeks to get it right and it was working perfectly. It's not easy, perfecting a wireless-controlled jet, you know."

"Jet?" I asked.

"Yes, of course – it's the UK's first ever jet drone."

"But nobody has told anyone here that you were sending a jet?" I said and called to our officers. But it was all too late.

In the post-mortems that followed, the question was asked time and again: why had they been working on a jet drone without ever telling anyone else?

I understood perfectly. It's an RAF boffin thing! Boffins are brilliant at solving problems but often quite lax at communicating their ideas to others. The whole day had been a disaster through people neglecting to talk to or listen to anyone else.

In 2010, the duke and I were both receiving honorary degrees from the Institute of Teaching.

When introduced, I said, "We've met before, sir." He asked when and I said, "1957."

He replied, "Good God. I won't remember that!"

But when I mentioned Aberporth, he said, "Oh no, the rocket launcher where they couldn't get the bloody rocket in?"

ABERPORTH AT EASE

My days at Aberporth were the first time I had mixed with really clever people, and I thought they were wonderful. They never embarrassed me by noting my lack of knowledge and were always ready to explain. More than that, they loved my desire and aptitude to learn.

The Aberporth social scene centred around the Ship Inn down by the key, where we raced woodlice for money. Friday night culminated in the village hall hop, where the local talent was waiting for us. Of this period, I have one truly memorable story to tell, and it has nothing at all to do with sex. It is all about the fateful night when, single-handedly, "I attacked RAF Aberporth!"

This particular night, I hit the booze very heavily. I did walk a local girl home, but she said, "Ta!" and slammed the door, leaving me to stagger the mile or so back to camp.

At the top of the hill, I looked back to see the moonlit sea behind me – it was a beautiful view. Walking on, I could soon see the camp and disused aerodrome to my left across a valley, with a dozen or so lights and buildings silhouetted against the sky on a high flat plain. It then occurred to me that a Russian SAS group could pop into Aberporth harbour at night, leg it up this road and across the fields and capture the camp and everyone in it. It would be a doddle. The road wound another half a mile past the camp, then looped back half a mile to the ever-open gate – but not tonight. Tonight, suddenly I was a Russian SAS commando, driven not by a love of communism but by Ship Inn alcohol.

In one bound, or perhaps three, I was over a five-barred gate and into a field, heading straight for the camp. I began running down the hill with my air Sten gun in my hands, determined to emerge up the hill on the other side and take the camp by storm. I was also wearing a smart pale-green suit with yellow tie and shiny brown leather shoes of which I was very proud.

I was running now at full tilt when suddenly something happened that I couldn't understand. I was flying through the air and turning head over heels. I landed on my back with a mighty thump on thankfully soft turf. Then all hell broke loose. There was wild frantic mooing all around me and I was in the middle of a stampede. Not being able to see anything below the horizon, I had run full tilt into a sleeping cow, which had taken me off at the knees. I had performed a near-perfect forward-flying somersault but got no appreciation at all from the lowing herd, legging it hastily o'er the lea.

So that was one obstacle out of the way. I was up again and quickly reached the bottom of the field. It was a bit marshy as any rain slowly percolated down to a high bank. Over the bank was a narrow farm track with another bank on the camp perimeter. On top of this bank was a two-strand barbed-wire fence – no problem for a highly trained Russian commando. I placed one hand on a post and a foot on the top wire. As I raised my left foot, my right foot on the wire started to perform a very fast pendulum movement like a circus slack-rope walker, only without the control. Sensibly, I dropped my left foot back to the ground. I steadied myself and tried again only to achieve an even faster pendulum wobble. In deliberating whether to come back or continue over, the decision was made for me and over I went.

By now, a real commando would have been cursing the people who did the pre-operation recce for not telling him that on the field side, the bank was eight foot high.

I could have hurt myself, but luckily a huge puddle broke my fall. Well, now at least I was a fully camouflaged commando. *Splosh splosh*, out of the mud and up the field I raced. Surprise was the order of the day. Get them before they even have time to get out of bed. Just a hundred yards to run! What could I do in the meantime? *Rattatat tat* – my air Sten gun strafed the water tower. I might fail to take the camp, but at least I could stop their toilets flushing.

At last I was in the camp and amongst the billet huts. A few imaginary hand grenades lobbed here and there, and the operation was over. I paused and caught my breath at my billet door. Quietly and soberly, almost, I found my bed, got out of suit and shoes and was asleep in seconds.

The next morning, I was awakened by, "What the bloody hell happened to you last night? Look at this lot."

Through bleary eyes, from behind a terrible headache, I looked! There on my bedside mat was a pair of Lovett green suit trousers, only, from the knee down, they were standing stiffly upright as though they still had legs in them. They were completely caked in dry mud and next to them were two great rugby balls of mud which I later found had shoes in them.

A CHRISTMAS PARTY

The climax of our Aberporth socialising with the opposite sex occurred on 18th December 1957 when we held a Christmas party. Instead of the usual handful that actually mixed with the local talent, that night the whole forty of us would be on hand.

The sizeable dining room was cleared and decorated. Rifle racks on a plinth, with an authentic footrest about 15cm high, made an excellent bar. Amazingly, the officers' booze store was handed over to us. The Ship Inn provided beer and other stock. The kitchen staff worked wonders with the food and coloured lights were strung all over the place.

The forty lads gathered for a pre-party drink, feeling amazingly nervous. What would our guests think of the lads who normally scooted home to mums or wives every weekend? What would the lads think of the girls that we were so proud to know? What if nobody turned up? In fact, who was turning up? The start was set for 8pm but at 7.55pm, no one had arrived.

We looked outside. Nothing. But outside the gate, a car and a couple of coaches and more cars and more! Then, in they came, gushing in, in a torrent, led by the ones we all knew best. Too nervous to be first, the girls had parked and waited for the clock to reach eight. But now they were here, looking fabulous in their best party gear, all two hundred of them.

Cardigan had a population of around 3500, but we had pulled every eligible girl in the county and a good few non-eligible ones who wouldn't miss this for anything. Every nurse, shop assistant and secretary was here, and we were the hosts, though outnumbered by five to one. Within ten minutes, one girl collapsed after downing several drinks in one. Was this to be the start of something? Well, no, as that was the only drink problem we had all night. The problem lay in being perfect hosts.

The regular socialisers realised we each had a pretty permanent girlfriend, but that wouldn't work tonight. Quickly we explained that, as hosts, we were duty-bound to put ourselves about a bit. So with their blessing, we did. As the hours passed and after most of us had disappeared outside several times for a snog, we made sure that not one single girl had been left out – and frankly, a few required another quick drink and a bit of courage. But we could happily say that we never left one single girl as a wallflower.

That night, I introduced Motorcycle Mick to a small effervescent blonde. From that moment, he was to spend the rest of his life in Cardigan.

A VERY CLOSE THING

There is just one other event that happened while I was at Aberporth. It's worth telling, as this one could well have ruined my life for ever. One Saturday bright and early, four of us shot off on a coach for Cardiff where Wales were playing England at football.

After the match and a pub crawl, we saw a cocktail bar sign outside a typical narrow city pub. At the end of the corridor down the side, we could hear loud jazzy music. On entering, we saw that the room was full of white girls and West Indian lads. This was no problem to us, and especially not to me, because over by the fireplace was a young Paul Anka lookalike beating the hell out of the bongos.

I grabbed a coal scuttle, turned it upside down, and we were drumming up a storm as we grinned at each other. I noticed a lad who was totally humourless. He suddenly rushed out! Then, while we were still drumming madly, all the black lads followed, leaving the girls, my three mates by the bar and the two of us.

"You'd better go, man – it looks like trouble," said Mr Bongos, still smiling broadly.

My three mates were already gone. I didn't feel threatened, but as I opened the door, down the long corridor, I saw my six foot three mate being kicked up the arse. He was out the front door like a whippet.

Two black lads were bringing the humourless lad back between them and were wedging the whole corridor. I was wearing a smart light overcoat, as we did in those days, with my hands in the pockets. As we got close, I smiled and backed to the wall to let them pass.

From behind me, a hand holding a broken bottle stopped two inches below my nose! He had come out of one of the side bars.

Without flinching, I said, "I'm causing no trouble!" and they let me pass. I didn't get the kick up the arse I had expected, and I walked out onto the street. Fifty yards down the street, I saw three heads peeping out of a shop doorway. At that moment, it was as if someone had thrown a full bucket of water straight into my face. Sweat just gushed out of me in every direction as the true situation hit me.

For months I had nightmares and moments where I wondered, why had I stayed so calm? It is clear that had I raised my hand even to knock the bottle away, I would have been too late, and my life might well have been scrambled for ever.

OVERSEAS AT LAST?

The RAF didn't keep you in one place too long, as there were always people coming and going. I was told a posting was due and I asked for somewhere overseas. I got my wish. They posted me to Northern Ireland.

Bishop's Court in Northern Ireland was a largish camp which won major prizes for the quality of its food, accommodation and facilities – and I hated it. But having loved Aberporth so much, I had taken no leave and was now told, "Take your leave or lose it!" So, on day two, I was off for two weeks' holiday, one spent at home and the other back at Aberporth.

When I got back to Northern Ireland, I was told I did now have an overseas posting, but not where. However, I must take two weeks' compulsory embarkation leave. So off I went again.

Next time I got back, I actually did do some work; in fact, in the eight weeks in total, I worked two day shifts and one night shift – but that was quite an experience.

The radar installation was some twenty miles south of Belfast on a headland looking out over the Irish Sea. Instead of one radar system, Killard had six, all on trial to find the best. In 1958, the IRA were a threat, although nothing like what was to come. Radar stations serve civilian air traffic needs as well as military aircraft so were not likely targets. But radar equipment was expensive and needed protecting.

Arriving for the sixteen-hour night shift, you drew a number which told you where you would be at any time. It might be radar watching or guarding the installations. I drew a short straw in that I was to guard the main gate from 2am till 4am.

On arrival at the main gate, the previous guard handed me the greatcoat, which might have been made of asbestos and which stank of sweat. I was also given 'the Gun'! This was a Sten gun, which was not really accurate even at twenty-five yards. In the pocket of the coat were two magazines, each only half full of bullets. A spring inside pushed the bullets up, so the next one to be fired was in position. But these had been dropped so many times, the jaws of the magazine had been damaged, and the bullets were held in with Sellotape!

Being on guard at night was a daunting experience, with the whole site in darkness except for all the major installations, including the main gate, which was floodlit. This didn't seem to make sense, as an IRA sharpshooter could look down on the camp from the fields around and, in the darkness, target the main gate, lit up like Blackpool Pleasure Beach, and me!

There was a guard hut, to shelter in, with a door and a slit window looking away from the site. But mostly I stood under the floodlight, a short drive from the Irish border at two in the morning, wondering whether the two-hour session would pass without incident. It wouldn't!

At around 3.30am, with dawn not far away, I was just beginning to make out the horizon line of the fields and suddenly there it was. I don't know what, but something moved on the top of the right-hand horizon. I nonchalantly walked around and into the gatehouse. Keeping well away from the window gap, I peered out. I then looked in other directions for a few seconds and then brought my gaze back to the direction of the movement. There was definitely movement.

I couldn't make out a shape, but something had come to the top of the hill where it could see the camp and me. Soon my eyes were aching through trying to see 'it' from my floodlit position. Then, in that first glimmer of dawn, I saw what 'it' was.

The cow and its mates had come over the hill to munch grass near the fence and the light. I had survived, but my nerves hadn't.

OH WHAT A NIGHT?

The only other escapade I had on the Northern Ireland trip was to leave strong memories that I have carried with me ever since. A bus took us up to Belfast, set to bring us back at 1am. We found a dance which was an eye-opener because already the Irish were producing brilliant show bands, while they were still unheard of in the UK.

As the dance finished around twelve, I asked to walk a very nice but quiet girl home. Her place was, I realise today, in Catholic West Belfast. When we arrived, she invited me in. This seemed like a good omen, but inside, I saw the tiny altar with candles, Virgin Mary and Jesus statuettes. My ardour got softer and in just a few minutes I was back on the street.

I arrived back at the bus station to see the back of my bus exiting at the other end. I was in Belfast for the night. I had around £16 in my wallet, so I was OK. I just needed a small hotel. Then there was perhaps the largest Sten-gun-carrying police officer I had ever seen.

"I think I need a bed for the night," I said, to which he said, "Right, come wit' me!" And I went wit' him. I must have tried to start a conversation, but all I got back was grunts as we passed dark satanic warehouses. Then, in the distance, we saw and heard a gate open and a fella push his bike out, shout 'goodnight' and cycle off in the opposite direction. The gate slammed and we heard a lock turning, the rattle of chains, bolts being thrown and a good deal of clanking to be followed by boots clattering away from the gate.

My companion never said a word till we reached the gates. He then swept back his cape and rapped on the door with his gun and shouted, "Hello. It's me!"

This didn't seem to me to be the most secure password imaginable, but it worked, because we heard the footsteps coming back and the unlocking rigmarole now in reverse. The small door opened, and I stepped into a yard. The big fella was suddenly behind me, but how he got through the gate without a lot of squeezing and levering, I'll never know.

I followed him across the yard and into a smoke-filled room where five coppers, all bigger than my fella, slouched over the furniture in a crazy maze of arms and legs.

"Got one here!" he said and threw his thumb over his shoulder at me.

They all looked at me with expressions that seemed to say they thought there was no one actually there at all.

My fella removed an old phone earpiece from a hook – it was straight out of a Sam Spade movie.

He dragged the dial around about four times and shouted into the mouthpiece, "Hello. Got one for you! Right! Cheers!" and put the phone back on the hook. He pushed past me without a word, and I followed him out. Five heads moved to look after us. By now, the other fella had finished locking the gate, only to see us coming. He sighed and turned to start all over again, as though doing sound effects for *The Goon Show*.

Once more we passed out into the damp and gloomy world and walked off the way we had come. Behind us, the rattle of bolts and chains played out its part. As we rounded the corner, a policeman on a bike passed us heading the other way, and I smiled, knowing it would all start up again very soon. My fella said nothing.

We arrived at a large building with a huge arched entrance and a dozen steps going up into it. Halfway up the steps, there was a sliding metal mesh gate. A fella appeared and unlocked the gate. I passed through and said, "Thanks," but my copper was already walking away. Now, I am usually a very chatty person and can engage anyone in conversation about any subject. But chat is a two-way thing and that copper made no indication at any time that he ever wanted to hear a word from me, ever. But I do wish we had chatted. For as we walked in, I was horrified to find I was in some kind of religious institution. There were stained-glass bible scenes everywhere.

The chap spoke. "It's two shillings a night, two and six for a cubitle."

"I'm sorry?" I said. "What's a cubitle?"

"It's yer own room; yer bed is in its own cubitle!"

Aha! I said I'd have a cubitle and gave him a half crown

or 12.5p in today's money. I was given a cup of dreadful tea as it slowly dawned on me where I was. I had £16 in my pocket, which would have secured a very nice hotel room, and my very smart suit suggested I had some pride. But thanks to the silent sleuth, I was now in a Salvation Army Hostel for the homeless drunks and down-and-outs of Belfast.

At the top of a winding stone staircase, we entered a large hall with perhaps fifty fellas sleeping on cots in three long rows. The smell was worse than anything I have ever experienced. There were enough grunts, farts, snores and coughing to waken the dead. In fact, those that made no sound might well have been dead, because surely no one could sleep through the racket? In the gloom, I could see smoke rising from some sleepless faces. I had never smoked, but I fancied one then – anything to combat the smell.

To the left was a line of 'cubitles', and I was shown to one of them. Thank God for my own room, except that the cubical was just like a toilet cubical, with walls ending six inches above the floor and rising to six foot six inches only. This was no barrier to the smell, but it did have its own window. After locking the door, undressing and getting into bed, I realised that there was only one chance of breathing comfortably. So I switched the pillow to the other end, opened the window a foot or so and, on a terribly cold night, slept with a blanket round my head, just six inches from the great outdoors.

The first light woke me, and I couldn't wait to get up and dressed. I stepped out of the cubical and shuffled along the hall and down the stairs to the tuneful accompaniment of the Belfast Coughing Old Farts Chorus. I refused another cup of tea, to which I was told I was entitled, while he unlocked the gate. But I was out like a rabbit, down the steps and off back towards the city. The first clock I saw told me it was ten past four in the morning – I had managed to stay in there for about two hours.

I have never spent such a terrible night. But it was not the last time I would be in a Salvation Army hostel and just four years later I was to be grateful for the experience.

After a few days I was rid of Northern Ireland, which I had liked, and RAF Bishops Court, which I hated. However, Northern Ireland was to feature quite a lot in my future life. But I was now off to serve Her Majesty in the fourth country in eighteen short months and at last abroad. I was off to Germany.

CHAPTER 5

A GERMAN EXPERIENCE

GO EAST, YOUNG MAN!

Everyone knows that you go south-east to get to Germany, except that you don't necessarily. I was headed for Jever, in Friesland, on the same latitude as Sheffield and Liverpool. It is a beautiful small market town famous for pilsner beer and just a few miles from the sea.

The Jever camp was built for Hitler's Luftwaffe in 1936, when Britain didn't even see Hitler as a threat. It had wonderful buildings, with spacious lawns and trees, and looked more like a US Ivy League university. Our three-storey home, Block 40, was in the shape of a large 'H' with three majestic, stepped entrances and stone corridors with beautiful quarry tiles reaching halfway up the walls. The rooms had gorgeous wood-block floors which would polish to an amazing shine. Despite the aircraft being one third of a mile away, we could hear nothing, as the double-glazed windows had a nine-inch sound-barrier gap.

My drums arrived but the flight lieutenant running the band was an average drummer, who still cornered the officers' mess with his small group. The Jade Basin Five Plus One, named after the local Jade Basin estuary, were a great trad group with no drumming opportunity there.

But I soon met 'Jock', a great Scots pianist, and Dave Cobbold, a base player. Our trio cornered the live music market in the large sergeants' mess, playing every Saturday night for a few quid plus overtime when the hat was passed around for us. Then we would get locked into the bar with their wives and daughters. Female company was scarce on a camp with two thousand blokes.

Soon we were also playing the married quarters in Oldenburg some ten miles away. We built up a repertoire of novelty numbers – my speciality being 'I'm Married to a Striptease Dancer'!

I found the amateur dramatics group and was immediately writing sketches for a new review. Thinking back, it amazes me that I had the confidence to be writing and performing so very early. The sketches went well, but I don't think there was anything worth repeating.

The Block 40 dramatics gang invited me on a night out in Bremerhaven. Now, British Forces were always sold cigarettes. A packet of fags cost a shilling, or 5p, and top-range fags like Sobranie, Passing Clouds and Player's No. 3 were 1/3d, or just over 6p. This had started as a gesture to the troops during World War One and the cigarette manufacturers were overjoyed, creating thousands of addicts to keep their business thriving into the future. You were given fag coupons for twenty cigarettes a day. Now, I had never even taken a single drag of a fag all through my school and teen years. It just didn't interest me at all. As J. B. Priestley said, "If God had intended men to smoke, he'd have put chimneys in their heads." But for this first special night out with the drama group, I thought I'd be sociable. So I lashed out 10p and brought forty fags so that I could at least 'crash the ash' as my turn came.

So when we met in the NAAFI bar, out came my fags and the cry, "No, look, have one of mine." My generosity was welcomed, but they insisted, surely I would have one myself? So, on this occasion, I obliged and lit up.

We got back in taxis at around 4am and realised that no one had any fags left. Having never smoked in my life, I had smoked forty cigarettes, as well as two cigars in one evening. The next morning, I could not speak at all and that lasted about a week. But I could smoke, which seemed to sooth my throat, and my thirty-a-day habit was established for the next ten years.

ON THE JOB

Before joining the RAF, my workmates had recommended, "Volunteer for everything!" And they had not been wrong. On arrival in Germany, I saw they wanted volunteers to spend a few weeks working with German civvies at Hanover Air Traffic Control. I was off for a fabulous two months. Just thirteen years since the war ended, Hanover had been rebuilt faster than any UK city. It was modern, vibrant and exciting but made me wonder why the losing side had been cared for far better than the UK.

While in Hanover, I met German activists trying to get East Germans out to the West. They showed me Russian educational material including a German-English language book, which was hysterical. The English was excellent and much better than my *Deutsches Leben* textbook in Bolton. They used 'hadn't' and 'haven't' and spoken English right from the start.

However, the book was complete, out-of-date propaganda. Everything in Britain was rationed, and of terrible quality. You had to queue for hours and almost everyone was on strike. The cinemas were so smoky you couldn't see the screen or hear the sound for people coughing. Holidays were just one day a year at the seaside in the rain. Gardens were allotments, essential as fruit and vegetables were too expensive for working-class people to buy. It made me feel quite homesick.

At Air Traffic Control Hanover, I stood behind the controllers as they instructed civil pilots of their desired height, direction and speed, and the exact time they would be at a certain point. I relayed this information to my home station so that our lads could identify every civil aircraft on the screen and where it was going to or coming from.

So, when I got back to Jever and our secret radar station, I was given the job of forming one of three teams who would identify every aircraft on the screen. To be honest, when I arrived it was a little hit and miss, but with a few other volunteers, we began to improve the system enormously.

We had the job of overseeing the northern Hamburg-to-Berlin corridor. We would also watch aircraft movements beyond the Iron Curtain, in East Germany. It slowly dawned on me that this was the Cold War and we were there to watch the Russians. Should World War Three begin, we would be on the front line.

So, we had the most important job there was! As a result, when we were finally demobbed, at least three of my colleagues went straight into air traffic control and one ended up in charge of Heathrow Tower.

WORKING WITH HEROES

Our officers were great blokes and many of them were heroes. Ginger Lacey, the British ace with the most World War Two scalps, played out the last of his RAF days with us, and there were many more. In the quiet hours, we would often get them to tell us tales of their exploits. Some would be happy to talk, but most would never revisit those times – they had probably lost too many mates to ever feel comfortable about it.

Occasionally we would have an exercise involving UK and NATO air forces. Once, in the middle of a huge exercise, everyone was enjoying themselves so much that the powers that be declared the game would go on for another sixteen hours. I was hit with a terrible feeling of dread. If I couldn't get out of our underground concrete rabbit warren for another sixteen hours, I was going to have to go more than twenty-four hours without a beer. This would be a terrible first!

In two and a half years, I had never gone a single day without a drink. Our duty officer saw the seriousness of the situation but could do nothing about it.

"Yes, you can, sir," I cried, "let me have the key to sick quarters."

"What do you expect to find in sick quarters?" our controller asked. "There is no brandy in there."

To which I replied, "No, sir, surgical spirit! With a lot of orange juice!"

Sadly, there was no alcohol of any kind, and I had to admit defeat. I made sure it didn't happen again.

WORKING THE SYSTEM

As our identification teams were so important, we were given extra bods to cover people being on leave. One of the lads we recruited made everything work out beautifully. He was a gentle giant of a lad and a farmer's son from the deepest West Country. As a result, dawn and he were bosom buddies – they always arose together to greet each new day, unlike me. So, once he was on our team, every morning he would be first at breakfast and dine well, after which he would pick up a mug of tea and pop over to my room and draw me towards a new day with a gentle nudge and kindly word. He would check that I had feet on the floor, as anything short of that and I would probably curl up and be oblivious again before he had closed the door behind him. Once I was definitely 'up', he would head back to the cookhouse. I would wash, straighten my bed, and don pants, shirt, trousers, socks and boots. I would then grip in my hand, wallet, collar studs, tie, beret, current book or project, and jacket. I would peak out of my first-floor window and, as the four buses started to pull out, stroll down the stairs and out to the open back door of the last bus. I would climb in, definitely the last man, and instantly off we would go.

Ensconced in the back-corner seat, I would then lay into a huge bacon or sausage and egg sandwich provided by my mate, along with another cup of tea. After that, I would finish dressing, including shoelace tying, and be ready as we arrived at Brockzetel to hit the ground running and work arguably as hard as any other person on site. Between us, our little group carved out a reputation for reliability second to none.

IT'S PANTO TIME

Eventually, our highly successful teams had so many extra bods we could take half our working time off if that was required, and for me it soon was.

The amateur dramatics team decided they would do a pantomime. Someone sent for French's basic *Jack and the Beanstalk* panto script as a template for our production. I immediately saw it differently. That panto required twenty-seven small scenes, but we did not have a well-equipped theatre; we had a cinema with great seating but terrible stage equipment. There were no pulley systems, and the curtains took twelve seconds to open or close. So, any scenery changes would involve hauling ropes over wooden beams. On this account, I explained that their plan would not work.

I waited for a call to the next meeting and, after two weeks, went round to them to find out what was happening. By now, four of them were halfway through a script, even though it clearly wouldn't work. It was a terrible affront to me, and I stormed out.

That night, as my six roommates settled down to sleep, I propped myself up in bed with a pad and a German Biro with a tiny lamp which shed a small pool of light on the page so I could write, while hindering no one. By the time I at last fell asleep, I had written the first act of my five-act pantomime – *Aladdin and the Genie with the Gamp* (a black umbrella) – in longhand, including a joke on virtually every line. I had done this in a temper. Perhaps it was a good idea to annoy me?

To cut down scene changes, I decided we could make do with just five scenes. 1. Pekin Street, 2. Cave, 3. Palace. Then, in the second half, 4. Street Scene and 5. Palace again.

The script needed to be finished within another ten days, and it was. I don't think I breathed a word about it to a soul. I lodged it with the sergeant who ran the amateur dramatics club late on the Friday deadline and waited for the meeting on Monday.

That Monday evening, the other crew breezed in, and some twenty people sat down. The sergeant announced that he had not one but two pantomime scripts and the whole room buzzed with surprise. Having studied them over the weekend, he saw that one was a good effort but not practical with something like twenty-seven different scenes. On the other hand, he had laughed out loud at the other complete script and saw how it would work; it included suggested castings and scenic directions, a chorus in which every character got a line or two, and a children's dancing chorus for the local school to get involved with.

"I think this is the one we should undoubtedly go with!" he said.

I felt, at the same time, terrible, devious and euphoric. This was so important to me and not some youthful jape. Moments after the sergeant's announcement, the other crew walked out. However, there was ample talent from those who stayed. We now had six weeks of production, and this is when I took the time off work. Amazingly, we hardly altered a single word of the first two scenes.

I was lead comic as the Genie with the gamp, and Aladdin, the principal boy, was the station commander's wife. Don't say 'of course' – she was both good and right for the part and fun to work half-undressed with, her in her tights and leotard and me in my pantaloons, bare chest and too small waistcoat.

The gamp, or umbrella prop, was my comic invention. Blackouts and flashes were difficult to synchronise. The flashes came from a slightly opened trapdoor centre stage. So I chose an athletic entrance. On the cue and blackout, I ran full tilt from the wings and took a flying forward somersault through a cloud of smoke. The flash might catch me somewhere in mid-air or even upside down. I slammed onto my back, which got a laugh and an 'ouch' from both cast and audience as the lights came up.

Where did I learn stunt work? I taught myself! As a thirteen-year-old, I had devoured the wonderful *Eagle* comic which had a strip on judo. The first issue taught 'how to break your fall'! As you land, you slam an arm or hand down to reduce the impact to the rest of your body. It was the only judo I ever learnt, but at Jever I expanded my stunt skills. I found I could fall backwards like a beanpole onto a stone floor or do a forward-role-dive onto my back as in the panto. I tried falling down a stone staircase and was amazed to find it didn't hurt once I learnt to relax, roll on one shoulder and tuck my head in to miss the stone steps.

By now, I was thinking 'comedy' almost all the time. Seeing Jerry Lewis at the cinema, I would impersonate him for laughs, but it wasn't me or what I wanted to be. As for the panto script, in all honesty it must have been pretty unsophisticated, but the show worked and entertained both families and 'the lads'. I had managed to be clean and funny at the same time for a forces audience, many of whom acknowledged the fact. Everyone in the show was happy with the material they had been given and, thinking of much later experiences, I don't remember professional pantomimes achieving that very often.

From now on, the idea of writing was always with me. I would even try to turn dreams into movie scripts, which would flounder after a while, as I was just too young and inexperienced to create characters and plots that would match the professional material that inspired me. I read all the comedy I could find; Mitford, Wodehouse and even John Osborne's *The Entertainer*, having seen the film with Laurence Olivier, which painted a futile image of life as a comedian. But it didn't deter me, as I couldn't relate to Archie Rice's worn-out persona. Unlike him, I had more energy than I could contain and a slowly growing confidence in myself. Now I realised that even the drums had been my adolescent idea of getting close to, if not into, show business.

A HAPPY MAN IN A BAR

Undoubtedly, a great amount of my Jever time was spent drinking. Our bar sing-songs grew and grew in stature. We had some very good singers and each of us had our own party pieces. I had several but always saved my speciality to the last. 'Little Drummer Boy' needed a broad, cockney, music-hall-before-microphones style. My raucous voice seemed to block out all other sound. People would heckle and catcall and place their hands over their ears, but they couldn't shut out the awful racket which increased in decibels right to the end. If ever you meet me, just ask for the first few notes of 'Little Drummer Boy' – that'll be enough.

Our finest singer was Taff Jones, who, with a headmistress mum and Sunday school superintendent dad, had sung as a boy soprano in most South Wales churches. He arrived at Jever having never touched a drop of alcohol in his life. Within a year, his liver and kidneys were gasping for breath. His mate, Taff Roderick, had dipsomania and would nod off after two beers. Then, just before time, Taff Jones would close the evening with 'Bless This House'.

Policing and uniformed discipline was quite light at Jever because there was never the slightest bit of trouble. However, a duty sergeant and corporal would tour the camp to make sure everything closed at the appointed time. On this particular night, we had a new and probably teetotal corporal on duty. With the whole room absolutely quiet, Taff Jones's beautiful falsetto voice cruised smoothly through 'Bless This House'. Then, suddenly and without warning, the bar double doors were thrown open so violently that one door hit the wall. At the same moment, in a raucous voice, the duty corporal shouted, "Alright, all out in five minutes!"

Taff Jones stopped dead. There was complete silence. The corporal saw that he had gaffed and turned to exit. As he did so, a pint glass shattered against the wall, missing him by a good yard. We urged Taff to start again, but he wouldn't, and a rumble of discontent filled the room. Suddenly, the doors were thrown open again and the duty sergeant appeared.

"A glass has been thrown at my corporal. I want the culprit outside immediately! Now!"

No one moved.

The sergeant, who was known to be a placid sort of bloke, didn't know what to do next, and then he spied Taff Roderick, who worked directly under him.

"Right, I want the bloke who threw the glass out here by me, immediately, or I will be forced to arrest one of you."

This was clearly out of order, but he compounded the issue by now staring straight at Roderick, who, like the dormouse, was fast asleep.

"Right, Roderick, on your feet and outside."

There were gasps, jeers and hisses as the sergeant and corporal lifted Roderick out of his seat and started to shuffle him to the doorway. It was the only time in three years that I saw a situation so out of order and close to violent mutiny. Several of us, like football players, gathered round and tried to talk sense to the sergeant. We explained that the corporal's crass behaviour had started it all. Eventually, as we stood on the NAAFI steps, the sergeant turned and addressed us.

"Roderick is under arrest. Whoever threw the glass must give himself up or Roderick will be facing charges in the morning. You had all better clear off back to your rooms or you too will be in trouble."

They moved off and someone said, "Come on, lads, they can't put us all in the guardroom." Sadly, that was me!

So we started to walk after them. Now, Jever is a large spacious camp, and the main gate and guardhouse were perhaps five hundred yards from the NAAFI, so as we wended our disgruntled way between residential blocks, our numbers decreased, so that when we arrived at the guardhouse car park, there were just seven of us.

Through the windows, we could see Roderick being checked in and we knew there was little we could do. Now, RAF Regiment Police are quite a different matter to a duty sergeant and when the police sergeant saw us, he came out to have a word.

We uttered thoughts on wrongful arrest and injustice until he got very close and looked straight at us. We shut up!

"Right, lads," he said, "your friend is in the cells for the night and there is nothing you can do about it. So, push off back to your quarters nice and calmly."

Nobody moved. Not a muscle.

"Right, I will count to three and if you have not moved away from this area, you will all be under arrest. Now, one, two, three – *move!*"

On 'move', just one of the lads moved, but not away! He started to revolve exactly on the same spot. As the policeman's brow furrowed, all seven of us began revolving on the spot. We might have rehearsed it for a week.

"Right, that's it, inside, all of you," barked the police sergeant.

So we shuffled forward, racking our brains for a way out. There was one chance. Someone knew that they were not allowed to put two people in the same cell. Perhaps they didn't have enough cells?

Sadly, no – they had exactly eight cells. With belts and shoelaces removed, we were allowed the loo and locked up for the night. We had all become suddenly very sober.

It was around 4.30am when we were woken and told to, one at a time, wash and dress. Then we were lectured about how to behave as official prisoners. We were to communicate to no one. We were to obey orders instantly and to the letter. We were then marched off to our billets. We were told to go in, speak to no one, and come out in our best blue uniform. We were then marched back and drilled severely for half an hour for marching sloppily. We were then marched back to our billets to change into working uniform. We were marched back and cleaned the whole guardroom area including our cells. We were then marched to breakfast, on a separate table well away from everyone else. We were then marched back to change into our best blue again and finally, at around 9.30am, we were delivered to the CO's office.

Taff Roderick was dealt with first and without knowing the outcome, we were marched in.

The charge was read out: "Unruly behaviour and refusing to obey an order!"

And we each had a fair chance to give our version of events.

Then the CO spoke. "So, although under the influence of drink to some extent, you had chosen to disobey orders on several occasions, thus becoming some sort of law unto yourselves and ignoring the very rules that you know are part and parcel of being in the RAF."

We all stood rigidly, feeling pretty dreadful. The groupie went along the line reading out the previous misdemeanours of each person. But for me, worse was to come. I had been in Group Captain Smith's company several times, including drinking and joking on the last night of the pantomime and the drama club's Christmas party. Suddenly, he was looking straight at me.

"Ball – I'm rather surprised you mix with this class of company? Right, you are all guilty – but a night in the cells is punishment enough. Admonished," (no punishment), "march them out, Sergeant!"

And that was that, except that as soon as we got outside, the lads repeated his words to me several times, which I thought would be the end of it. But no – the lads sent me to Coventry for a week and refused to speak to me in the bar, which was the only place I ever saw them. One week later, to the very hour, they released me – but it was suddenly my round.

LADIES TO THE RESCUE

It was around that time that a whirlwind hit the camp in the form of two very smart and attractive uniformed women's voluntary service, or WVS, ladies. Being on several committees, I, with a couple of others, was chosen to show them round. Next to the adequately furnished bar, there was a larger totally empty room.

They asked, "Why?"

We had to admit we didn't know.

"But," they said, "this is your 'airman's lounge'?"

We sniggered.

Next we were in the corporals' mess, which was hardly used, as, when promoted, lads still chose to drink with their mates. The place was devoid of people but full of furniture. Next we called in at the sergeants' mess, which I knew very well; then to the officers' mess, where we were asked to wait in the hall. The WVS ladies came out of an office after a couple of minutes smiling broadly, while the officers' mess secretary was looking very worried.

The explanation came next day as several trucks arrived at our NAAFI door, from which emerged loads of leather settees, easy chairs, tables, reading lamps, carpets, pictures and even potted plants. The large empty room was soon the most comfortable lounge you could imagine, with an information desk featuring all kinds of sports and activities that we were entitled to but never knew about. The WVS girls had shaken the tree, and the equipment was redistributed according to regulations. The corporals' mess shrivelled up and died. The next weekend in the sergeants' mess, there was certainly a lot more room to dance.

The lead WVS lady quickly disappeared, probably to tackle the next station down the road as their chief trouble-shooter. Another girl arrived and through the two, we were made aware of the perks we were entitled to, like assisted trips to Amsterdam and Copenhagen for weekends. Trouble was, a weekend in these places was expensive, especially if all you did was drink.

NEVER SPILL A DROP

In Copenhagen, I discovered a way to make money. I had perfected a bar-room feat that few others could manage. I could lie on my back and balance a 'full' pint on my forehead. Then, without touching the glass or spilling the beer, I would slowly stand upright. Do try it! So, in a Copenhagen cellar bar, with a quick demo from myself, we soon had half a dozen American servicemen lying on their backs and spilling beer all over the place, at five bucks a go. At the first try we raised three full rounds and then moved bars.

DOWNTOWN JEVER

Jever had a club on the south side and away from the main town called the Deutcher House which was mostly frequented by British RAF lads. The German band was quite jazzy, and I would sit in for the drummer on Friday or Saturday nights and we became great pals. In those days, the cartoon symbol for Germany was a hedgehog called Mecki and as I had a crew cut, I became Mecki to the band and club owners.

Surely my most memorable night in Jever was on my twenty-first birthday. We started in the NAAFI bar as usual and towards time, it was insisted that the birthday boy execute the ritual known as Cardinal Puff. Starting with a full pint, you recite a progression of lines, with certain table taps, gripping the glass in a certain way and taking one drink, as large as you liked. There were three rounds to get through but the slightest error in the ritual and your glass was topped up and you started again. By the time I had got to the end, I was so full of beer that I could only dip my lips into it. So I stripped off my white vest and shirt, tipped the full pint over my head, dried myself with the vest, threw it away and put my shirt back on. Then, after 'Little

Drummer Boy' and 'Bless This House', it was closing time and we staggered to our rooms to change for the Deutcher House.

One of my best mates was a Scouse with a heart of gold, named Cheetham, who boxed for the RAF. He was a good centre half and would pick me as centre forward. All I had to do was hang on the shoulders of their defence and wait for Cheetham. Suddenly, he would emerge unscathed from a scything tackle, where he had probably done the scything, and charge upfield leaving bodies in his wake. Eventually, he would pass to me and, with the goal at my mercy, I would usually cock it up.

Cheetham and I perfected a film fighting routine that usually fooled everyone. I would throw a right hook towards his head, which he blocked with his left forearm. I would immediately throw a left hook which he would stop with his right forearm, while his open palm was close to his face. Now I would throw another right hook, and people would hear the *smack!* He would reel away holding his face and checking his hands for blood from his nose or lip. In actual fact, my third haymaker hit his right hand, close to his face, to produce the *smack*. It looked great – or awful, for those who didn't like violence. So, at the bar on my twenty-first night out, I suggested we do the routine by apparently starting a row. Cheetham was not keen, seeing that I was as fist as a part (it's a spoonerism), but at last he agreed.

So the row started. "Listen, Bally, just 'cos it's your f—in' birthday, don't think you can drink my pint."

"Don't be the stupid scouser you usually are, Cheetham. I haven't touched your pint," etc.

The lads around tried to calm us down, but suddenly I threw punch one, punch two and… I think I sort of lurched just a little, as the third punch never quite arrived at his waiting hand. It hit him smack in his Adam's apple and Cheetham fell back onto his behind, gasping for breath. I collapsed in hysterical laughter. It was the funniest thing I had ever seen – it's a lad thing.

Ten minutes later, when he had recovered, I suggested we should try it again and I would get it right this time.

"No f—in' way," came the reply. But it was my birthday and Cheetham reluctantly agreed. We moved to the bar, where a small and definitely non-aggressive lad was standing with a small beer in his hand. We started the argument, over nothing. But the lad tried to calm us down.

"Come on, lads, don't quarrel. It's his birthday."

"Birthday? I'll f—in' birthday him."

It was time. I threw the first punch, and he blocked it perfectly. He stopped the second one, but now was watching me like a hawk. As the third one set off, he decided that discretion was the better part of valour and clearly moved back away from me. But I saw what he was doing and reached further with the punch. But I couldn't reach, and the wild hook missed his open hand – and, totally out of control, collided with the nose of the 'definitely non-aggressive' lad! His nose just burst and Cheetham and I, being as drunk as we were, could not stay on our feet for laughing, while the lad tried to understand what had just happened. After that, we did all we could to patch him up. Happily, this was the only time in my life that I have actually hit anyone.

I GO INTO BUSINESS

Besides my roughish drinking mates, there were also some friends who saw life in a more sophisticated way. One mate was slightly older than the rest of us, having joined the RAF at around twenty-five. Clive was public-school educated, very witty and musical. He once took one of the WVS girls on holiday to Corsica. Clive had a strong theatrical side and would use all the standard quotes of Oscar Wilde and Noël Coward. He became part of my theatrical education.

We started a coffee bar together in a large empty room in Block 40, which helped cut down our beer intake and earned us a few bob. Soon we were making and selling around 150 cheese or German sausage rolls a night between 7.00pm and 9.00pm. We would then go to the bar or stroll out of camp to the pub about a mile away for a nightcap, talking about music and theatre. He knew that I wanted to write for film or stage and his musical knowledge helped me tremendously.

At the largish pub restaurant, his upper-class charm would ooze forth as he greeted the landlord or Henry, the ancient white-haired waiter. We would have a couple of beers and then Clive would invite Henry and the landlord to Schnapps. Four glasses and a bottle would appear, the landlord would pour and, "Putt Putt," the glasses would be emptied. We would probably savour that one, but in less than a minute, I'd say, "My round," and the bottle would tip four more times. We generally didn't move on to another bottle, but we always finished that one, with the landlord generously taking about half the hits.

Walking home, we often had trouble staying on the heavily cambered German road.

MY RAF TIME DRAWS TO A CLOSE

My forces experiences alone would truly fill a book, but that's about enough, except perhaps to tidy up and bring my forces days to a close. One day, Don Crockett and I were called into the adjutant's office and told that we were being made up to corporal. It was a lovely gesture and the fact that it would be 'acting unpaid' didn't seem to make any difference – our efforts had been acknowledged.

It was quite a surprise when the very next day we were called in again.

"I've got some terrible news for you, lads, I am sorry. They are posting a huge bunch of corporals out to us, so your promotion has been rescinded."

Well, this was the forces, and you came to expect things like this.

Then he said, "Oh, by the way, Ball, you will be teaching four of them everything there is to know about aircraft identification!"

Soon enough, my two years and eleven months in the RAF was coming to a close, with a month demob leave given as a matter of course. Suddenly, it was our last night and Sam Fish and I decided there had to be some celebration, so just the two of us called for a taxi. On the way out, we saw a one-way street road sign that had been hit and practically uprooted, some two hundred yards from the gate house. Sam and I spent the night in Jever town and on the way back in a Mercedes taxi, we remembered the sign. So we stopped the taxi. We got out and lifted the huge four-metre long pole with the sign on one end and a huge concrete block on the other and tried to stick it through the taxi windows but the taxi driver didn't like the idea, so we paid him off. Sam and I carried the sign on our shoulders all the way back to Block 40. We intended to leave a mark. So, right in the middle of the central flower bed, we dug a hole with our bare hands and planted the one-way street sign. We just about got it to stand upright and left it.

As Sam and I entered Block 40, we heard a loud voice. "Oy, you two – Ball and Fish."

We came down to the hall and doorway to see an SP in slashed brim hat walk around the flower bed, as regulations insist, to catch us on the steps.

"What 'ave you dun wiv the road sign?" he asked.

"What road sign?" we asked.

"You have been reported by your taxi driver as 'avin

purloined a road sign. You will report to the guardroom at 6.30 in the morning, in best blue!"

It was now around 2.30am – great!

We started to climb the stone stairs to the first floor and had a natural view of the SP through the window on this very dark night. Previously he had walked around the flower bed, but this time he thought, *Sod it* and took the shortest route, stepping over the white rope to walk diagonally across it. Unbelievably, like in a cartoon film, as his left arm swung forward, so his right leg shot out in front of him, and he walked slap bang into the sign – we even heard the *clang*. The sign slowly fell over, and he hopped and yelped out of the way. He rubbed his head, cursing, put his hat back on, then, with great difficulty, lifted the four metres of steel and concrete 'evidence' onto his shoulder and staggered off into the night. Sam and I collapsed on the stairs and rolled about laughing till we probably woke up half the block.

The next day, we checked in at the guardroom where they informed us that charges had been lodged and we were to report to our adjutant at 10am. We were marched in, hatless, and the adjutant found us 'incredibly guilty'. However, any punishment would have meant a great deal of paperwork and required us to miss our demob train and ship home. Too much work. So we were admonished and marched out.

Then came the shout. "'Ats on and get back in there!"

This time the adjutant came around the desk smiling broadly. He shook us both warmly by the hand. He had nothing but praise for what had been a fabulous group of lads, which was sadly now breaking up. He merely confirmed our own sadness that we were at last leaving.

Jever was a far happier place than I had ever known and would not only stay in my memory for ever, but would also repeatedly remind me of the things I learnt there, the sum of which made me a better and more rounded, confident and mature person by far. That is how important it was. Jever truly was my university.

CHAPTER 6

CIVVY STREET –
LAUGHS AND LEARNING

MEETING A NEW LIFE

I had loved every single day in the RAF, and it had broadened my outlook immensely. But the sadness of leaving was very brief, as I was looking forward to being in charge of my own destiny once again. This was hopefully to be the start of my career and the realisation of my ambitions.

While I was in the RAF, my parents moved to Cleveleys, seven miles north of Blackpool. But I found them again and got home on leave several times. The first thing I did on arriving home was to write to Butlin's asking for a job as a Redcoat. The quick reply said they would need people for the summer and would come back to arrange an interview around April. It was certainly not a knock-back.

Socially, I enjoyed Cleveleys and got some good drumming in. Blackpool Jazz Club at the Raikes Hotel on Wednesdays was widely known with the likes of Don Rendell, Tubby Hayes and other British jazzmen guesting each week. It was possible to 'sit in' as guest drummer, but the club had a few seriously good drummers who generously gave me a few numbers every week.

But it was comedy and not the drums that filled my dreams and ambitions. There was a late night ITV review in which Barry Took, in heavy horn-rimmed glasses, played a cocktail barman and delivered a short topical routine, which I quite liked. Then in the local paper I saw the job at The Cliffs Hotel, Blackpool for a cocktail barman. I went round to the hotel that very day and found the manager. Our conversation was very brief.

"Hello – I've come for the cocktail barman's job."

"Every worked in a cocktail bar before?"

"No!"

"Can you mix a Manhattan?"

"What's that? Er, no?"

"Why have you applied for this job?"

"Well, I reckon with a bit of practice, I'd be funnier than Barry Took."

"Sod off!"

THE BUTLIN'S INTERVIEW

After a couple of months, salvation arrived. A letter from Butlin's asking if I would attend an interview at the Palace Hotel, Manchester a few days later. Would I?

I arrived at the Manchester hotel feeling as frisky as a mountain goat. A porter led me down the corridors to the interview room. I begged a lend of his comb, flicked back the hair and asked him how I looked. His expression said, *Bloody awful*, but, "OK!" came out. I knocked and went in.

There were five soberly suited gents behind the table, of which two seemed to be in charge; a generous and warm-hearted man called Frank Mansell, and a tall, affable, bald chap called Johnny Johnson. They asked what skills I had.

Well, I could sing well enough to run bar sing songs. I'd had a good apprenticeship in the forces. I loved people and I couldn't think of a single other job that I wanted. In fact, it had been my sole ambition since I had seen Des O'Connor as a 'Red' at Filey seven years earlier. Des was now a TV regular and a huge hero in Butlin's circles.

"I also play the drums," I added.

"Do you have a kit?"

"Yes," I replied.

"Is it professional? Would it look OK on a band stand in front of a few thousand people?"

"Yes, certainly," I lied.

There was a bit more banter and Frank Mansell said, "We'll consider you and be in touch soon."

I must have looked crestfallen, for as I turned for the door, Johnny Johnson saw my reaction. "Don't worry, lad," he said, "you'll look great in a red jacket!"

I rushed out, beaming all over my face, and was soon in a Manchester music shop. In five minutes, I had put down a deposit and signed a HP agreement of £2 per week for three years, and I was the owner of a gleaming light-blue pearl Trixon Drum Kit, with fabulous cymbals and delivered free to Cleveleys forty miles away the next day. Soon the dreamed-of Butlin's letter arrived; I had been accepted – heaven!

BUTLIN'S – YEAR ONE

At last the day arrived and I boarded the train which delivered me to Butlin's Pwllheli Station, way out at the west end of North Wales. Also on the train coming from Wallasey was Ken Frost, who was to become my friend for life.

Ken and I agreed to share a chalet. But very soon Ken was doing more sharing than me as he almost instantly sorted out a chalet maid as a regular companion. Ken's sex life took no account of time at all. If he had an hour free, at any time of the day, that was time enough. If I came back to change, Ken would look round as he lay in bed, face down, and politely say, "Oh, hello, John. Y'alright mate? This is Gwen."

We'd swap hellos and, for decency's sake, his behind would stop pumping up and down for a minute or two and he would chat to me as though there was nothing under him but the mattress!

A couple of weeks into the season, Ken's girlfriend turned up with her mate, as arranged by Ken. Within an hour, my virginity had gone at last – what a relief.

In these days before Spanish holidays, Butlin's was the place where every teenager went to sample sex for the first time, for better or worse. Sex with a Redcoat was a desirable aim and so it was often more difficult not to pull. But the sex-crazed burst only lasted a couple of weeks, and soon most of us sought a more meaningful semi-permanent relationship with a member of staff.

In my first year, the established 'Reds' had the pick of the jobs and we 'first years' often had quite mundane tasks like snooker tournaments. The first time I did this, I saw that the equipment in the twelve-table hall was a mess. So I told my boss, Johnny Johnson, and together we ordered and re-equipped each table with short and long rests, cues, etc. It was very clear the boss appreciated someone actually thinking from the camper's point of view.

ANOTHER DRUMMER?

My drumming was confined to playing with an organist and for the *Redcoat Show*; all rather mundane. Then, one scorching hot afternoon, I found myself on Rock and Roll Ballroom duty.

With the sun cracking the paving stones outside, the place was empty. I then saw that the drummer's sticks were just lying there with the kit. So, I sat down and started to play. Soon I was running through jazz numbers in my head, culminating in the most influential of all my records – *The Drum Suite* – which featured four drummers sharing solos and drum breaks. With the orchestra and soloists blowing frantically in my mind, I played through all six movements, while the sweat flew in all directions.

In the middle of all this, a lad with a short dark beard came and sat in the seats directly across the dance floor. I just carried on and ended with a long period of solos, reaching a huge climax.

As I finished, the lad got up and headed for the stage.

I said, "Hang on, you can't come up here, mate!"

To which he replied, "They're my f—in' drums!"

So we chatted and he asked, where had I learnt all this technique? I explained that, besides copying records, tutor books had taught me to read music, which widened the possibilities immensely.

So he asked, "Could you teach me to read?"

I said, "Yes, of course!"

But I never did, and we never even discussed it again. Perhaps if I had, one of the greatest stories in pop history would have turned out differently. But the lad didn't need my help, as he was already a solid rock drummer.

His name was Ringo Starr.

A week or so later, early Sunday evening, I heard a Tannoy call, "Would Johnny Ball go to the Rock and Roll Ballroom immediately?"

When I got there, the problem was obvious. Rory Storm and the Hurricanes were without their drummer. They had Saturday off, so every Friday night, at 11.15pm, they were in their old banger cars, heading back to Liverpool to squeeze in a Saturday night and two lunchtime gigs. On the Sunday they had to be back for their eight till ten slot. This night, they had all made it except for Ringo.

The kit was all there, so I sat in. I had never played rock before but knew the majority of the numbers and coped pretty well, with the base guitarist shouting, "Tom toms," or, "Double time!"

Ringo made it for the second session and for the first time I watched him and the group. They were great and the kids loved them in their slim-cut pastel-shade suits. As the set drew to a climax, tall slim Rory gave them every Presley movement and more. To picture Rory today, think of a young Rod Stewart. If Rod didn't copy Rory's style when he started out, I'd be very much surprised. The hair was identical.

THE END OF YEAR ONE

I loved every minute of the first year as a 'Red' and burnt the candle in the middle and at both ends. But I had one big problem – getting up in the morning after only three hours' sleep. If I was on first sitting for breakfast, Ken would wake me and kick me out of the door. If he was on first sitting, he would drag me off my top bunk and stand me on the floor before he left. But still, I would fall asleep again standing up and find myself late for the 8.55am Redcoat meeting. But that was the major no-no in the Redcoat rule book.

One morning, over halfway through the season, I made the meeting, but five minutes late. The Reds sitting facing the door saw me arrive and tried to signal for me to get out, as I had not been missed and the meeting was nearly over anyway. Johnny Johnson saw their gestures and turned to see me. He said just three words: "Goodbye, Mister Ball!"

I turned and walked out of the door in a daze. I did not

know what to do next, so I started to walk back the way I had come. I had been sacked on the spot!

Then I heard, from the doorway, a shout: "Ball!"

It was JJ – the very man who, at my interview, had told me that I would look good in a red jacket. I turned with tears running down my face. This may sound wimpish, but you can't know just how much I loved this job. Johnny Johnson waited until I was close, and we were alone.

He then said, "Give me one good reason why I shouldn't sack you on the spot."

I shook my head, because I couldn't think of one. Thankfully he could.

"Because you're a f—ing good Red. That's why. Now get back to f—ing work!"

Phew!

That wonderful first season was sadly soon over, and we were all on a train leaving Pwllheli.

The question for me now was, how was I going to survive the winter?

PENNILESS IN LIVERPOOL

I arrived back in Cleveleys, and I quickly found a job at Blackpool Pleasure Beach, where the season went on much longer. When that came to an end, with my drums and a suitcase, I left for Liverpool, with just two friends' phone numbers – Pwllheli's rock star Rory Storm and his drummer Ringo Starr.

Straight off the train, I rang Rory's number. Iris, Rory's sister, explained that the Hurricanes were now in Hamburg with some other band, but she invited me round to the house where she would help me find digs. I stuck the drums in left luggage, hopped on a bus and half an hour later I was at their house in Broadgreen Lane.

Iris and her mother, Vi Caldwell, welcomed me with open arms and I had the first cup of Vi's weak tea that I was going to get so used to. I couldn't then have guessed that Vi, or Ma Storm as everyone called her, would play such a pivotal role over the next year or so in all our careers. There were student digs around the corner but when we found they charged £3-10-0 a week for bed, breakfast and evening meal, Vi said, "Well for that you can stay here and have Rory's room till they come back from Hamburg."

So I moved into the tiny three-bedroom semi with a lounge, kitchen and tiny hall which my drums almost filled. Pa Storm was a very gentle Bible-reading occasional window cleaner who completed the household which I was yet to learn was the most amazing show business magnet.

Vi and Iris assured me Liverpool had dozens of groups and that I would soon be drumming. But I needed money coming in immediately and so, next morning, I walked into the Liverpool Labour Exchange and asked for 'any clerical job'. The interviewer said they had dozens of jobs, but the wage would be around £8 a week and as I could not live on that, I would soon leave and go home. So I was advised to, "Go home now!"

But through a temp agency I did take a job with the almost Dickensian West Coast Stevedoring Co., where I copied lists of ships cargoes from paper sheets into a ledger using a fountain pen only. The boss asked if I had any other way of earning and when I mentioned the drums, only then did he give me the job, at £8 per week.

So, £8 less stoppages was £7, less digs at £3.50, then £2 for the drums and £1.50 for cigarettes left zero, and I hadn't even got on a bus yet. Luckily the office gave luncheon vouchers. Immediately, by agreement, my drum payments were put on hold. Meanwhile, every morning I got the bus at 8.15am and got back at about 6pm in the dreariest time of my entire life.

Iris was great fun though and kept me amused. One morning, I got to work wondering why everyone on the journey had been behaving strangely. As I hung my mac on a hook, I saw her mother's old grey bra and knickers hanging from the back.

Iris knew the Liverpool music scene and took me to the Mardi Gras where the Swinging Blue Jeans were resident. They also used trad jazz bands and soon I was getting a few gigs. However, the 30/- fee went on taxies and a pint. I bought my own beer, as not standing your round with musicians is a no-no.

Then, one night at Stormville, in stormed a real-life Bobby Darin (whose name escapes me) with clicking fingers, neat suit, stylish hair, a Scouse-American accent – oh, and an American Jeep parked outside.

He took me to the Latin Quarter in the centre of town, which was a death trap, with the only entrance down the tightest spiral staircase. Soon with the trio, he was singing Cole Porter's 'Let's Do It, Let's Fall in Love' where he ad-libbed, "Hey, you there, in the corner, don't go winking your eye, stop behaving like little Jack Horner, take your finger out of someone else's pie."

The drummer said I could have 'the worst gig in Liverpool' and I was there Tuesday and Thursday from then on. Soon I was 'fixing' the bass player and pianist, as no one stayed long. The eight till twelve gig paid £6-10-0 between us, with one twenty-minute break and one free Coke.

I didn't know any Liverpool musicians, but my Jack the Lad pal trawled through his little black book and found me about a dozen pianists and three or four bass players. Fixing that first week, I spent at least £1.50 in the corner phone box. So Jack the Lad came to the rescue and taught me how to 'tap a phone'. With the old dial phones, your finger dragged the dial round to a stop point and let it go. The dial, dragged back by a spring, dialled that number. The length of the return journey indicated the digit – one was the shortest return and zero the longest. But if you tapped the rest bar at the same speed as the dial return, while counting, you could fool the phone into dialling each number without inserting any coins.

Some nights, I would make twenty or thirty calls, all for nothing. When pianists refused the job, I asked for other pianists' numbers and soon I had around forty numbers in my book, none of which I knew, or if they were any good or not, so I was skating on very thin ice. But I finally sorted out a couple of trustworthy pianists who were as desperate as me for money, plus a regular bass player, who was great but a hypochondriac, especially where ultraviolet light was concerned. At over six foot tall, his head was practically rammed into a fluorescent UV tube, so he was probably right to be worried. But he became part of the club decor as his dandruff lit him up like a Christmas tree. Many years later, I saw him playing bass at the London Palladium and when I ran down for a chat at the interval, he practically leapt out of the pit to greet me.

NEW FACES?

Then suddenly, amazing events began to occur at Stormville. Rory and the Hurricanes were coming back from Hamburg. It looked like I was going out of the door, but Iris was leaving for Christmas panto rehearsals, and I just swapped rooms, and everything dovetailed.

The Hurricanes arrived and piled their kit in the hall on top of my drums. The through door from hall to kitchen was now impossible to get to. Then another group arrived, and their kit was piled on top of the rest, reaching right to the ceiling. That was the way it was going to stay, as the other group didn't have parents who saw rock and roll as a sensible career path, so they hardly ever seemed to go home at all. The group was called The Beatles.

Life at Stormville was suddenly one long series of people coming and going and chatting and laughing and guitar strumming and Ma Storm making awful tea and her husband tut-tutting and smiling to me about the antics of 'this younger generation'.

I was introduced to everyone, but when they heard I worked in an office, I became almost invisible. No one then knew that in Hamburg the seeds had been sown and John, Paul and George had started to see Ringo as a more suitable drummer than Pete Best. I'm afraid I can't remember Pete Best at all. But his mother was pro this lifestyle and had even arranged early Beatles gigs. Pete must have been there sometimes, as it was to be over a year before Ringo swapped groups.

I remember John Lennon so well because when he said anything, it stayed said and we all understood. He could be very blunt, but then again, he was so playful. If there was ever a lull, he would clap his hands on his knees to a count of four and shout a word, any word, and look to the person next to him. They had to come back with an associated word by the next count of four and it went around the room. With John driving, the game just happened.

Paul was more likely to have a guitar on his knee and be talking tunes and chords and winking at Iris. It was totally clear that Iris had been waiting for Paul, but also apparent that he didn't see the friendship going anywhere.

One event happened that perhaps gave an indication of Paul McCartney's personality and determination. Iris met up with Australian singer Frank Ifield, who had created a name for himself with 'She Taught Me To Yodel' and 'I Remember You' with the 'ooo' going into high falsetto. Frank had been playing the Liverpool Empire and one day Iris picked up the phone, chatted a little, blushed and then said, "Give me half an hour." She shot upstairs and came down looking fabulous in a white leather mini coat with fur trimmings, white leather boots and her glorious blonde hair and said to Paul, "Can you give me a lift into town? I'm seeing Frank off at Lime Street Station."

The silent reply from Paul was, *No chance!* and as no one else moved, she left in a temper to catch the bus. A few minutes later, a solitary Beatle also quietly left Stormville.

At Lime Street Station, with Frank leaning out of a first-class window and press all around, Iris stretched up, with her leg cocked into the air, to kiss him goodbye. It was a beautiful picture, and the cameras flashed.

Then suddenly a figure burst through the posse of cameramen with his short black leather jacket pulled up over his head. He lurched forward in a crippled Quasimodo stagger and grabbed Iris's hand, with the words, "Come, Esmeralda, it's back to the dungeon with you, hahahahaha!"

Iris screamed, "No, no, you're ruining it all."

But Paul McCartney wouldn't listen. Even if he wasn't quite that serious about Iris, he was jealous enough to let her know how he felt about her being friendly with an Australian yodeller!

I was still a little shy in the presence of nine lads all a couple of years younger than me and all chatting, gagging and squabbling. George was the most likely to be sitting quietly and we would talk about anything and nothing. The fact that I would arrive from work in an office suit and tie did little to help me mix easily with them. Also, I think those months of desperate poverty in Liverpool had made me more withdrawn than I have ever been before or since. My belief that there was no money in rock and roll didn't go down well with them either.

Iris eventually came back from pantomime and I at last had to move out to the student digs around the corner. However, I popped round to Stormville every couple of nights to see how they were all getting on. Then I got a great drumming job, and I too joined the Liverpool rock scene.

A NEW JOB IN NEW BRIGHTON

Someone at Stormville saw an ad in the *Liverpool Echo* for a drummer and I was soon in New Brighton in a very dismal place reeking of stale beer, sweat and urine, over Burton's Tailors.

The band looked rough with no uniform or presentation like the Hurricanes or Beatles. Besides bass and rhythm guitars, they had two lead guitars: a lanky chain-smoking teenager with a Duane Eddy twangy guitar style and a balding middle-aged chap with an amplified acoustic guitar straight out of a museum. But boy, could they play!

After just two numbers, I had the job! The two leads exchanged choruses and went for a high-energy sound, playing all the numbers in the current hit parade. Many top-twenty hits had orchestral or brass sections, so the two guitars would fill in. But now they saw that I could fill in with drum breaks. It felt tremendous.

The paunchy middle-aged boss took their cue and offered me the job at £7.50 for Friday, Saturday and Sunday night. The first night went so well that, from then on, they placed me front left, with the two lead guitars to the right and the other two guitars behind them. They wanted me on show.

By they also had five great singers. First, a smooth cocky lad in a dark jacket and open-neck white shirt who could swing through the Bobby Darin, Kenny Ball numbers. The next lad covered Elvis and Cliff numbers, including all the moves. Then came Ginger Jim, under five foot tall with a mop of red hair, doing all the 'Good Golly Miss Molly' screaming numbers. Then we had a beautiful Chinese girl who sang all the female tracks popular at the time.

But to top all that was another singer. He had a wild stare and a stutter, but he could impersonate all of the others and could sing everything they could – only better. His name was

Freddie Starr. Freddie was both fabulous and trouble. The boss caught him with a youngish girl in the beer cellar. Freddie was sacked and never got paid for that weekend. The next week, pleading for his job, the boss put him on trial, not paying him for the first night. Then he was back again and the following week he would get sacked again. This was in the winter of 1960.

It was in 1965 that I found Freddie Starr again, now penniless after Brian Epstein had snubbed all has advances. But I told him cabaret and variety was just waiting for him. I gave him my agent's number and within weeks Freddie was a true variety star.

Although our new band looked terrible, the sound was incredible, and we packed the place. Other groups heard about us and would arrive expecting to pass in, as musicians usually did, but not at our place. The nasty boss wasn't having anyone not paying. The band stand was set over the stairs and the bouncers held the top of the stairs. So visiting bands had to stand near the top of the stairs and crane their necks to see me and my drums and the heads of the rest. But they could certainly hear the sound we were creating.

Now I was getting a name for myself. Liverpool's music shops somehow knew, and I would be given drumsticks free of charge! But rock was just an essential money-spinner for me. I was still, at heart, a jazz drummer and I met a group called The Mersey Jazz Sextet, all music teachers connected to Liverpool University who wrote half of the material we played. We met on Sunday afternoons and Wednesday nights, but for practice only. Liverpool gigs with modern jazz was nigh on impossible, though we did once play the Cavern, at three in the morning.

But they were wonderful. I played brushes for practically every number and would use only snare drum and high hat, with my drum pedal thumping my equipment box. We swung like mad in the American West Coast style. It was pure heaven.

BLEAK HOUSE AND THE TROUSER SAGA

By now, with both Rory and Iris at home, I was in student digs at Bleak House, just around the corner. How bleak was this place? Well, my mum and dad came to see me, and Mum took one look and cried, begging me to come home. I was looking so gaunt and thin, living on less food each week than I had been eating every day in the forces.

There would be eight or nine around the dining table. There was no central heating, and the huge fireplace had a two-bar electric fire – and this was winter. The food was awful: cottage pie or shepherd's pie; or sausage, beans and chips; or chicken at weekends. Whatever it was, we would race to get it eaten and then dive for one of the four places on the tiny settee or easy chairs near the fire. Those who missed out had to find another way to keep warm. So we would make a newspaper ball and play football around the table – just to keep from freezing.

Bleak House was so cold that the Liverpool University students would work in bed, as the only place they could keep warm, wearing mittens with the fingers sticking out so they could handle their pens. We did have shilling in the meter gas fires, but they were expensive.

I had an even bigger problem. Being at Butlin's and always in uniform and then penniless, I hadn't bought any clothes. This was in the days before jeans, and I had one suit which I would wear to work every day. Then I would stuff a sweater on and a mac and get to New Brighton wearing the same trousers. I would then beat the hell out of the kit for three and a half hours and get home still damp with sweat. I was wearing my pants out from both sides at the same time. But I still had to wear them for the office. So I would put them on a hanger and hang them half out of the slightly opened window, so the fresh air would hopefully get rid of the sweat. The freezing cold would wake me before first light, and I would get up and close the window. I would carefully place my now frozen trousers under the thin mattress to thaw them out with the heat of my own body as I grabbed another couple of hours' sleep. This also pressed them, so they looked reasonable for work.

The next problem was getting enough food. After a gig, I would arrive home with everyone else in bed. There would be a few biscuits and processed cheese triangles or spam and perhaps some bread. So I developed sandwich-making creativity, augmenting what I had with what I could find. So, brown sauce and salad cream with processed cheese could be heaven along with other weird and wonderful concoctions. But some nights the gods smiled on me as there in the fridge would be a cooked chicken meant for the following day's evening meal. Of course, I couldn't just knock slices off it, as I would be discovered, and no food would be left where it could be got at ever again. So I taught myself a great wheeze. I learnt to carve a chicken like a gynaecologist, going in through whatever aperture was available. I could take out enough chicken for a double sandwich and not alter the outward appearance of the bird in the slightest. It required breaking off a couple of inner ribs and losing them in the waste bin. But I went to sleep still with a grin on my face.

STORMVILLE AGAIN

I would often pop back to Stormville to see how things were going and have a late chat with Vi as she toasted her mottled legs on the two-bar fire and we drank her awful tea. This was a habit that would last few a good few years. But Vi was such a natural wit that even Ken Dodd would call round occasionally.

One night, Iris and her friend decided to have a Ouija board session with an upturned glass, letters of the alphabet in a ring, and the words 'Yes' and 'No' at top and bottom.

Of course, I didn't really have time for all this nonsense, but I played along. Amazingly, the spirit kept spelling out words of a sexual nature, with the girls giggling and Vi tut-tutting. I accused them of forcing the glass, which they denied. So I set a test. With all our fingers in contact with the upturned glass, I mentally asked a question. Then I removed my finger and waited to see if the spirit could give an answer. The glass was slow to move, but then it went to the letter 'K'. It waited and then went to the 'No' and started again. It went to the 'K' again and then to the 'No'. It went to the 'C' but again slid to the 'No'. Then it went 'K', 'A', 'R' – then 'No'. Then 'K', 'A', 'K' – 'No'. The girls gave up and asked what question I had asked. In looking for something obscure, I looked down at the dog at our feet. I then mentally thought, *What colour is the dog's hair?* But the word I thought of was the army uniform colour, 'khaki'!

Both girls later said they were not sure they had even heard the word khaki and definitely had no idea how to spell it. So how come the glass had repeatedly tried to spell it out? Of course I don't believe in these things – but!

Soon it was April 1961 and my Liverpool winter was almost over. From being totally broke in November, I was now earning over £20 a week and my drum payments were up to date. I also had a new suit, shoes, shirts and a couple of pairs of trousers. I had loved Liverpool and the wonderful scousers. But once more it was Butlin's time again.

I knew that leaving the drumming job in New Brighton would upset the boss, so I advertised in the *Liverpool Echo* and got half a dozen replies, some from drummers in groups that would make a name for themselves over the next few years. Still, when I announced on the Sunday night that I was leaving, the boss went berserk and told the bouncers to throw me and my drums down the stairs.

They baulked at that but carried the kit down and placed it on the pavement, in the rain. I asked these really tough fellas just how they could be so subservient to such a ruthless bleeding idiot. They said, "Sorry!" but left me to pack my drums.

CHAPTER 7

MORE SMILE SCHOOL AND COMEDY BEGINS

REDCOAT PROMOTION AND A WINTER OFFER

Back at Pwllheli, Ken Frost and I shared a chalet once more and it was as though we had never been away. The first week of the season required only one dining hall and two houses. For the second week, dining hall two would open, requiring four house captains, which of course were the star Redcoats. Three 'old hand' Redcoats took three of those jobs, but on the Friday of the first week, at the Redcoat meeting, a totally new house captain was to be announced; but who? Johnny Johnson announced that for the second week, Gloucester House would be captained by... Johnny Ball. The girls and a good few fellas applauded and cheered. But a whole set of male Reds went very quiet and I saw that being good at my job did not necessarily win many friends.

The captain's job entailed making sure that every camper knew that you were there to help. Some fifteen minutes into every mealtime, the house captain would mount the podium, grab the gong and beat out *bong, bong-a-bong, bong* and the campers came back with a *clap, clap*. This was followed by *hi-de-*

129

hi and their answer *ho-de-ho*. It was honestly never as corny as the TV series made it, except perhaps for my new house slogan: 'If they ask, "Which house is boss, sir? Tell them proudly, the House of Gloucester!"'

My job was to encourage some 1500 campers to enter competitions and compete for house points. I found a wonderful group of Londoners who entered everything and on the Friday we realised that Gloucester had won the House Cup. I was carried shoulder-high around the village green – just as we had done with Des O'Connor, some eight years earlier. I was a very happy bunny.

As house captain, I got the top bar sing-song job, which was reminiscent of my RAF days. My drums prevented me being involved in Redcoat sketches, so comedy ideas would just have to wait. Though I did compère the hour-long *Grundig Tape Show*, where eight audience members were coerced into impersonating major stars, with a brand-new tape recorder going to the winner.

The season went swimmingly and just over halfway through, I was asked if I would like a winter job at Butlin's Metropole Hotel, Blackpool. What could be more perfect?

WINTER IN BLACKPOOL

So, at the end of the season, after a week with my parents in Cleveleys, I travelled the seven miles down the promenade to start the winter at Butlin's Metropole Hotel and arrived in the middle of a crisis.

As I walked in, the entertainments manager asked, without hesitation, "Can you do an act?"

"No," I said.

"Shit," he said, and the tale unravelled. The summer Reds had gone and we were starting up the winter season. But the hotel had no lull between summer and winter. There were guests who needed entertaining, but with whom?

Principle comedian Freddie Davies was on honeymoon and a second comic hadn't yet arrived.

"Are you sure you don't do an act?" asked Vince in desperation.

"Well, I do know an act!" I said.

"Great," said Vince, "you're doing it tonight."

For the past two seasons playing drums for the *Redcoat Show*, I had watched the very funny, never-changing comedy spot of Ricky McCabe's around sixty times. Of course, I knew every word.

It opened with, "Hello there. Will the lady with the lucky ticket come up and get me?"

So, that very Friday night, having no option, being the only person available, I was top of the bill. I was very nervous, but once the first few gags had got laughs, I relaxed, and it went quite well.

"Fabulous," said Vince, "same again tomorrow night!"

I pleaded no, but, of course, the guests changed over on Saturday so I would have a totally new audience. This time, with more confidence, it went very well indeed.

Right after the show, one of the girls came up and said, "Great spot, Johnny. Oh, the new Redcoat has just arrived – he says he knows you. His name is Ricky McCabe!"

I was rooted to the spot in shock. But, plucking up courage, I rushed into the lounge to find Ricky.

"Hello, mate," he cried, grinning from ear to ear.

With no sign of a smile, I guided him to a table and said, "Ricky, I've got to tell you something terrible. I've just done your act."

The smile drained from his face! I quickly explained that I hadn't volunteered to do it. They had nobody else, and I had admitted that I knew his act, having watched it so often from my drums. Ricky went through the act, and I confirmed, "Yes, I did that. Yep, that too." I had missed nothing.

Ricky was in complete shock. After a few 'bloody hells!' or similar, he resigned himself to the situation and started to work out what he would do for an act the next night, with me trying to help.

In a couple of days, Ricky had forgiven me. What's more, he was to be a major catalyst in both forming and guiding my career – and it all started here. At no time did Ricky ever mention the event as being an act of stealing on my part. I had had no alternative.

Within a week, the winter team was in place and there was no immediate need for me to perform. Freddie Davies came back from honeymoon and took over as light entertainment manager. It was in this season that he found a gag about a budgie and developed the Parrot-Face character, which was to make him a star within a few years. Ricky McCabe settled in as second comic and was soon back to doing a version of the act that I had borrowed.

Ricky's room-sharing partner was our organist, Dave Nicholas – a brilliant exponent of the Hammond Organ. But Dave also had a tool-strewn modelling table on which was emerging a highly detailed replica of a green Birkenhead double decker bus! Ricky was one of the smoothest 'pullers' and would grab the time when Dave was organ-playing to lure young ladies to their room. Ricky had the bottom bunk, but Dave would not only model at the table, he would also model in bed. As a result, there was a slow but constant shower of balsa wood shavings raining down on Ricky's lower bunk. Now, balsa wood is quite soft and pliable, but it can still cause discomfort when it comes into contact with an amorous young lady's nether regions. Somehow, Ricky suffered all this with equanimity, until one day, things took a turn for the worse. The young lady of the hour screamed, and Ricky had to remove the modeler's exquisitely sharp razor blade from her bum and surreptitiously seek medical attention.

The Dave and Ricky saga came to a wonderful conclusion when, at long last, Dave completed the excellent Birkenhead bus. Ricky cheered up enormously as there was a lull in the modelling.

Then, one morning, as we all breakfasted together, Dave arrived, grinning and rubbing his hands – a habit he had when he was pleased with himself.

Dave said, "Guess what? I'm going to build a fire engine!"

There was a short stunned silence. Then Ricky casually looked up from his bowl of cornflakes and simply said, "Well you'd better hurry up. 'Cos I'm going to set fire to your f—ing bus!"

FIRST COMEDY STEPS

As a team, we all became great friends at the Metropole and Ricky helped me write my very first comedy act. I had been collecting gags by the hundred since I was eleven, but jokes in a book do not make an act. It was Ricky and his experience which solved this problem.

For some reason, I had never had a good haircut. Ricky saw that as a lead in – as a comedian, you have to explain in the first instant just what kind of person you are. I was incredibly nervous and unsure of myself, so that had to be the tack.

With Ricky, we produced my very first comedy routine. Are you ready for this? Here we go:

"Hello, excuse me, I'm not well. I'm just recovering from a very bad haircut. Have you seen this? The Tulip Cut. Looks like somebody just tiptoed through it. I went to the barbers. I said, 'Do something with my hair.'

"He said, 'Like what?'

"I said, 'Well do you think some grease will be any good?'

"He said, 'Hang on, I'll go and scrape some off my bike.' He rushed out. I rushed out after him. There was the hairdresser, in the middle of the road, with his bike over his head. He was shouting, 'What we want is constitution, restitution and prosperity.'

"I said, 'What are you doing with the bike over your head?'

"He said, 'I'm holding a Raleigh.'

"I dragged him back in the shop. I said, 'Do something with my hair.'

"He said, 'I will! I'll give you something that no one else has not got.' And he did. He gave me a sideways cut. It came up at this side like a man's in front and came down on this side like a woman's behind – like the back of a woman's. It was very nice. I was back two days later.

"I said, 'You'll have to change this – the sideways cut.'

"He said, 'What's wrong with it?'

"I said, 'I'm fed up with people coming up and whispering up my nose.'"

And that was that. The start of JB's first ever act – and quite amazingly, it worked. But I was still seeming nervous on my entrance, so Ricky suggested I carry a brown paper bag, slightly inflated, and arrive on stage visibly shaking. At the microphone, I would say, "Hello. I'd like to start by, er, start. I'd like to commence. First of all, I'd like to say, to start, er, first of all!" Then I would stop and point at the quivering bag and say, "Bag of nerves!" It always got the laugh and often applause and I would throw the bag into the wings and come back smiling. The ice was broken and away I went. I soon became known as 'Bag of Nerves'!

Soon my spot in the *Redcoat Show* grew along with my confidence. Freddie Davies got me a date in a Blackpool working men's club, which required four short spots. For a comic, this system was terrible, as you have to first 'get' the audience and then build on the atmosphere to sustain it. Stopping every seven minutes kills all that.

I got to my club and was incredibly nervous. But the Bag of Nerves and the hair gags went well. I started another routine which didn't go so well, so I cut it short and lapsed into another one. That was worse, so I started another. I ran over time and came off to muted applause. Worse than that, I had now destroyed all my material. Three more spots would be totally impossible!

The secretary saw my nervousness and said, "Don't worry. They all liked you. Have a breather, as I'm going to call a couple of houses of bingo."

I spotted a lifeline. "I can call the bingo. At Butlin's, I'm one of the best."

He looked at me and said, "OK, don't go too fast – they don't like it too fast." He announced the bingo and that I was going to call it. So, I started and over an hour later, I had ad-libbed the whole Butlin's bingo repertoire, plus all the gags I had planned to 'use in my spots. They giggled all the way through, and my success exceeded my wildest imaginings. I was so pleased, I left without picking up my fee and the chap delivered it to me next day.

SEMI-FINAL TIME

One of the main attractions in the winter schedule at the Met was the semi-finals of the Butlin's competitions, when sixty-four summer winners would arrive for a free weekend to be whittled down to the sixteen who would go on to the grand final in London in the early new year. It was a major ploy in Butlin's advertising their next summer season.

First came the People's National Talent semi-final. Most were musical acts, but one comedian really impressed me with the sheer audacity of style. This was Mike Coyne and, in dinner jacket and bow tie, his totally dead pan and humourless opening went something like this:

"Good evening. I've got a surprise for you. Me! I tell jokes. They're not funny jokes but they make you think. They make you think they're not very funny. I'll give you some idea what I mean. I'm going to do a trick with this handkerchief," (whipped out of his top pocket), "you can do this trick with any colour handkerchief you like, as long as it's a white one. Notice while I'm doing this trick there's nothing up my sleeve," (the handkerchief has now disappeared), "except my elbow, and there's no 'arm in that, is there? This gives you some idea what the rest is going to be like. Eight minutes of sheer – bloody – misery!" Mike's slick routine got him to the final.

Little did I know we would meet again and become great friends.

The next free weekend group were the Holiday Princesses – sixty-four cracking-looking birds. However, they were all very young with mothers or boyfriends in tow and spent so much time on hair and make-up we hardly ever saw them.

Next came the Glamourous Grandmothers – some still under thirty! But whatever age, they were a load of laughs, and late-night lounge sessions would go on till four in the morning.

Finally, we had the Miss She Best-Dressed Woman semi-finals. This time, sixty-four real 'lookers' descended on us. Everyone in Blackpool knew about them. Remember, my home was just seven miles north, and on the Saturday, I got a message that friends in the public bar wanted a word.

My Cleveleys mates explained, "We've got a great house for a party tonight. Can you pull any birds for us?"

I asked how many fellas were expected and was told up to twenty, but that many girls might be a tall order.

"Oh, by the way, it's fancy dress – but that's not compulsory!"

I checked that they had cars enough to get any girls there and back and said I'd see what I could do.

An hour later, I had a dozen beautiful girls in a dingy cellar going through the Redcoat prop baskets for costumes. One tall girl found a guard's uniform with skintight trousers and thigh-length boots. Word spread and girls whose whole life was dress and presentation started inventing ways to tog themselves up for a party with a bunch of fellas they had never even met. The pick-up was for 10.30pm when around thirty stunning girls and a load of very excited fellas met. It was electric.

At the party, in a quite spectacular house, more girls arrived and all those without costumes were whisked up to the bedrooms to reappear in bedsheets and a few pins looking like Grecian sprites, though the lads were more interested in inadequate cover than authenticity. Then girls started to notice that prop-basket costumes are not exactly spotlessly clean and at the first whiff of stale perspiration, it quickly became something of an 'out of costume' party.

BUTLIN'S SEASON THREE

Suddenly, the long hotel winter season was replaced by the new summer season and Ken Frost and I began sharing our chalet once more.

The *Redcoat Show* was very good, but the two comic spots naturally went to new compère Jimmy Tarbuck and Ricky McCabe, and I could see no way of breaking through. I played drums for the show and, as usual, Ken and his then Welsh girlfriend Mair were all part of an excellent hour's entertainment.

At one point, Mair was discovered onstage in a crinoline dress and began a light operatic number, 'Brightly Dawns Our Wedding Day', which the audience loved. But something was not quite right. Every time she hit a high note, she reached up with her head – and it stayed there. As she sang, she slowly grew till she was about eight foot tall! On the final note, as the applause rang out, she hitched up her crinoline to reveal the bare, hairy legs of Redcoat Big Brian, who carried her off on his shoulders.

Then Ken Frost was onstage for his circus solo number. In pathetic clown face and costume, he began a song so melodramatic the words have to be seen (or heard) to be believed. Ken repeated the last line to a heart-rending finish and there wasn't a dry eye in the house! But as Brett Creswell, our producer, said, "A show always requires pathos before a final uplifting and celebratory ending." And it always worked brilliantly, until one fateful night.

On this night, as I sat looking up from my drums, Ken came onstage and looked at me with a mischievous twinkle in his eye. He was planning something! He went into the song, and it was perfect up to a point. The audience was spellbound, but, either intentionally or by accident, Ken's next line changed. Instead of "As from the sawdust ring, my broken Rose was taken!", Ken sang, "As from the broken nose, they took my sawdust bleeding!"

I guffawed and collapsed over my drums. Sticks clattered and cymbals splashed, and I was fighting to keep my laughter silent. But by now Ken had 'gone' as well and he continued, "A voice said, 'Joe-oh-oh, the show-ho must still go on.' I tried to laugh like the clown in *Pagliacci*-hehe," (and in the most serious part of the song), "but the laugh in my heart had gone – teeheehee."

He was now totally uncontrollable. Somehow he got to the end and walked off. The audience didn't understand just what had happened, but I didn't stop just aching for ages.

SINGING IN THE RAIN

On days when Butlin's woke up to a rainy morning, the Redcoat meeting would plan a *Singing in the Rain* show starting at 10am and running until or even through lunchtime. The Tannoy would constantly remind people of the show, as, in rain, it was one of the few things people could do.

For each hour, a particular Red would be the compère, with an organist or pianist on hand. The next available Red would be introduced and do their act, with sometimes no idea of how long they would be on. If no one else turned up, that could be some time. Singers sang, instrumentalists strummed, and people tried things out. We did standard 'crossovers' that had been used at Butlin's for years. Someone would run on screaming, "There's a fire, there's a fire."

"Where?"

"In your eyes, you sexy beast." Exit.

In the *Singing in the Rain* shows, I got the chance to give my act a run out. It must have been a particularly wet summer, because I got quite a bit of practice, and it was getting stronger all the time. Then there came a very momentous moment.

For some reason, Ricky McCabe and I were walking up the aisle of the main theatre and Johnny Johnson, the grand boss, came to meet us. He looked very serious as he started to speak.

"Ricky, I watched the last *Redcoat Show* and frankly I was appalled. Blue gags are creeping in everywhere. You know the Butlin's policy. No smutty material; the parents don't want it, the kids don't understand it and we won't have it at any price."

Ricky smiled in bemusement. "I haven't done any new gags. I'm doing the same gags I did last year."

The boss came back, "Well, it's filthy. Sorry, you're out of the show. Johnny, you will take over his spot!"

I was totally flabbergasted and blurted out, "You can't do that. Ricky doesn't do blue gags."

JJ came back, "Nope. That's it. He's out. You're in."

I came in again, "No, you can't do that. It's Ricky's spot."

And now Ricky chimed in, "Listen, mate, it's just the chance you've been waiting for. Don't worry about me. You do it. You'll be great."

Johnny Johnson was already walking up the aisle. I was nonplussed.

Ricky kept on, "Go on, John. Take your chance, mate."

It was a terrible situation. As a pit musician, I played the audience in and out before and after each of the three, one-hour *Redcoat Shows* and so I was never backstage with the rest of the team. So I didn't really know what everyone thought of the new situation, although I did know that, without exception, everyone thought Ricky had been dreadfully treated.

I'M A COMEDIAN AT LAST?

The die had been cast and the following Wednesday, in the middle of the first *Redcoat Show*, I left my drums and scurried backstage. The organist played the previous act off while I changed jackets and puffed up my 'Bag of Nerves' before being played on. The spot went well, and with nerves more under control, it went even better in the next two houses – perhaps too well?

On the following Sunday night, Ricky rushed up and called me to one side. "I've just been watching the *Sunday Night Variety Show*, John. Our compère has just done your act!"

This was a terrible situation. The camp's main compère, who wore a navy-blue blazer rather than a Redcoat, also had a *Redcoat Show* spot, just a few minutes after mine. He had made it known he felt Ricky shouldn't have been dropped. But we all agreed with that and, after Ken Frost, Ricky was my closest mate. Ricky had knocked my act into shape and taught me more about stand-up than I had ever known! So it was no secret that I was not happy taking his spot. But that was not how the camp compère saw it!

That week, with Ricky's help, I cobbled together another seven-minute spot, and the three *Redcoat Shows* went well once again. But that weekend, for the Saturday night show, the compère did some of my new act, and on the Sunday, repeated the stuff he had stolen the previous week!

Perhaps I was wrong at the time, but I never confronted him. I felt so guilty over Ricky being dropped and I couldn't face a confrontation when what had happened was not my doing. Also, I had made no secret of my first doing Ricky's act at Blackpool. In fact, I told everyone what I had done and why I had absolutely no alternative at the time.

As I recall, after a few weeks, the compère, who was destined to become one of Britain's most well-known comedians, went back to his own material and I settled down to mine and steadily improved. But those antics were something I have never forgotten.

A TYPICAL WORKING DAY?

The *Redcoat Show* was just one aspect of the Butlin's job. The majority of my time was taken up being a house captain and cheerleader and I ran everywhere from morning to night. On top of that, with beach parties most nights, I never got more than four hours' sleep, if that.

Perhaps my Wednesday PM schedule might give you some idea of how full on it all was. After lunch, I would assemble a few of my house Reds on the village green in the centre of the camp and, at exactly 2pm, we would start to march to the sports field, two thirds of a mile away, carrying our house banner to encourage many Windsor or Edinburgh holidaymakers to join us as we were led by an aged London busking band who played around the camp each day. The march was no more than a saunter, but we cheered and encouraged every step of the way.

On arrival at the sports ground, as far away from the centre of camp as could be, we quickly set up the equipment and scoring tables and started activities at 3pm with the one hundred-yard dash heats. I would spot those from my house and, on the word 'go', I would run with them to encourage them, in every heat. Around halfway, I would let them run on, still cheering, and then get back for the next heat, which followed as soon as was possible, with four or five heats. I would do the same thing for the single-lap four hundred-yard race and this continued until the last ten minutes of the hour-long session. I would by then have spotted eight hefty or overweight men from my house and tipped them off that I would need them later.

Now, for the tug o' war I would get my team out, sort them into heaviest at the rear and give them fail-safe instructions on how to win a tug o' war. You take up your position, get the rope tightly under your arm and, on the command, take the strain, lean back so your body is absolutely straight, with no bend at the waist, with the pressure on your straight left leg and bent right one. On the word 'pull', you did absolutely nothing! You simply stayed put and held your ground. The other team would strain and tug until they started to get out of shape. Only then would I shout, "Ready now – one!" My team, if they obeyed my instructions, would straighten their right leg and bring the left one back, straighten that, and stop; nothing else. After several spaced out single tugs, the opposition would hopefully be showing signs of strain and start to wobble about, and I would start the, "One... one... one," each getting closer until we simply walked back and won.

The sports hour was over at 4pm, and we quickly gathered all flags and markers, got the rope in a tea chest, and I would then run for my chalet. I would shower, if there was time, or wash and shave and change into my evening gear of red coat, white trousers, clean shirt and black bow tie. It was tight, as I had to be in the theatre pit at my drums at 4.50pm to play the audience in for the first *Redcoat Show* at 5pm.

The one-hour show would include my seven-minute spot, and the organist and I would play the audience out at the end, till 6.05pm. But at 6.20pm we would start to play the 6.30pm house in. At 7.35pm, after playing them out, I would run to the nearest bar for a well-earned pint but be back at 8.20pm for the third, 8.30pm show which ended with us playing the audience out till 9.35pm.

But now I had twenty-five minutes to clear the stage and set up for my own one-man *Grundig Tape Show* at 10.00pm until 11.00pm. By that time, I had not had anything to eat since lunchtime! But the only late restaurant, five hundred yards away, stopped serving at 11.15pm. I only missed being served once, and after that, they always had my steak on the grill at 11.15pm as their very last order.

IS THERE LIFE AFTER BUTLIN'S?

The season was nearing its end when, in the last week, Ricky introduced me to a tall, dark, shy young man.

"John, this is Mike Hughes. He'll get you started in the clubs in Liverpool!"

Mike was to be my agent and would help my rise as a professional comedian. Older Ricky had already decided to quit stand-up and had agreed to join Mike Hughes as his assistant.

A few days later, I said goodbye to Butlin's after three quite glorious 'smile school' years where I learnt a lot about comedy but so much more about people and character. It was a fitting topping on the cake after my wonderful forces experience.

MERSEYSIDE IS SO FULL OF COMEDY

I was soon back in my old Liverpool digs at Bleak House. Until I could earn enough from the Liverpool clubs to pay my way, I needed a day job. So I joined Islington National Assistance Board, or the NAB. This job and the Liverpool spirit were to be a comedy education in itself.

They do say that Liverpool is full of comedians, and sure enough, on my arrival at the Islington office, I got a tap on my shoulder and the question, "What are you doing here?"

I turned and immediately recognised Mike Coyne, the comedy magician who had won the People's National Talent semi-final in Blackpool. I asked how he had got on in the final and he beamed. "I won it – mind you, I also won it two years previously with a different act." Mike would never turn professional, as his father had sight problems. So he always maintained his semi-professional status. But he also became the senior north of England social security officer.

EVERY DAY, COMEDIANS!

On my second social security day, while shadowing a client interviewer, suddenly someone shouted, "Form!" I thought they were asking for one of the many forms we had stacked in small shelves to one side of our desks. But everyone else was pushing their chairs back in panic and I looked up to see that an Irish interviewee, just released from Walton Jail, on being told he could not have any money, had picked up an eight-foot oak form with iron legs and, while smiling broadly, was about to lob it over the wire mesh grill at us. He was talked out of it.

Soon I was interviewing on my own. One person, who resembled Rigsby in *Rising Damp* and had a whelpy-looking dog, had just agreed he had not had any employment or money from any source over the past seven days. So, as is the custom, I wrote *No change* in the declaration box and returned it for him to sign. However, our manager and main troubleshooter, Les Clydesdale, happened to be coming down the stairs behind us and, seeing my client, shouted, "Eric bloody Wilson? What are you doing here?" He grabbed the form which Eric had just signed. "No bloody change? You cheeky sod! You tried to sell me twenty fags off your tray outside Lewis's only yesterday. You're getting nothing. Get out and take that bloody dog with you."

Eric got up to leave but at the door he turned and said, "I'm going, and I'm going to get rid of the dog and I'm going to buy one with buck teeth!"

We all wrinkled our brows as Les said, "Buck teeth?"

"Yes," said Eric, "buck teeth. So it'll come back and bite you through the f—ing grill."

With that, he left, while half a dozen officers just dissolved in laughter.

PAYING A VISIT

It was customary to visit clients claiming social security money to check that their situation was exactly as they had declared. So I would take about a dozen cases home and visit them from around 7.30 the following morning, slowly working my way to the office where I would then write up my notes.

Each client had case notes and warning stickers might be added to the cover. A red crescent might indicate violence, or a red star might mean violence to an officer, etc. One morning, on the second floor of a huge block of flats, I knocked on the door and recalled that this case had a 'full house' of stickers. He had just been released from Walton Jail! So I was slightly surprised when he opened the door. In his hand, at face height, he held a hatchet!

I backed off to the wall behind me with a two-storey drop behind that. "OK, it's NAB?" I shouted.

He looked at me and then at the hatchet, and said, "Oh, sorry. No, don't worry, come 'head!"

I followed him in. The flat had no skirting boards, only two interior doors and, in one bedroom, no floorboards at all. In the lounge was an upright piano, which he was in the process of turning into firewood, as both gas and electricity had been turned off for non-payment.

When I told him he could not destroy his flat, he simply said, "They'll rehouse me!"

I pleaded with him that somewhere along the line he had to meet 'them' halfway and stop being impossible. He agreed, though whether he ever changed or not, I don't recall. But I have to be honest and say that I actually spent a very bright and cheerful ten minutes with someone who was dead-set against the system but was definitely not a nutcase!

MY FIRST LIVERPOOL GIG

Mike Hughes was true to his word and arranged my first ever Merseyside club date at a small club in New Ferry, south of Birkenhead. I arrived to find the pianist had excruciating toothache, but that was his problem. My problem was that there was a billiard table in the room where I was to deliver my performance. But worse still, my performance space was on one side of the table, while the audience was on the other, and I had to look at them through the gap between the table and the huge shade hanging over it. So I had only one option! I performed both my spots in a Groucho Marx squat, so my torso was still upright but my head was low enough to be seen by them all. Amazingly, it worked, and it went so well that by the end they were cheering, and the pianist had laughed so much he had forgotten his toothache.

So, my new career looked like a doddle. How wrong could I be? I died at each of the next nine clubs I played, and had it not been for that opening night, I might have given up.

AGENT MANIPULATION

Slowly, I turned my performances around and learnt the tricks of keeping the audience on side and building a rapport with them. This change of fortune arrived when I learnt to relax and appeared to be enjoying the audience's company from the first minute.

The 'Bag of Nerves' gag worked ever better and my style became one of almost asking the audience for their approval before I could carry on. I would soon slip in a slightly bluer joke and immediately ask for their approval. So, rather like Max Miller, I was apparently giving the audience what they were asking for and only ever as rude as they wanted me to be.

The improvement was surprisingly quick, but the fee was stagnant at £3.50 a night. In conversation with Mike Coyne, who had a good few years under his belt, I tried a ploy that might give me some fee leverage. I turned up one Sunday lunchtime at Ozzie Wade's club.

Ozzie Wade's club featured in the classic Albert Finney film *Gumshoe*, where Albert played an amateur sleuth while also compèring a working men's club on the side. The big feature of the club was the resident band of fellas, all well past their best but still knocking out great trad jazz. They called themselves The Saturated Seven!

On Sunday lunchtime, all the minor club agents gathered, and new acts got a chance to impress them, or not, as the case might be. In my case, my spot went very well, and I was immediately surrounded by half a dozen agents. So I took half a dozen Saturday or Sunday bookings all at a £4 fee. Then, on the Monday, I rang Mike Hughes and told him the dates that were no longer available. He displayed his annoyance as disappointment, but up went my fee to £4 minimum and at last he began to take me seriously.

Soon I was offered 'a week' at The Garrick, Leigh, where I was told the previous two comedians had been sacked on the first night. This heightened my nervousness, but I was a great success.

Soon I had enough money to buy a brand-new Mini van, which besides having room for my drums also came with no purchase tax, at around two thirds of the normal Mini price. It cost £400.

I CEASE TO BE A FALL GUY

On arrival at each club, I would eye up the band position and if the drums were set so that the whole audience could see them, I would chat up the drummer and get permission to finish my second spot on drums for a high-impact finish.

But to lead up to this, I devised a routine that involved both the drums and my acrobatic falling skills. I created a film routine which eventually lead to 'Red Indian' jokes while with one hand I played the steady tom-tom rhythm so familiar from old Western films. I would relate a film where the drums started *bum bum bum bum – bum bum bum bum*, etc. Then in every western, very soon, you see a puff, and another puff, a stream of puffs coming over the hill – Freddie and the Dreamers.

I knew Freddie and there was nothing gay about him or his group, but Freddie's style was perfect for the gag. Then I would reach the climax where, at last, someone would shout, "Indians!" With that, I would slam the drumstick into my chest as though hit by an arrow. Having mapped out the layout of the stage, I would then fall backwards like a beanpole. This tremendous finish worked every time. The secret was in my upper arms taking the shock.

Then, one day, while at my social security desk, as I nonchalantly leant on one elbow, a pain shot through me. My elbow was severely bruised. I then accidentally leant on the other elbow and practically screamed, as that too proved to be very bruised indeed. I was damaged. But the real problem came that night when at last I arrived at the well-rehearsed drum routine. On the shout of, "Indians," I once more began falling. But this time, I was so aware of my bruised elbows, that I made sure they did not hit the stage. Instead, it was the back of my head that took the full force and tears spurted from my eyes, and I nearly passed out. I took my bow, while in terrible pain. But the trouble wasn't over, for I had another club and another performance to come.

This time, at the climax, I began to fall but was now determined I wouldn't bang my head again. So, in compensating, the contact was not with my upper arms but fair and square on my sore elbows. I screamed with pain. The audience gasped! The drum routine was never repeated again.

A SPECIAL STORMVILLE MOMENT

Though I was now in the Bleak House student digs permanently, I did pop round to Stormville from time to time for a chat. One night towards the end of 1962, I arrived to find George Harrison having a cup of tea with Ma Storm and Iris and her mate. Soon I had a cup of tea in my hand too as we chatted and Vi kept us laughing.

Sometime later, there was an urgent rapping on the window and we could see it was Paul McCartney urgently beckoning us to come outside. We rushed out to find him back in his car, with the window down, listening intently to the radio as it blasted out 'Love Me Do'! It was the very first time they had heard themselves being broadcast and it was all very exciting, but it was significant in that Paul kept shouting, "Listen to Ringo, listen to Ringo!" That only became significant some time later when it was realised that, though there was nothing wrong with his drumming, George Martin did not like Ringo's drum sounds and got session drummer Andy White in to give the sound he wanted. So Paul was secretly appreciating Andy's drumming.

I was to meet Andy White a few years later and got the complete story. This only happened at one session, for Ringo immediately quizzed Andy and made changes to his kit so that George was always happy with Ringo's sound from that session on, and it never happened again.

A SAD FAREWELL

As the end of 1963 approached, I found myself earning at least £40 every week from clubs, which dwarfed my earnings from social security. I was also working almost every night and getting very tired at the office. It was time to leave. But I had loved every minute working for social security, helping people with genuine difficulties and making it harder for those just trying to play the system.

I had also had some terribly sad experiences. I often visited clients who were not just in a desperate state, but who were incapable mentally of improving their lot. More than once I had to report people totally unable to look after themselves properly. Several times on arrival at the office, I would consult the boss and then ring special services. On two occasions, when they arrived, an infant I had seen alive the past few hours had now passed away.

It was around then that Harold Wilson became prime minister. One of the things the new Government did was take a lot of decision-making out of the hands of social security officers. This led to far more system abuse and allowed many more people to bleed the system while evading their own responsibilities – a terrible error!

When I finally left to turn professional, the staff bought me a music case for my musical arrangements or dots, as Mike Coyne had said it was what I would need. As I said goodbye, I cried bitterly and felt not a little shame that I was leaving them all to carry on their vital work.

The bouncing Balls

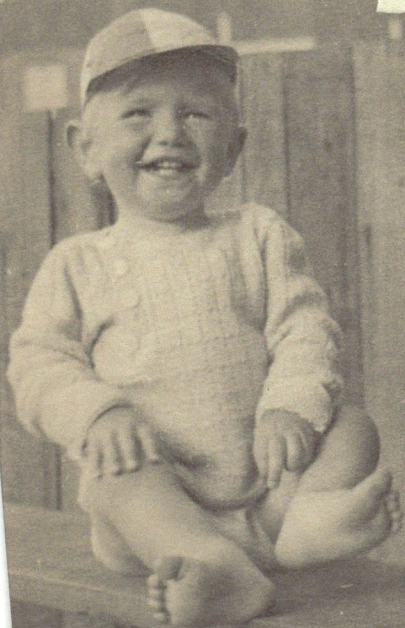

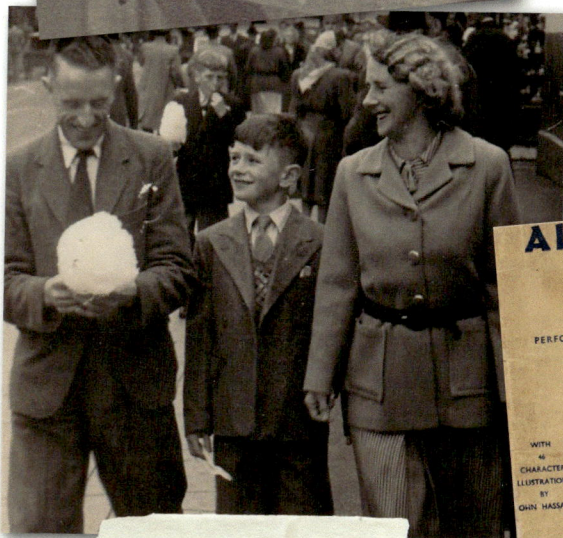

The book that hooked me
onto comedy.

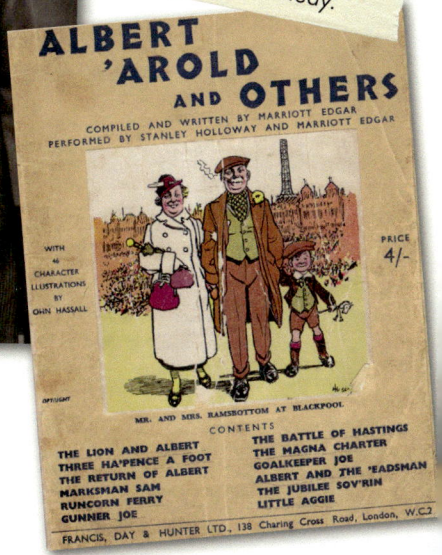

Dad's candyfloss lasted
longer than mine!

ALBERT 'AROLD AND OTHERS

COMPILED AND WRITTEN BY MARRIOTT EDGAR
PERFORMED BY STANLEY HOLLOWAY AND MARRIOTT EDGAR

WITH
46
CHARACTER
ILLUSTRATIONS
BY
JOHN HASSALL

PRICE
4/-

MR. AND MRS. RAMSBOTTOM AT BLACKPOOL.

CONTENTS

THE LION AND ALBERT
THREE HA'PENCE A FOOT
THE RETURN OF ALBERT
MARKSMAN SAM
RUNCORN FERRY
GUNNER JOE

THE BATTLE OF HASTINGS
THE MAGNA CHARTER
GOALKEEPER JOE
ALBERT AND THE 'EADSMAN
THE JUBILEE SOV'RIN
LITTLE AGGIE

FRANCIS, DAY & HUNTER LTD. 138 Charing Cross Road, London, W.C.2

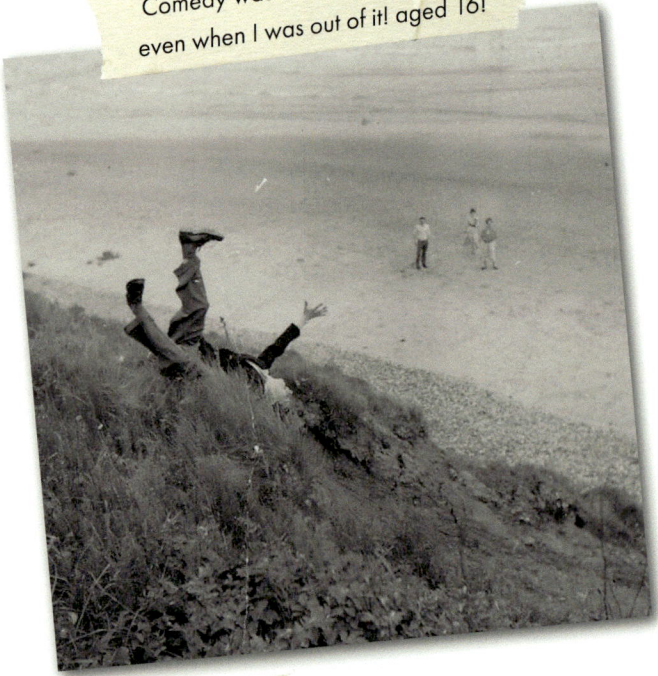

Comedy was always on my mind, even when I was out of it! aged 16!

My only picture in RAF uniform. The photographer asked why we were always so happy?

My first written work. "Aladdin and the Genie with the Gamp!" That's me, dead centre. But all the principles got laughs.

First dream achieved. I'm a Butlins Redcoat.

First picture as a comedian – a cigarette was part of the act.

Impromptu stunt – was I pushing the trolley or dragging it?

Two early tours, 1964 – one a total joy – the other a screaming nightmare.

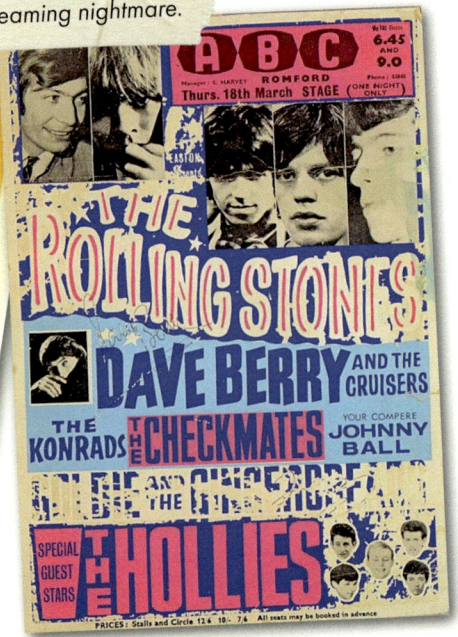

On stage and totally at home!

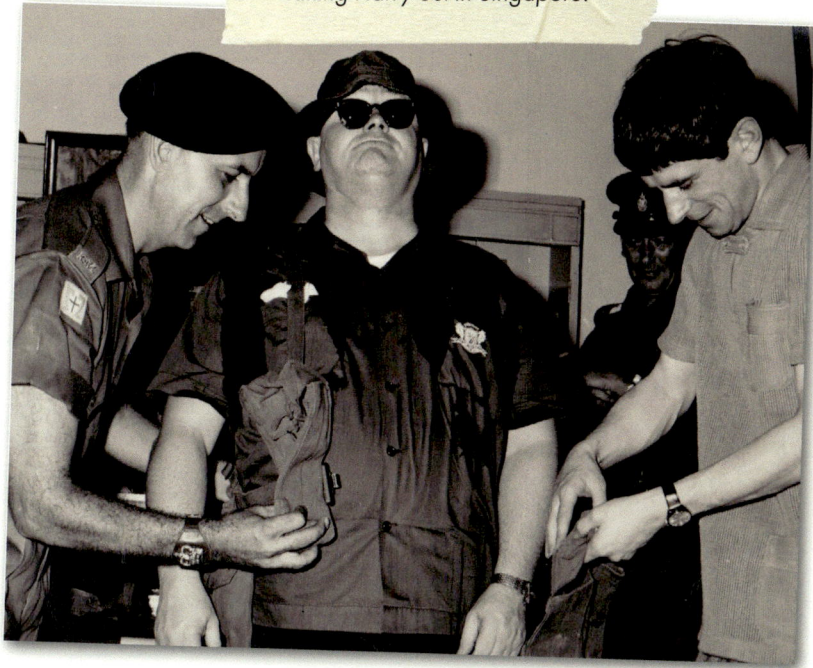
Kitting Harry out in Singapore!

Playschool – a new and surprisingly happy place to be!

Playschool was a perfect fit.

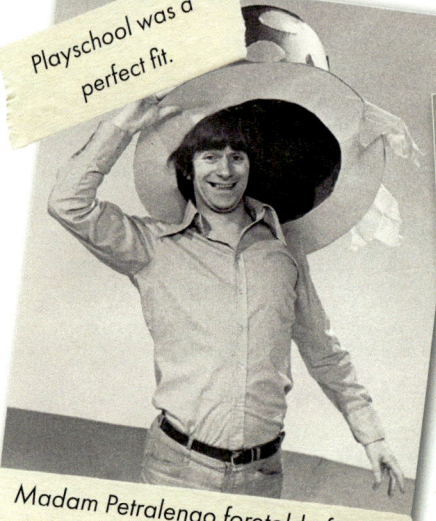

FOR "THE KING WHO LIKED BEANS?" Cutting the legs off the chair was part of the story.

Madam Petralengo foretold of great change, JUST one hour into the future?

WHEEL of FORTUNE.

Night out with Di and her Show Pals. They were on wages – me? – a celery?

The girl I fell for instantly – and snuffles who didn't approve!

And Zoe came too!

Think of a Number has Lift Off!

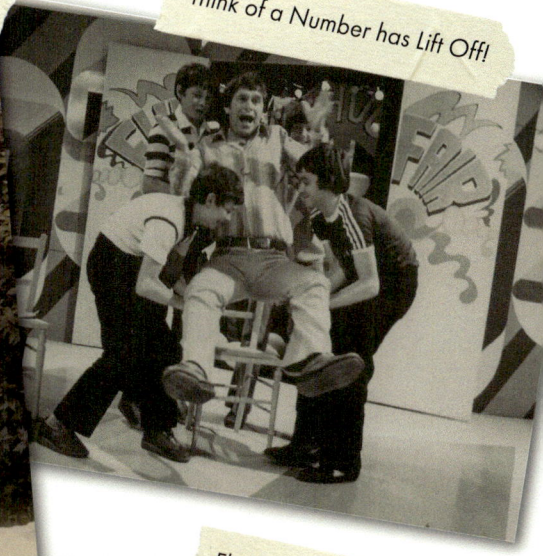

Floating on air!

"Think of a Number" with a rattling good chap.

Let me show you a trick!

All home made – that includes the cupboards!

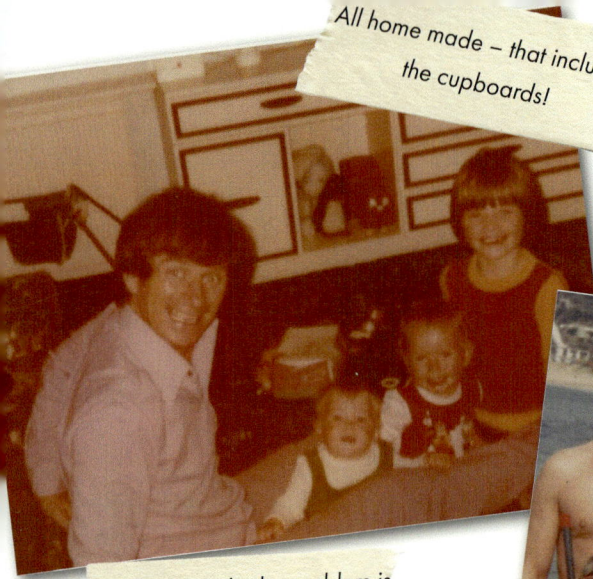
It is not assured that all your kids will be good looking.

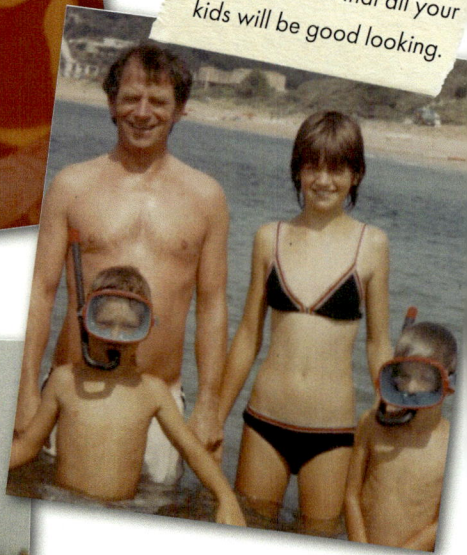
With three kids, the problem is always "the upkeep!"

My Fab Four!

MY PREVIOUS LIFE IN COMEDY

PART TWO

CHAPTER 8

THE PROFESSIONAL COMEDIAN, 1964-1966

EAST BY NORTH-EAST

The first Sunday in 1964 saw me pointing my little green Mini van north by north-east over the Pennines for my first professional gig at La Strada, South Shields. By now, The Beatles were the biggest thing on the planet and Liverpool was their famous home. Now I was part of the new Liverpool comedy sound, following Mike Burton, who, unlike me, actually was from Liverpool. He had been well received, so I was hoping I could do as well.

I needn't have worried, as on the first night it was clear that there was a freshness about our Merseyside-honed material, quite new in Tyneside. Rising to the top in Liverpool, where everyone is funny, was a sure sign that we had something to offer. In fact, I found the audiences beyond Manchester starved of fresh and reasonably clean comedy, so it was a very happy experience.

After my opening show, I ventured out to explore Newcastle's La Dolce Vita, then reckoned the best club in the country. I introduced myself as the comedian at La Strada that week and, with great politeness, I was asked to take a seat in the elegant foyer. A minute later, two identical and very dapper Jewish gents came out of the office, beaming all over their faces. They were the Levi brothers, the club owners. One wore a mink bow tie; the other had mink shoes. They had heard of my success and ushered me to their private table, overlooking the stage/dance floor. I was introduced to Joe Baker just before his spot as the week's star comedian. Then they left me with the instructions to order absolutely anything I fancied; food or booze. If this was to be everyday life for a professional comic, bring it on.

On the Tuesday, after pottering around the shops, I got back to the digs around 5.30pm to be told there was a visitor waiting for me in the lounge. I walked in and a very elegant brunette in a smart business outfit said, "Hello. I'm Norma!"

"Wow!"

Norma was the personal secretary to Stan Henry, who, together with his partner, ran the Bailey Organisation, based in South Shields, and the best club circuit in the country. Norma had called to say she would be at the club that night to catch my spot. We hit it off immediately.

After my spot, each night we called in at the Cavendish, Wetherall's or other Bailey clubs in the area. I never got to sleep before four. If the pace was to be like this every week as a pro, I would be retiring with exhaustion by the time I was thirty. The Bailey club designs were far better than anything I had seen outside movie sets. On top of that, everyone was so very well dressed, which suited me, as I had three handmade suits with matching shoes and ties, besides my stage suit, all in the back of the pathetic Mini van.

To my complete surprise, Norma and I became an item. After that initial week, wherever I was in the country, Norma would check the Friday train times from Newcastle and meet me in Birmingham or Manchester or Leeds ahead of my show and be with me over the weekend.

Through the week, I was 'the comic' and club managements were usually fine, but not over-gushing. Then, on Friday night, I would arrive with Norma on my arm, and everything changed. We were on the owners' table and the booze and food was just there as we wanted it.

Norma knew everyone. When I first met Bob Monkhouse, he said, "So you're Johnny Ball?" Meanwhile, I was getting stronger as a performer all the time.

A MINI CATASTROPHE

If there was anything holding me back it was the Mini van, which didn't suit the 'very smart couple' we had become. Then one night it really did let us down. We arrived at a major junction, leaving Salford for Manchester town centre. It was around 8pm, drizzling, and the traffic was horrendous. As I reached the middle of the junction making a right turn, there was an almighty *bang*. We both hit our heads on the roof as the car stopped dead. Right in front of us, we saw my offside front wheel roll forward and revolve like a spinning coin before rattling to a stop. We both burst into hysterics and couldn't move. All traffic was stopped and while we tried to control ourselves, two bus drivers jumped from their cabs, picked up the front end of the Mini like a wheelbarrow and wheeled us backwards to the curb. Now we really were incapable.

The next thing, there was a rap on my side window. I slid it open, and a Manchester accent said, "Give us yer 'and."

I poked my hand out palm upwards and he put four wheel nuts and the hub cap in it, while the other chap had picked up the wheel and laid it on the pavement. I clearly needed a new car. But the Mini was to outlast Norma.

We were both at a nice country club in Selby one night with the Joseph brothers, who owned Leeds City Varieties. After my spot, a waiter said someone wanted a chat, so I went over. The fella was a doctor and had enjoyed the act very much, but was now curious.

"Could you confirm that you were born towards the end of May?" he asked.

I told him my birthday is the 23rd, to which he replied, "Absolutely, you are a strongly typical Gemini – as was Noel Coward – it just beams out of you. You are at times totally confident and brilliant and at others desperately unsure of yourself."

This was spot on. Although he didn't believe in day-to-day horoscopes, he firmly believed in personality characteristics that indicate birth days or perhaps reflect the time of conception.

Norma joined us and after I explained what had happened, she asked him, "So what sign am I?"

Immediately he came back, "Oh, you are clearly a Capricorn." Spot on again. He then enlarged on her characteristics and eventually I asked him what he thought of our relationship.

He pondered for a moment and then said, "Well, I can tell you she is absolutely the right sort of person you want at your elbow, especially in your profession and at this time." Then he turned to Norma and said, "But you need him like a hole in the head!"

Oh how we laughed – but that was the cue. On the Sunday, still the best of friends, we parted for good.

POP TOURS

On the strength of my successes, I soon had my first taste of the pop world. I was to compère the Dusty Springfield nationwide tour. This seemed right for me, as I enjoyed young audiences.

The opening night was at Edmonton on the London North Circular, and I parked the humble Mini well out of the way and strolled in to meet Dusty, Brian Poole and The Tremeloes, Dave Berry and The Cruisers, and a new name to me, Peter Noone with Herman's Hermits. The opening band was The Gobbledygooks, who were unknown then and unknown again shortly afterwards. We opened and, surprise, surprise, they had a compère who got laughs. I had written a host of gags to suit the young audience – one example was, "What is worse than having a Beatle in your bed? Having a Searcher in your underwear!" It was cheeky and fresh, and the kids loved it.

After the show, I was a showbiz rarity, being almost the first comedy compère to be mentioned in glowing terms in the musical press. After the buzz of the launch party, I quietly walked back to the Mini van and headed two hundred miles back to Liverpool. What other option was there? The very next night, we were booked for the Liverpool Empire!

The night after that, we were in Exeter, then Worcester, Leeds, Glasgow and so on – the tour-booker's mother must have been frightened by a bluebottle. However, from Liverpool on, I travelled on the tour bus, spending most journeys chatting with the wonderful Dusty.

Dusty would have been a wonderful comedian. She talked gags and used goon voices all the time. A highlight of her spot was impersonating Kathy Kirby and other female stars hilariously. For the barefoot Sandie Shaw tag, she popped her head around the curtain and began, "I walk along the city street, I used to walk along with you, daa aaa." And on until, "Oh how can I, forget you, when there is—" She then burst onto the stage in huge grotesque plastic joke feet, with the line, "Always something there to remind me."

It was a wonderful three weeks, and I was always sad that I never worked with Dusty again.

By the second week, my own success was rewarded, as I got news that I would be compèring the first ever Rolling Stones nationwide tour! The two tours were to be as different as 'In a Monastery Garden' and a Fat Boy Slim gig. Once again, opening night was at Edmonton but at a different cinema, right on the junction with the North Circular Road. I got there around 2pm and found the Stones recording 'Little Red Rooster', with Andrew Oldham producing.

The idea was to record with quality sound in the empty theatre, then see if the music could be mixed with the live show in the evening. When Andrew was satisfied, the Stones left, to return later for the show at 8pm. However, by 7pm, the theatre was full and so was the entire main road junction outside, jammed with thousands of screaming teenage girls.

I got us through the first half of the show, but this time I was getting very few laughs from the very young and screaming girl audience. The Searchers closed the first half, but we now had a problem. Every road was completely blocked, and the Stones couldn't even get through! Goldie and the Gingerbreads opened the second half and then I was thrust back on stage to announce the Stones, which was kind of crazy as they weren't even in the building.

The girls screamed and screamed. I managed to get some kind of order and threw a couple of gags at them. There were laughs, but not for long, as the chanting started all over again, only louder, "We want the Stones. We want the Stones." What could I do?

As they chanted, I conducted them and made them go faster until it all broke up. Then I started thanking them for screaming at me but complained 'the Stones' was the wrong name, and I spelt my name on the tabs in big hand-drawn letters. After a while, Dave Berry brought me some crisps, which I threw to the audience. They threw sweets and gum back at me. I had created some kind of rapport, and they weren't actually lynching me.

After just over thirty-five minutes, there was a loud stamping behind the tabs – the cue. The Stones had arrived and were ready. When I got to the wings, their tour manager, Eric Easton, congratulated me on a brilliant job and, as a token of his thanks, handed me a ten pound note as a bonus.

There then followed a two-week tour in which, frankly, no one ever heard a word I said. In fact, I spent more time on stage putting girls back in the audience than actually compèring. At Manchester Opera House, the girls pushed a solid row of bouncers back until the great oak rail around the orchestra pit, with eight-inch wide posts, snapped like a twig. I looked up and saw a girl standing on the very front edge of the upper circle rail. She was leaning out at forty-five degrees like the girl on a Rolls Royce bonnet, with two ushers holding her arms frantically trying to stop her jumping.

One girl had jumped from the dress circle and smashed her leg on landing. They got her into the foyer, with the bone sticking crazily out of her broken leg. I got her a seat and rushed to get an ambulance man. A minute later, she was gone, back into the theatre, and no one saw her again.

That was the end of my pop tour adventures, as I refused other offers. I just didn't need the hassle when I could work comfortably in the clubs with audiences that wanted to laugh.

A BBC ENQUIRY

By now I was having more and more success and felt sure that a break would come. Then we had an enquiry. Frankie Vaughan was planning a new BBC series and needed someone to link the show together. My name had been mentioned.

I was booked at Southport's Prince of Wales Hotel – surely a good place to be seen? The BBC would drive up to catch my spot.

So, with Susan Shirley, a Liverpool singer, we arrived and got a bit of a shock! The event was a 'Young Farmers' Union Annual Ball', and though we were not required until around 9pm, they were all totally plastered by 8pm. Susan was introduced and some four hundred drunken farmers and girlfriends oozed out of the bars, flooding the ballroom.

As Susan began singing, a drunk tried to dance with her. She neatly sidestepped the old fool, not missing a beat. I rushed on and coaxed him back into the crowd. Suddenly, a large table was pushed over and glass splashed across the dance floor.

Susan cut a few numbers, and it was my turn. I had no idea whether the BBC people were in, but that was no longer my concern. How was I going to work this totally drunken mob? The first few minutes were bedlam, but I focused on a crowd of girls, playing them against the fellas, and the laughs started coming. After around eight minutes, I had got them quiet. I did around half an hour and got off to solid applause. I was highly chuffed with what I had achieved!

I went to the foyer and enquired. Yes, three people had arrived from London. They had seen the show and had left immediately afterwards.

A few days later, Mike Hughes rang to say the TV job had gone to Peter Glaze. I thought he was as suitable a partner for Frankie Vaughan as Muffin the Mule was for Red Rum.

Around that time, I had a friend in comedy magician John Wade, whose billing on the stage back page was 'the Patter of Magic Feats'. Shortly after the Southport episode, John wandered into the grade office in London and mentioned my name and his thoughts that I had great potential. The reply came back quite unequivocally, "We hear he's blue!" It was clear that in quelling an almost impossible crowd of drunks in Southport, I had blackened my own name!

LEEDS CITY VARIETIES

One place that almost all club comedians worked in the '60s was the Leeds City Varieties, which featured on BBC TV's *The Good Old Days*, where the audience would book years ahead and arrive in elaborate Edwardian costume. For the normal weekly acts, it was not quite so glamorous.

The City Varieties was the last of the old music hall theatres and reeked, or rather stank, of tradition. Each week, the show featured a stripper and carried titles like *Sunset Strip* or *The Nine O'clock Nudes* or *Bare With Us*. Usually, a music act topped the bill while a comedian acted as compère. The show ran for exactly one hundred minutes with a twenty-minute interval. Despite there being six other acts, that first week, I was on stage for fifty-six minutes of the eighty.

On the Tuesday night, just before the interval, I got a heckler in the circle. I somehow knew the voice, but I waded in and held my own very well, and then pleaded he let me finish, as he was stopping everyone getting to the bar for the interval. As soon as I was offstage, I rushed up to the circle bar to find Bill Maynard, who was filming *Heartbeat* in Leeds. I had never met him before, but the grin told me he had been the culprit. He told me how upset comics would get with his heckling. But, there and then, we worked out a couple of gags which would fit a routine I would be doing in the second half. We did an apparently impromptu exchange which brought the house down.

On the Friday, I got a heckler almost immediately from one of the side boxes. Coming off, I was told Friday was student night. So I ran up to the box during the next act and suggested we meet in the bar at half time. By then, I had written down half a dozen gags for them to heckle at me and the cue as to when to start and, more importantly, when to finish. It worked a treat and slowly I started creating bits in the act which prompted members of the audience to chip in.

This extended the 'Bag of Nerves' opening, which was now a trademark. My style was unique as, through my gentle opening, I was asking the audience for their approval and then building on that. I appeared to slowly gain in confidence as the audience encouraged me that I was actually funny.

A TASTE OF LONDON THEATRE

I realised that however well I did in the northern clubs, it would eventually be London where I would make my name. So I started getting down there at every opportunity.

I caught Frankie Howerd in Sondheim's *A Funny Thing Happened on the Way to the Forum*. Zero Mostel had played Lurcio on Broadway, to great acclaim. But Howerd took it a stage further. It was his greatest career success, resulting in many *Up Pompeii!* spin-offs! An example of his brilliance occurred in the middle of the second half. His eunuch stooge, Kenneth Connor, constantly got everything wrong for which Lurcio always got another laugh with the put-down. By now he had done every eunuch joke. "You don't want to be a eunuch all your life," and, "Just a moment? I wasn't cut out to be a eunuch." Surely now the theme was exhausted? But no! After another Connor gaff, Frankie gave the audience a look as only he could and squeezed out a long slow, "Oo-recently!" The huge laugh was followed by a very solid round of applause – and all for one single word. Now that, as they say, is comedy!

A WELSH ESCAPADE

I was by no means a 'camp' performer, but after seeing Frankie, I found that any slight 'ooh' or 'ah' or 'oh, no!' got a laugh where no laugh had existed before.

In the following week, just one person said I reminded them

of Frankie Howerd. However, I soon found how to maintain the laughs, having dropped the impression – all that was left was an inflection that I owed to Frankie but was now part of my personal comic artillery.

A similar trick was to use local accents when, by the Tuesday, my now slightly localised jokes went even better. This happened when I first travelled down to South Wales, where so many comedians died and hated the place. My first week was to be memorable for several reasons.

I was directed to a pub in the village of Nelson, a dozen miles north of Cardiff. I had my itinerary but the names of the places I was to get to made no sense at all – Ystrad Mynach; Bargoed; Bedwas; all sounded like something from *Lord of the Rings*. But in the pub, two fellas insisted on showing me the way to each club – as it turned out – for the entire week.

They were both very funny – when I could understand what they were saying. One had been a club comedian and singer but had retired. The other I'll come to in a minute. As we arrived at each club, they acted as official translators. We'd have a pint before my first spot, and another before the second and perhaps another afterwards and a few more back in Nelson. They were now my bosom buddies, but they hadn't put their hands in their own pockets, even once.

My chaperones helped me become quickly acclimatised to the accents and pace of the valleys. By the Tuesday night, I was dropping Welsh inflections in everywhere and storming every club, even the notoriously difficult ones. The rising tone at the end of each sentence – "See?" – was so similar to the Frankie Howerd "Ooh!" and another lesson in how to make a very average line much funnier.

A QUITE AMAZING STORY

On the Wednesday lunchtime, I was playing dominoes with my ever-present pals in the Nelson pub when a truly amazing situation developed. By now I had learnt that the pal who hadn't been a comedian had a rather unusual occupation. He was 'the Village Thief'! He never worked and existed by stealing anything anyone wanted, to order. When he told me this, he said it in the same matter-of-fact way as he would had he been an accountant.

Suddenly, the pub door burst open and a chap swaggered in with a surly grin on his face. The Village Thief slammed his dominoes down and said, "Well, you can f— off right away!"

It took me a few minutes to understand what was going on. The intruder was another thief. But this chap wasn't fit to lace the boots of our thief. Our thief could out-thieve this thief any day!

Insults flew, until my thief suddenly jumped up from his dominoes and moved towards the other fella! But, at the last minute, he turned sharply left and out of the pub door. The interloper was now like a stag who had just won a rut. He strutted and scoffed at my mate, mostly in relief, as he had thought he was going to get a busted nose.

In no more than two minutes, the door burst open and our hero returned with a large ledger. On the domino table, he started to flick back through the pages. Everyone was at first flabbergasted and then convulsed. Our man had run over to the police station, popped his head in the door, nipped in and nicked the police charge book! Now he was thumbing through it, highlighting the other chap's entries, which occurred regularly, proving our man was the better thief by far! He then popped out and returned the book. Surreal, but absolutely true!

One last note on my Welsh valley chaperones. On the Thursday, as I put my hand in my pocket to pay for the first round, they stopped me dead in my tracks. They had their dole money, and I wasn't allowed to buy a single drink all night. Halfway through Friday evening, when their cash ran out, they said, "Your turn again now, John lad!" with two very generous Welsh smiles.

That triumphal week saw a sea change in my understanding of how to get inside the minds of club audiences. It was imperative you spoke the same language. So the next week, in Newcastle, I adapted the Welsh accent into a Geordie twang, as both have strong similarities. The responses I was getting began to improve rapidly. It also explained why TV name comics often found it difficult outside London. One exception was the master of stand-up comedy Bob Monkhouse.

BOB MONKHOUSE – THE MASTER

Bob first saw me working a big rough club in Manchester. He arrived looking very out of place in his dress suit with tissues tucked around his neck to stop the make-up reaching his Persil-white collar. He caught me as I came offstage and complimented me on my timing and the fresh new style I was developing. He ended with, "Now watch me get up there and die on my arse."

I watched, and for an hour he paralysed them. That night, he was at the Manchester Cabaret Club, and he did it all over again. Ken Dodd was in to see him that night. Now, Ken achieved more laughs per minute than any comedian, ever. But Bob was the greatest comedy technician I would ever see – the consummate master.

From Bob, I learnt that when you are coming to a major punchline, you make sure you are moving towards the audience on the tag, or lighting up your face, or changing it to a frown – anything with a dynamic impact. This learning process wasn't about stealing – it was about learning the many ways that a performance can be improved and adapted. I feel that in many ways I took to stand-up more like an actor at RADA, exploring every way of turning words into laughs. I was on a long learning curve and the only danger I saw was in my being categorised as a particular type of comedian. The last thing I wanted was to become a comedian you could sum up in two words.

A major asset I had was that I actually loved audiences and could adapt to suit them or persuade them to adapt and join me in my comic world. We were beginning to enjoy each other's company. Surely this was going to be a huge asset for my desire to progress upwards?

Sadly, the truth was quite the opposite. Being able to conquer the majority of clubs, including the rougher ones, by adapting my performance to local requirements was to actually hold me back.

FOURTH IN A FOUR-HORSE RACE

In late 1964 (still my first year as a professional), Mike Hughes called his four principal comedians to Liverpool for a photo call. He had marketed us as the Liverpool Comedy Wave and it worked, even though only one of us hailed from Merseyside. The quite awful picture showing Mike Hughes in the centre with the four of us grouped around him appeared in the 1965 *Stage Yearbook*, as 'Four Up and Coming New Stars'. That we thought it was a terrible idea clearly shows on our faces.

Besides myself, there was my old Butlin's mate Freddie Davies, already an *Opportunity Knocks* success with his Parrot-Face character. Mike Burton was a Liverpudlian who, with his almost skull-like face, could get laughs from incredibly simple comedy ideas. Mike would often temper his Scouse accent and adopt an incongruous posh one.

"I was coming here today and this beautiful woman said, 'Hello, handsome!'

"I said, 'Oh, do you think so?'

"She said, 'Yes, could you tell me the way to the optician?'"

Now, surely that is not very funny? Well it was for Mike Burton, who created genuine warmth with his audience.

The fourth comic was Mike Newman, also ex-Butlin's and the most Irish of Irish comedians, who would screw his face up into grotesque shapes as he talked about the little people and phantom tomatoes. But Mike had gone to school with Con and Dec Cluskey of The Bachelors. From that link, Mike Hughes persuaded The Bachelors' agent Dorothy Solomons to take the two Mikes and Freddie as part of the permanently touring Bachelors show. I was left out in the cold. This wasn't a problem for me, as each time I worked a theatre show I found the far shorter spots left me feeling I had sold the audience short. So, I was happy still working clubs. Many were fantastic, while a lot required all my guile to make a success of them.

All three also appeared on *Opportunity Knocks*, but I refused to even consider it. Everything about it smacked of amateurism. I remember one of them appeared on the show sandwiched between three schoolgirls singing 'Three Little Maids' and a taxi driver from Walthamstow who played 'the mouth organ'. Of course, the show did make stars of Freddie Davies and dear old Les Dawson, who I knew well.

I had met Les on the club scene in Manchester, where he invariably died a death. He was a comedian's comedian, and we all loved his material despite the fact that it didn't get many laughs. His flowery vocabulary was very entertaining to us, but club audiences weren't that enamoured with his total lack of energy. What club audiences wanted was vitality. What Les gave them was lugubriousness. He was a droll and his style suggested a dismissal lack of care for everything, including his own act.

On two occasions, I recall talking Les into carrying on in the business. But I honestly didn't think he would carry on much longer. Then came *Opportunity Knocks* and his static comic style made him an instant star. Les was absolutely perfect for television! Producers loved him, as when Les was on, the production had a rest. BBC's *The Val Doonican Show* was all dancing and movement, and the comedian was the BBC's equivalent to a commercial break – ideal in giving the music and movement a rest.

Meanwhile, I was in such demand in the clubs I still had every confidence that I would get a major break very soon. *The Stage* newspaper's respected James Towler, in his 'Yorkshire Relish' column, featured the four Mike Hughes comedians, ending with, 'But the one with most potential is most certainly Johnny Ball!' Only time would tell.

MY FIRST FORCES TOUR

Meanwhile, I soon got the chance to branch out in a different direction which was to give me enormous pleasure. I was asked to do a British Forces tour and was soon on a plane for Cyprus. Wonderful! I was heading back to the forces I loved, though now with some acquired skill.

The chap in charge of the Combined Services Entertainment (CSE) group was Derek Agutter, who had been a major during the Cyprus trouble. On one occasion in married quarters in Nicosia, an unarmed Derek, with his wife and young daughter Jenny (who was destined to become a huge film and TV star), had sheltered under a kitchen table for over twenty-four hours until they were relieved.

However, the Cyprus trouble wasn't over when I arrived. We stayed at the Curium Palace Hotel in Limassol and on the first morning, I was awakened by a chanting mob marching around the hotel shouting, "British out, British out." It worked – it got me out of bed far quicker than normal, but after it subsided we had no more trouble.

I loved working for forces audiences from the word go. Quite surprisingly, I was asked to keep it clean, which I did. Forces language is pretty rich and their humour brash, broad and basic. But what they wanted from us was a taste of home and good professional entertainment and that is how the shows were designed, with a top of the bill, two musical acts, and two comedians, one of whom did the compèring job – which was to be me.

After each show, we would be entertained at officers' or sergeants' messes, and around the bar, the gags would get pretty racy by the end of the night.

The first show went wonderfully well and after working the west end of the island, we arrived for two nights in Famagusta in the east. Straight after the first show, I was confronted with a young blonde officer's daughter with the devil in her eyes. This isn't really a book about my conquests as a young man, but these next two stories, I think, are worth telling.

The girl was enormous fun and was back again on our second night. We talked about me flying out next morning and agreed we might see each other again, sometime in the near future. The next morning, we arrived at the military airport to find some kind of a hitch. After almost an hour, our coach was allowed in and we were taken straight to board the plane, as we were now behind schedule. It was as we buckled up that the crew told us what the delay had been. Some young blonde major's daughter had tried to stow away on board! It might have been understandable had we been going to England, but we were off to Libya, for heaven's sake, and that was to be the scene of another sexual encounter, but this time in a location where sex was as rare as wooden horse manure.

This story took place long before Gaddafi, when the old King Idris was still ruler and a great friend of the British. He befriended any military personnel who did anything for him and would usually hand them a Rolex watch. A road was built from Tobruk on the coast, stretching south through the desert to El Adem, an airstrip and military base, built there ostensibly for British desert training. In fact, it was there to act as a buffer to protect the King's traditional desert village, a little further south.

El Adem had one women's voluntary service officer, very near retirement age, but who looked younger every day, and one WRAF officer. So imagine my surprise, as we unpacked, when Derek Agutter came in with a broad grin and said, "Well, that's you fixed for tonight!"

I could get no more out of him until just before the show. The officers' mess set-up was settees and easy chairs at the front for the senior officers, dining chairs for other officers and NCOs, and the lads arranged in rows at the back. We had a screened 'wing' area, and as I looked along the front row, my eyes popped out of my head. There, almost exactly centre, was a fluffy petticoated pair of legs in high heels to die for.

"Who's that?" I cried.

To which Derek replied, "I think she's yours."

The show opened and I was on, and the laughs were flowing beautifully. I did a double take on seeing the girl and the whole room cheered, as up till now they had been looking at nothing else. She was about twenty and gorgeous, and next to her was a quite elderly chap in civvy evening dress, with his wife alongside. Everyone loved the show and at the reception afterwards, Derek beckoned me over to meet the threesome.

There was some confusion as we started chatting, as they were under the impression I belonged to a wealthy family in the jam and preserves industry, and I was just having a fling as a comedian before I took over the family firm. In just a week,

Derek and I had become great friends and were constantly kidding each other along.

What this family were doing in El Adem soon became clear. The gent had been a senior RAF dentist and had served King Idris and his family for years and had the Rolexes to prove it. Now he had retired, but the king had summoned his personal friend back for more high-class tooth sculpting. The British Government were keen to keep close to the king, so he was allowed back with his wife and daughter in tow.

After ten minutes, the old chap yawned and said, "Can we leave Clarissa in your capable hands?" And they trudged off to bed, leaving me with their precious daughter. In a minute we were surrounded by RAF personnel, like wasps round a jam pot. I asked if there was anywhere else we could go and we ended up in a tiny officers' cocktail bar with a steward wiping glasses and nearly dropping them when a cocktail-dressed twentyish girl walked in – in female-bereft El Adem? The four young officers already there were immediately around the girl like bees round a honeypot and soon the jokey banter was flying. I was coming back with heckler stoppers and keeping things sort of orderly when the door burst open and in walked two enormous SAS lads just back from survival training. They had been dropped in the desert with no map, just basic rations, and told to get to El Adem, which, with some difficulty, they had done. Now changed, shaved and showered, they were seeking liquid refreshment, until the moment they saw the girl and suddenly alcohol was the last thing on their minds. Here was a very rare, solitary desert dolly bird, but she was stuck with a jumped-up civilian. What was going on?

I found the only way I could protect the lass was for her to stand with her back to the bar while I placed my hands on the bar, either side of her. She was pale but smiling and I was feeling ever more on shaky ground. I managed to keep the situation under control, just.

Then one Flying Officer Kite shouted, "I know what's required. Barman, bumper!"

The steward dived into the fridge and out came a bottle of champagne. Kite took the bottle and started to unwrap the foil. Standing in the centre of the room, he loosened the cork and took aim at the clock in the centre of the bar display. There was a loud *pop* and a groan as the cork hit the ceiling and bounced off somewhere. It was a terrible miss, but now there were glasses for everyone. The steward was used to this regular tally-ho clientele and seemed to be on my side.

Another bottle was ordered, fired and missed, and I spied my chance. As a Butlin's house captain, each evening I had presented a lucky table with a free bottle of Butlin's champagne (really Pomagne and worth about four shillings – 20p – retail). But to complete the ceremony, I would fire the cork into a bucket held by another Redcoat four yards away. Now it was me crying, "Bumper," and buying the next bottle. I started to remove the foil and the wire cage. The room fell silent. The cork was lively, and I had to hold it in place till I was ready. Then, *pop* – the cork flew through the air and hit the clock just a fraction off centre. Hurray!

But what happened next? That was the real surprise!

The assembled officers cheered to a man and then went into a cod ceremony where they presented me with the girl! We toasted each other all round, said our goodbyes, and I walked out of the bar with the girl on my arm. Now that's British fair play for you!

TOURING WITH HARRY SECOMBE

The very next day Derek Agutter came back from the communications room and said, "How would you fancy doing Singapore?"

"What?"

They were so pleased with me that, two weeks later, I was off to the Far East with Harry Secombe. Yippee!

I had first met Harry only a year earlier, in Malta, when I was doing a week's hotel cabaret. I blagged my way into a British Forces theatre where Harry was appearing and was introduced as he waited to go on. It was very dark backstage, and I asked if he could see his way.

He came back, "Don't worry, lad – I've got brail feet!"

Now I was with him on a prestige tour, as the combined Commonwealth Navies were assembled in Singapore Harbour and needed some entertainment. Harry was at the peak of his popularity. We also had Anita Harris on board, as well as Billy Burden, the West Country comic whose opening line was, "Evening! I'm a son of toil. The boss said I look more like a ton of soil!"

Harry's reputation for never uttering a straight line was both daunting and exhilarating, and I was determined to joke along with him from the moment we met. So I read gags for several hours every day right up to our meeting. Now, whatever Harry said, I would come back with an extension of the idea. Within two minutes of our meeting, his eyebrows raised in recognition of what I was doing. He loved it and we hit it off immediately.

As our military aircraft had gone 'unserviceable' at the last moment, we had been stuck in an airport hotel and early next morning we were at Heathrow Terminal 3 and ushered to their VIP lounge. As Harry and I ascended a short flight of steps, side by side, the VIP manager, watching through the frosted glass, whipped the doors open expertly and cried, "Johnny Ball! Hey hey!" and thrust out his hand in welcome, completely ignoring Harry. The fella had been the Italian maître d' at the Pink Parrot Club in Blackpool. Never watching TV, Harry was a complete stranger to him, while I was a comedy star.

It was in that lounge where they broke the terrible news. The only aircraft that would get us to Singapore in time was a Bristol Britannia aircraft, which, instead of jets, had propellers made in Bolton, where I had worked as a sixteen-year-old. What? Surely, flying by prop aircraft to Singapore was lunacy? It was! Thirty hours later, after three eight-hour legs and two refuelling stops, now totally exhausted, we were met by an army officer who, it was soon clear, was having a genuine nervous breakdown. He was excused normal duties and doing anything important. So they put him in charge of our show. He was to prove a bloody nightmare!

Firstly, though arriving at eleven at night, we were whisked to a private restaurant and fed a full three-course dinner which ended, on our insistence, at 1.30am. We got to bed at 2am and were awakened at 6am and told to muster in the hotel lobby in fifteen minutes. We thought there must be a fire, but no – our officer in charge had arranged for us to rehearse! But we required no rehearsal. As compère and with Harry, we had worked out the running order together, timing and music with our pianist on the flight and everything was settled. But we couldn't get back to our rooms, as we were whisked off to an artillery regiment who had been told to show us what they did for a living at 9am. Then, at 11am, we were dragged around the Singapore Forces Hospital, not to see the patients or staff but to see where the Japanese had butchered every allied inmate in their beds when Singapore fell in February 1942.

Then we were whisked to an officers' mess for a 12.30pm lunch and a round of, "Hello and what do you do?" and, "Which one are you?" and, "Can you earn a living doing this sort of thing?" That all stopped when Harry casually told them, in round figures, what he had earned in the previous year.

Now, extremely knackered, we got ready in rugby changing rooms for the first show, at 2pm, to an audience of four thousand. The stage was a boxing ring without ropes, under a huge roof over a fully chaired parade ground. On three sides there were sloping grass banks crammed with navy from the UK, Canada, Australia, New Zealand and goodness knows where else, plus British army and RAF. The temperature was in the steamy nineties.

I went on and the laughs were enormous, or so I thought until I introduced Harry. His reception was like a pop concert, and we were deafened. Harry had decided to work in dress trousers, shirt, black bow and cummerbund, and I had fallen in with that. The noise was so loud that all Harry could do was mime, so he pulled his cummerbund up to look like a bra, struck a gay pose and started dancing with me while the pianist played a waltz. As we danced, completely unrehearsed, I grinned as an idea hit me.

I held Harry tighter and leant forward.

"You're leaning on me, you bugger," he breathed at me.

I danced us to the side of the stage, unhitched myself, ran to the mic and shouted, "Don't stand at the side, Harry. The stage will tilt." I got my laugh!

The show was a breeze. Afterwards, we blocked any invitations and insisted we lie down. They found us other people's beds and we all slept soundly until the fabulous evening show.

At the crack of dawn next day, we were on another prop aircraft heading for Kuching in Borneo. Still dog-tired, right after lunch we went to bed. Seeing how exhausted we were, they cancelled the road transport to our next show, in the middle of the Borneo jungle. Instead, they flew us over the thick forest in two helicopters with huge side doors open. The choppers swirled and danced around each other, across dense jungle.

Our audience that night was an all-male group of hardened fighting soldiers. Just before going on, someone came to me with a stick insect about a foot long, with a body exactly like a huge rubber-plant leaf. It was fascinating, but it gave me the shudders. Then it was showtime, and the piano and drums struck up. As I walked on, a chap in the front row bent to pick something up from between his feet and threw it my way. Four long legs splayed out as the creature travelled through the air. My feet had to jump in opposite directions as the 'thing' landed where I had been standing. It was the most enormous toad. The lads gave a huge cheer. I paused to get my breath. Then I stamped hard on the stage, just behind the toad. Almost reluctantly, it hopped about eight inches forward.

I turned to the all-male audience and said, "Well, enjoy that, lads! That's the only jump you're going to get tonight!"

That got a huge cheer, and we were away with a show, entertaining soldiers fighting in terrible conditions.

After Borneo came Thailand and Penang. On the eleven-day trip, we flew sixteen times, by which time we were back in England. But oh, what a trip!

A FATEFUL LONDON GANG SHOW?

Back in the UK, I was now getting frustrated, as although I was very successful in major clubs, I was getting no breaks at all. I was offered a summer season in Jersey, but I turned it down as being 'off the map' in career terms.

Then my agent rang to say that he had got me a week in London so the London agents could see me.

Great, I thought, but he continued, "It's at Mr Smith's in Catford."

I gasped. Mike Hughes clearly did not watch TV news and had missed the shooting at Mr Smiths, Catford on 7th March 1966. It was one of the most momentous events in gangland warfare! My pleas for sanity were ignored. I even rang the club to check it was even open and they told me that the police couldn't close it down until it's license came up for renewal.

So, a month later, I arrived at Mr Smiths and a bouncer escorted me in. It was Monday afternoon but there were people gambling. The blonde on the roulette table gave me a welcoming smile.

I asked, "Who's the blonde?"

He came back with, "Don't ask about the women in here, John. Mark your card – don't even ask."

The band told me their version of what had happened on the night of the shooting. The club owner, Manchester's Dougie Flood, had apparently asked Eddie Richardson and his pals to 'mind' the club as he used their gaming machines. On this particular night, a group of five or six Kray associates dropped in. Then Eddie Richardson and Frankie Fraser arrived with another three or four mates. Shortly after 3am, when the club was supposed to be closed, Eddie asked Dickie Hart and his mates to leave. A fight started and Hart drew a gun. One witness said it was like the O.K. Corral. Hart shot Harry Rawlins in the shoulder. Frankie Fraser knocked the gun out of Hart's hand but was shot in the thigh either by that gun or one brandished by Billy Gardner. The injured Fraser started kicking Hart in the head, and Gardner shouted, "You're mad, Frankie, f—ing mad!"

Fraser was known as Mad Frankie from that moment. This was a fair assumption, as Fraser was unarmed and fighting several fellas with guns. Hart was soon dead, and his mate Peter Hennessey had a bayonet wound in his head.

Somehow Fraser and Eddie Richardson got themselves out, into a car and to hospital. When the police came round, they said, "Fight? What fight?" A few days later, Ronnie Kray shot George Cornell at point-blank range in The Blind Beggar pub in the Old Kent Road, many believe as direct retaliation for the death of Hart. Reports indicated that the Richardson Gang's reign of power ended then and there.

Not true, at least from my experience. On my opening night, even before I got going, I had a heckler from the bar. As a defence against this kind of thing, a comic has 'heckler stoppers' in mind. But to use insulting gags on a heckler in this place would have been crazy, so I used it on myself – "You're right. I have got a big mouth. Last time I saw a mouth like mine, it had a hook in it." Within a few minutes I had built a routine out of heckling myself.

It worked and a got a better response every night – even on Thursday, which was memorable. As I started my routine, I noticed a single fella at the bar, wearing a light, black, leather overcoat, pork pie hat, dark trousers and an open-neck white shirt – oh, and in the waistband of his trousers, for all to see, he had a rather large gun. He was just marking out the Richardson territory. Needless to say, no London agent came anywhere near.

MY FIRST TV APPEARANCE AS WRITER-PERFORMER

I seemed to be getting more and more second-rate clubs, mostly because I'd recently worked all the good ones. One Tuesday saw me at a club in Darlington with just seven people in the place. The opening got no response and so I started a salvage operation with gags like, "Why don't we all get in a taxi and go to see a show?" or, "You should have been here last night. Well, somebody should have been here last night." The silence was broken by giggles and then laughter and it all got very silly and we had a ball.

Afterwards, in the gents', a fella took the stall next to me and said, "You were brilliant. I'm a TV producer."

He was lucky I didn't turn and pee down his leg. In fact, I ignored him, so once out of the loo, he explained. He produced a fifteen-minute show called *Late Date* which ran around 11.15pm on ITV in the north-east. It featured club singers like Dusty, Joe Brown, Matt Monro and Dickie Valentine. He'd never used a comedian before but wondered if I'd like a try. The set was a deserted night club, with the performer running through their material with the camera eavesdropping.

I agreed to have a go and wrote a short solo play in which, in the deserted club, I asked myself, "Why didn't they laugh at this then?" I'd then do a joke or two and then question whether it was funny and what else I could have done. In my musing, I found a Polo mint in my top pocket, lit a cigarette and treated each as new comedy inspiration. I then turned my attention to the musical instruments. I tried to lower the support strut of the double base by sitting on the floor and balancing the whole thing on my knees and then loosening the strut. I then stood up to play it and put the pointer through a knot hole in the floor. After another gag, I fired the butt of my fag off a string, timing the gag to it hitting the floor. I put a cymbal on my head and did Chinese gags – political correctness was not an issue in those days, but neither was I insulting; it was all for fun. The show ended with me still musing as the credits rolled.

The producer loved the script and the date was set. But when I arrived, they didn't have a clip-on microphone, just four stand mics dotted here and there. So rather than wander at will, I had to block the whole piece so that I was always near a mic at any time. In sorting all this out, we used up all the time. So, without rehearsal, I did the fifteen-minute show in one take.

But it worked. I remember Colin James of the Morgan-James Duo saying they thought it was something very special. Other than that, I don't think anyone noticed. But it was my first telly – I had secured and created the job myself and it was both original and totally different.

I NEEDED TO WRITE AND CREATE

I had achieved success in the clubs by moulding myself to what those audiences required. But really what I wanted to do was create something that was totally me and not shaped by others. As I had said aged sixteen, "I want to be a writer!"

One original routine came to me while I was stuck in a traffic jam on the Shepherd's Bush triangle with comedy magician John Wade, who I stayed with on occasion. John mentioned an American comedian talking about calling things what they are instead of giving them fancy names. For instance, why even call a heart a heart, when all it is really is a pump? That was all I needed, and in that traffic jam I wrote this routine:

"Why do we use confusing technical terms? My uncle invented a 'Streptotrap', which is used in hospitals for catching streptomycin. But why do we need complicated names for things? Even the heart? Why call it a heart? It's a pump. It pumps blood round your body, down your arms and up your legs, oops? Call it what it is. It would change things, but you have to change with the times.

"Song titles would be different. You'd have tunes like, 'You're Breaking My Pump, 'Cos You're Leaving' or 'We Are In Love With You, My Pump and I'," (then rising in intensity), "or 'From the Bottom of My Pump, Dear' or Cilla's 'Anyone Who had A Pump!' Pump, pump. Or what about The Bachelors hit," (big finish), "'Love Me With All Your Pump'?"

Immediately, the heart routine proved extremely strong; so much so, just about everyone nicked it. Johnny Hackett used on *Sunday Night at the London Palladium*. Then, at the Talk of the North, I got no response.

"Who did this last week?" I asked?

"Frank Carson," came the reply.

Eventually, I knew of six female acts alone who made it part of their act. What price originality?

BBC RADIO EXPERIENCE

I was called in to do radio spots for Geoff Lawrence at BBC Manchester, which improved my comic creativity hugely. My third show was a BBC *Blackpool Night*, and halfway through, I was clearly the hit so far. So, from the back of the theatre I watched the last comedian, Albert Modley, who was well stricken in years and surely past his best? Really?

He came on and began in his broad Yorkshire accent. "I were walking past this pub. Hee hee. I were walking past this pub. And I thought, this can't be me walking past this pub? And it weren't – I were inside! Eee, it's grand when you're daft."

The effect was electric. Within three minutes, I was laughing so much that I slid down the pillar I was leaning against. But what was I laughing at? Gags like calling through the microphone, "How are you all in Scarborough? I once bought a bike in Scarborough. You can't go wrong – all't roads are downhill. Hee hee!"

Modley's comedy was totally effortless. He got even more laughs when he forgot a line or messed it up. It was his love of his audience that beamed across the footlights at you. You could do nothing else but return that love and good humour. When he went, "Hee Hee," suddenly, so did everyone else.

I loved and understood Albert Modley and Ken Dodd and Frankie Howerd – but I envied none of them. I wanted to be me, but my problem was, I didn't want 'me' to be so simple and two-dimensional. I wanted to do more – to be more multifaceted.

Well, as 1967 dawned, we entered a year when I was to get not just one but several opportunities to break new ground. It was to prove a most fateful year.

CHAPTER 9

1967 – A VERY EVENTFUL YEAR

HAPPY IN THE CLUBS

1967 came in with an impossible task. Alan Williams was thrilled with my stand-up success and booked me for a New Year's Eve spot at Liverpool's Blue Angel, as I was working a club just out of town. At 11.30pm, I was ready to go on, but the stage platform was just six inches high, and the low-ceiling cellar room was one solid mass of revellers. Alan said it was pointless for me to try the act, so sadly he couldn't pay me.

"What?" I grinned at him!

So I shuffled my way around the floor, grabbed the mic and performed, while looking straight into the eyes of people just a foot away from me. I got order amazingly and got some good laughs till, running close to midnight, I wished everyone a Happy New Year. Alan paid up.

One of the most amazing successes as a club in those days was Greasborough Miners Welfare Club, Rotherham, which I played with Matt Monro as top of the bill. As with all miners' clubs, the week started with the Sunday noon show in which ninety-five per cent of the audience were men who downed copious pints and then went home to recommend, or otherwise, the six acts for that week.

I arrived around 10am, and I was talking to comedy magician Mark Raffles, who was already quite well stricken in years. Mark asked me to come to the bar with him as the miners started to arrive. When he explained why, I realised that my presence might well be matter of life and death. Besides being a magician, Mark was an expert pickpocket who would relieve helpers of their watches, wallets and braces without them noticing, while the audience saw everything. But with Sunday lunch audiences, it was impossible to get volunteers to come onstage. So he needed to force them! So, beforehand, he would mix and mingle near the bar and quietly steal a few items so that later he could entice the owners onstage to retrieve them. I was needed because, as good as he was, if he was caught, a hulking great miner might not be too happy with a posh-accented southerner nicking his belongings. But Mark was so good I wasn't needed and inside two minutes, he had a watch and a couple of wallets.

OK. I was billed second top just before Matt Monro, but a couple of acts ran over their time and I was told I could only have seven minutes – or not go on at all, which sometimes happened during the shortened lunchtime performance. I begged ten minutes and told the organ and drum backing to play my intro music extra fast. On I went and, cutting out all the padding, I machine-gunned just the gags I knew would work well. It was a riot and over in eight minutes, but the applause took another two minutes. The staff thought it was wonderful and declared I would be doing that act every night.

Soon I was using the shortened act ploy on Friday nights in young-audience clubs, where I could hit the hen parties for six and then get off before their concentration span collapsed.

A MISSED OPPORTUNITY

Well, as 1967 unfolded, so did the direction of my whole career, and what promised to be a high-achieving year gradually turned into one that wasn't going to be very pleasant at all.

Firstly, a phone call came. Harry Secombe had a one-hour BBC TV show devoted to our far-eastern forces tour and they had a spot from me – my first national telly. However, my agent, seeing I liked forces audiences, had booked me to tour American bases in Germany and Italy. I had heard about dreadful American bases and never wanted to go anywhere near them – people only worked them if they couldn't get work elsewhere. Sadly, the London agent wouldn't release me from the US troop tour, even though they neither knew nor cared who I was. This was a major black mark against my agent.

Harry and the others talked about me and showed still shots of me working in Singapore, but not so there was any impact. The cast all wished me well via the TV screen, but it was a golden opportunity missed.

The US bases tour was a fiasco, and I hated every minute. Officers and NCO mess audiences were OK, but the other ranks were pretty much animals. After the first night, I sat down in my hotel room and wrote an act especially for them. It worked and I survived. The gags were crass and brash – "What a terrible place! Even the 'john' attendant has left. He couldn't stand the smell from the kitchen!" To break the boredom, I hustled US troops at pool each night, only ever losing one game. Three weeks well worth forgetting.

RADIO LEADS ME TO TELEVISION

By now I had done quite a few radio shows for Manchester producer Geoff Lawrence and he had become a great friend.

One day, Geoff got a call saying that BBC Children's TV was looking for a suitable northern performer. Thinking the show had to be *Crackerjack*, he instantly recommended me.

So, I arrived at the same Manchester hotel where I had clinched my Butlin's Redcoat job, and I was once more absolutely up for it. I breezed in and could tell from the smiles and reactions that BBC Producer Peter Ridsdale-Scott was sold after a few moments.

As I paused to take a breath, he said, "Oh, I think you'll be wonderful in *Play School!*"

I stopped dead! I asked, "*Play School?* What's that?"

He said, "It's a programme for under-fives on BBC Two…"

I was off for the door, but he followed and persuaded me to stay. He explained that the show went out at 11am Monday to Friday on BBC Two. But no one I knew even had BBC Two! It was just about in its third year and the take-up was very slow. So I'd be practically unseen.

Peter explained, "Every time you are booked, you do a week of five shows, so the money isn't bad."

Most predominant among my thoughts was the fact that it was television, and I knew I needed more experience of how TV worked. So I agreed to do their audition.

At Tyne Tees, I had kept asking what the shot was. Close up, medium or a long shot. When the producer asked why I wanted to know, I had replied that whatever part of my body the audience can see, that part needed to be working. That was to wrinkle the brow of more than one TV director in the years ahead. At the London audition, I found myself amongst half a dozen actors.

One chap was pacing up and down saying, "Humpty and I are going to sing you a song!" And then, "Hrrmph. Humpty and I," (smile to non-existent camera), "are going to sing you a song!" This was another world.

As I waited, I realised that I was the only one not in jeans and trainers. I was in a tailor-made suit with Russell & Bromley shoes in a matching shade. I took my jacket off and loosened my tie. Then it was my turn.

I was shown the set and basically they wanted me to draw a tree in a field and some branches, and, while doing it, introduce a song called 'And the Green Grass Grew All Around', which surprisingly I already knew. I fixed my key with the pianist and awaited my turn. What was I doing with these actors who mostly looked like they were on the dole? I was earning £150 a week with never a week out. Why try something so totally opposite to what I was getting ever better at? So, as the job meant absolutely nothing to me, unlike the others, I was totally relaxed and at home with myself, if not with the toys scattered around. So I began drawing on the blackboard:

"This is the story about a tree in a field, with a branch on the tree, and a twig on the branch and a nest on the twig, but I didn't need to tell you that because it's all in the song!"

In the absolutely silent studio, I could hear strong laughter coming from the control room upstairs.

I was the only person at that audition to get the job, purely because I was the only one who didn't need it – it's a situation so common in every branch of the entertainment business. You can always get the breaks you don't really need.

The first recording date was only a month away and after ordering two pairs of cavalry twill slacks to go with my three Singapore handmade shirts, I booked into Snows Hotel on the Cromwell Road for the week. This was a 'pros' hotel and several comics stayed there, including Billy McComb, 'the Talkative Trickster', and Chic Murray, who was to become a great drinking buddy. It was a very lively, heavy drinking hotel.

Play School recorded daily from around 10am until 3.30pm

and I would be back at the hotel half an hour later, with the rest of the day my own. What could be nicer? Haha!

My co-presenter Miranda Connell was blonde and petite but surprisingly nervous, which was not conducive to a good working situation. In fact, she was on Valium, and I was on glucose tablets through exhaustion. The pianist, Jonathan Cohen, kept geeing me up with, "You're jolly good!" But I knew that the twee script was jolly bad. In the pub across the road on the Friday, I asked the floor manager how I had faired actually. He said, simply, "You were f—ing diabolical!"

They gave me a second week and I improved, but there was something holding me back. Give me a song or a story and the TV camera and I was OK. Get me to do a duet, while holding Little Ted and Hamble, and I just couldn't relax. At last, my new boss, Cynthia Felgate, took me to one side and said, "When you are happy with the material, you are brilliant. But when you get it into your head that the material is below you, you are terrible. So you are letting both yourself and us down. So go away and think – 'do I want this job?'"

I realised that it was only my mental block that was spoiling everything. I also saw that though I adored working the big clubs, I could do without the 'not so good' clubs, which accounted for two thirds of my club work. Now, with this TV work and the forces shows to break it all up, I could ask agent Mike Hughes to bypass the bad in favour of the good. It cut no ice, and I still got saddled with bad clubs all too often.

One of the reasons for this was that anyone could work the good rooms but comics that could be successful in the Social Toilet Clubs as well were highly sought after. In the North East, I would walk on top of the long tables, trailing my mic lead and avoiding the glasses, just to get order. If the gents' was close to the stage, which was surprisingly often, I would sometimes follow a chap in there and continue the act, oblivious of how it was going with the audience, only to come back and find that it had worked a treat. But is this what I wanted?

After a few days, I called Cynthia. Yes, I wanted strongly to stay with *Play School* and even help broaden the scope of the programmes. What clinched it was the total integrity of Cynthia, Peter and the rest of the *Play School* team. It was a totally different world to the clubs, but one I was beginning to like more and more. I had no conception then that I would stay with *Play School* for sixteen years and the BBC for over twenty.

HARRY NEEDS HELP

It was still quite early in the year when I got a call from Harry. After Singapore, I wrote him a few gags when he had a record in the charts. The lines need Harry's Goon-type voice, but among them was: "I've got a new record out. It's plastic, you know – waterproof, you can play it in the bath. There's even a hole in the middle to let the water out!" He replied with thanks and a cheque, which I sent back, as I felt I had learnt more from him than vice versa.

Now I had a message that he had something that might be of interest and for me to call him at the Theatre Royal Drury Lane. By coincidence, that night it was the birthday of Carol, my Cyprus stowaway pal, and we were already in London. I picked Carol up and we popped in to catch Harry in his dressing room.

It was a very strained atmosphere indeed and clearly they had problems with the previews for *The Four Musketeers*, a new big-budget Delfont musical with Harry playing the hapless D'Artagnan. Harry welcomed us with open arms and introduced me to Jimmy Grafton, who kept the Grafton Arms in Victoria, where *The Goon Shows* had first been hatched. Harry was clearly worried about the script and insisted we stay to see that night's preview, which would be a birthday treat for Carol. But Harry made such a fuss and asked that I come back in the interval. I insisted he'd be too busy, and he replied, "Not for you, come back at half-time. Seriously!"

Jimmy Grafton then said, "If you can think of any gags that might work in the show, let me know!"

That was a surprise, but Harry's reaction was even stranger. "Yes, and you'll f—ing pay him for them!" The tension was enormous.

We sat in the stalls behind the director's working desk with Jimmy on my right and Bernard Delfont, then probably the most powerful man in British theatre, on our left. Along the row were writers, director and the designer Sean Kenny. There was a saying in those days: 'At a Sean Kenny musical, you come out whistling the set.' *Musketeers* was no exception.

Drury Lane is the largest stage area in London. It had no problem landing a full-sized helicopter every night for *Miss Saigon* some years later. But Sean Kenny was much more ambitious than that and the sets were enormous. A fight scene had Cardinal Richelieu playing a honky-tonk piano, forty feet up in the air. Then, from that point, someone was hit and fell to certain death, only to land on a cushioned bed, rolled out in the nick of time and pulled offstage again. The Musketeers retained their original characters: the lover, the gambler and the drunk. The leading lady wooed each in turn around a huge bed. For the lover, the bed became a pink and sexy boudoir; for the drunk, an alcoholic's paradise of dangling bottles; then for the gambler, a giant casino. When romping in bed, the gambler's leg hits a lever and they are showered with coins. The line, "I think I've hit the jackpot!" should surely have got a laugh? It didn't.

We went backstage at half time and Harry wanted my thoughts on everything we had seen.

The second half had even greater problems. Harry's big solo, 'This Is My Song!', which was to reach number two in the charts, was drowned by the squeaking and squealing as a huge ship swung in to fill the stage, with the rear end far up stage left, while the prow of the ship and figurehead reached over the orchestra pit and the people in the fourth row of the stalls.

After the show, back in the dressing room, Carol and I were pressed into service, serving drinks for Harry's visitors, including John Profumo of the Christine Keeler scandal and his wife. They had gone after half an hour and suddenly Harry and I were surrounded by the writers and producers, standing in a circle.

Harry turned to me and said, "Tell them what you told me about the bed scene."

I gulped with embarrassment but explained that a three-sequence gag might work but the four-sequence gag was not and at least two of the early sections were getting nothing at all, thus dragging the whole thing down. So when Harry eventually got on stage, he had to build the audience back up again. Then just as he started getting laughs, the scene was over.

Later still, when most people had gone, Harry grabbed Bernard Delfont and I by the shoulders, so we were eye to eye, a foot apart.

Harry said, "This lad is brilliant, you know. I'll take you to see him work."

Delfont replied, "You'll be working here."

And Harry came back, "There's bloody Sundays!"

I found it totally embarrassing!

A week later I was back, and the Musketeers' parts had been trimmed to the bare minimum. However, the leading lady's main song had been cut and she had left the show. That night, I had just a few ideas for Harry and after the show, Sean Kenny joined us and the three of us got pleasantly plastered, which was the tension relief that Harry needed.

Eventually, the show was knocked into shape and ran for just over a year. But I had experienced a big star fighting for the sake of the show, but most especially for his own reputation. It's tough in show business, even, or perhaps especially, when you are at the top.

A GLIMPSE OF THE TOP?

Around that time, I got a close look at how things look from the top when I toured with Judith Durham and the Seekers in spring '67. We did theatre one-nighters usually on Thursday to Sundays. Judith was lovely and in Norwich she had a friend in tow, who I got chatting to.

Next thing, I'm driving the girl, whose name was Jacquie, back to London. I asked her how she knew Judith and she declared she was connected to show business in that her dad was George Black junior, and I had to hang on tight to stop swerving off the Norwich road. George and Alfred Black had preceded the Grades as Britain's most successful impresarios. They owned Yorkshire-Tyne Tees Television and, since the Crazy Gang days, were still major producers of top UK shows.

So, we had become something of an item, and I called in to see her at Blackpool's Clifton Hotel, where she was staying with her family! When Ken Dodd was mentioned, I realised they were producing his summer season at the Opera House and it was opening night. I asked why they weren't there. Five minutes later, we were, as Jackie and I just passed in and watched from the side aisle.

The show was all Doddy, interspersed with dancers and Diddy Men. But Doddy was never offstage for more than a few minutes. Besides watching Doddy, I watched the audience. They would sway backwards and forwards like a field of wheat in a high wind in August. Some older people had to be helped out before they did some permanent damage. I just needed that one experience. I then started to aim, in my own act, to roll the audience, then let them rest, then roll them again, in the same way. I was learning from the King of Comedy.

Back at the hotel, we joined a worrying discussion about another star. Tony Hancock was compèring the Saturday night BBC TV special from Blackpool's ABC Theatre. But here the story was quite different. He was difficult, unhappy and, frankly, dying on his feet. This is when I first met Tony's brother, Roger, who had been managing the family hotel in Bournemouth until Tony had started suffering such awful nerves. He had sacked his writers, Simpson and Galton, and jealously complained about everyone in his shows and especially Kenneth Williams, who got gales of laughter from even straight lines.

I later learnt that his most celebrated TV shows almost failed being made. The schedule meant studio recording start at 8pm for a half-hour show and ended at 9.15pm or 9.30pm latest. For one TV show, he had declared the script totally unfunny after a week's rehearsal and refused to come out of his dressing room until gone 9.15pm. At last, he emerged and recorded *The Blood Donor*, recognised even today as possibly his and Simpson and Galton's finest ever episode.

As it turned out, the Blackpool problem got worse. Tony later took an Australian winter tour but told Roger that he had suffered enough so he would do this tour without him. It was on that tour that Tony Hancock sadly committed suicide.

AT LAST, A MAJOR BREAKTHROUGH

Meanwhile, in early September, Mike Hughes mounted a shop window show in London. These shows had been successful for others in the past, but now it was my turn. There were around eight acts in each half as comedians alternated with music acts. But the prized spots were me closing the first half and Freddie Starr closing the show.

By now, I had enough experience to tackle this kind of audience. TV production people are not at all generous with their laughter – for those in TV, comedy can be a very serious business. However, when my spot came, I mixed my surefire material with some coaxing and ice-breaking and it went better than I could have anticipated. My BBC Children's TV people were impressed by my 'other self'. But most impressed was a group of three people on a table to my right – and with them, I really cracked it.

After the show, they called me over and introduced themselves. Sid Colin was Head of Variety at Rediffusion Television. He introduced the producer and director of a show called *Down at the Old Bull and Bush*, which had been using the camp Ray Martine as compère. They had a ninety-minute Christmas Eve special lined up for recording in late November, and they needed someone new, having turned down several past compères from *Sunday Night at the Palladium*. Now they wanted me, after which they would be planning thirteen shows running up to Easter 1968. Suddenly, it looked like being 'my turn'!

MEANWHILE, WHAT'S IT LIKE IN A WAR ZONE?

In early November, a story hit the news that Hughie Green had gone out to Aden where our troops were having a very rough time. He gave them a sort of *Opportunity Knocks* revisit, with a few inexperienced winners in tow. Suddenly, without warning, Hughie Green cancelled the final show for our troops in a very tight situation so he could get his film back in time for his live *Opportunity Knocks* show. The tabloids slammed him. This was, of course, disgraceful!

Hearing the news, I picked up the phone right away and apparently my call was a second behind Harry Secombe's. In a couple of days, we had a show ready, and next day, arrived in the Aden action zone.

At Aden airport, as we boarded our bus, the driver asked if I played football. I thought he might be suggesting a five-a-side between the show and the lads. I was wrong.

I dropped into the seat behind him and said, "I play a bit. Why?"

He said, "Sit there and when a hand grenade comes in through the door, you side-foot it out again!" He was deadly serious.

The heat was stifling at around 110F and so all the coach windows were open but covered in chicken wire for protection. The driver's mate stood by the open door, with one hand on the lever to close it. As we went past a souk, it would be easy for anyone to nip out, throw a grenade, nip back and be lost in the alleyways in no time.

We were soon in the safety of the base. By lunchtime next day, we learnt that an officer and an NCO who were returning from leave and we had been chatting to on our flight had been killed at the checkpoint into Crater. The officer half searched an Arab and then turned to give an order. The unspotted gun was out, and they were dead – the rest of the crew blasted the attacker against the wall, but that was little consolation.

Harry and I passed through that very checkpoint a few hours later, with escort, of course. Crater was too dangerous for an actual show and no one else in the cast came with us. Crater, as the name suggests, is in an extinct volcanic crater, like an inverted cone. The volcanic rock is so craggy you could hide a hundred snipers, who could pick off people in the tiny town at their leisure – that was, until Mad Mitch brought his Command of Argyll and Sutherland Highlanders in to sort things out. They commandeered a bank, as the toughest building in the place, and the lads worked eight-hour shifts, on and off, and slept on the marble floor when off duty. From there, Mitch gave his orders. He highlighted snipers he wanted removed and sent small parties to ferret them out. Several of the lads complained that he was ignoring a sniper who was actually very close.

"That bastard couldn't hit a barn door with a banjo!" he said. "We'll leave him till last."

The operation took a couple of days and Crater was secure and much safer.

Harry had been sent for, but they hadn't said why. We were gagging around with the lads, who were in remarkably good spirits, mostly because Mitch had proved to them how bloody good and professional they all were. Then we arrived at the bank. New toilets had been hastily built and Harry was shown a tartan ribbon ready to be cut. Without a pause, he ducked under the ribbon and into a cubicle. He yanked the toilet chain and said, "All cisterns go!" He then cut the ribbon, saying, "May God bless her and all who *thrrrrup* in her!" blowing his celebrated *Goon Show* raspberry. Scotch whisky flowed like… well, whisky as we and the troops grabbed the opportunity.

Our show had been thrown together quickly and Harry's pianist was not available, but the Diamond Twins (a pair of beautiful blondes) had brought their pianist, Les Baguilly, who Harry knew of old. What Harry didn't know was that Les had filled the intervening years on the sauce and was in a pretty sorry state when we met, leaving England. Out in Aden, Les kept downing pints to cool down in the heat, which, as anyone will tell you, doesn't work. He was becoming a liability. Then we had a show at 2pm to about 1500 lads in an improvised open-air theatre set between a couple of two-storey barrack blocks. The stage was on a platform at the end, facing into the sun, which was nigh on overhead. The breeze that blew between the blocks did nothing to lower the temperature, which stood at about 105 in the shade, which we didn't have.

On these tours, you only ever needed to ask, and a drink would be in your hand in a few seconds – the forces are wonderful hosts – which leaves it down to you yourself to control what you are consuming. No amount of explaining this had worked with Les and he was in a sorry state as he sat on stage at the second-rate upright piano for Harry's spot. He plonked his full pint on top of the piano and sat in his saturated shirt, sorting the music, while I filled in easily with gags. We conscripted two lads from the audience to hold the music as the warm wind blew straight at us.

When all was ready, Harry walked on to tumultuous applause and the laughs followed as always. As a hush fell just before Harry's first song, an excited lad in the front row shouted, "Go on, Harry – give us a song."

Harry walked over and, standing directly over the lad, he looked down and said, "Settle down now, young fella, settle down, or I'll fall on you!"

Harry's showstopper, long before The Three Tenors' success, was 'Nessun Dorma'. So he began – "Here is a song – well, it's an aria really, but then I am Aria Secombe – ha ha. It's a song written by Fred Puccini – tall thin fella with glasses – entitled 'Nessun Dorma', or 'none shall kip', or 'sleep'."

Les struck up on the old but in-tune piano and Harry launched into the song. As always, the crowd were enraptured! Then they reached the middle eight bars where the piano restates the tune and builds to Harry's final verse and big finish. Harry looked over to the bare-headed Les, who was sweating so profusely that spray was flying in every direction, though he was playing all the right notes. His shirt was sticking to his flabby flesh and the wind was blowing the music around while he was broiling like chicken on a spit in the relentless sun.

Soon he came to the music bridge, which ends on four huge, loud, echoing chords – come on, you remember 'Nessun Dorma'?

La dada dada, dump da dada, la dada dada, dump da dump, (chord), bump, (chord), bump.

Now, in perfect time, Les grabbed his full pint and emptied it over his own head, put the glass back on the lid and hit the four chords as Harry's intro – *bang bang bang bang!*

But no note came from Harry. He had collapsed in laughter, and we were both totally helpless for a couple of crazy minutes. Eventually, Harry regained his composure, tried to ring Les's shirt out while he was still wearing it, and at last picked up again from the piano for the big finish. As usual, the lads went wild.

While in Aden, we were privileged to be invited to the Governor's Palace where we were waited on by liveried servants as though it was still the era of the Indian Raj. The view over the sea from its high clifftop position was wonderful, but what was most memorable was the conversation. The senior officers told us what they thought of the situation. These weren't squaddies grumbling about what their idiot officers had them doing. These were very senior army and diplomatic personnel, and they were ragging at the Wilson Government and the alcoholic George Brown's decisions, which, just a few weeks later, had the British Forces evacuating Aden 'backwards' with guns at their hips, like defeated cowards, when, had anyone been adequate for the job of negotiation, an agreement would have been easily achieved where the Brits could have marched out of Aden with bands playing and banners flying.

MY FIRST MAJOR TELLY

Slowly, the Rediffusion show got closer and at last the cast was confirmed. Scott Walker of the Walker Brothers was to be top, joined by The Bachelors, with Kenneth McKellar, Bud Flanagan, Aimi MacDonald, Kiki Dee, Tommy Bruce with two buxom girl singers – and knitting it all together would be yours truly.

Rediffusion's Head of Comedy Sid Colin was always on hand and had booked two writers – Barry Cryer and Dick Vosburgh. They had never seen me, and running my routines to them in a coffee bar was something I could not get used to. I was seeming, to them, rather unfunny! They both spotted my self-effacing style, and Dick came up with two gags: "I don't have to do this for a living. I could be a detective. Yes, I've always had a nose for something crooked – and something crooked for a nose." Or: "I don't have to do this for a living. I could have been a reporter. Yes, I've always had a nose for a scoop – and a scoop for a nose!"

I looked at Dick and simply said, "You wrote those gags for Bob Hope, didn't you?"

Barry offered this opener: "Hello, I'm Kim Philby. No, seriously, I'm Johnny Ball."

In retrospect, there was a gag of sorts there, if I had said, "This job should have been done by Kim Philby, but he missed his flight back from Moscow."

I have been friends with Barry ever since. But sadly they never came up with a single gag I felt I could use with confidence.

So, I wrote some good gags for me with Kenneth McKellar and Aimi MacDonald, but the real treat was to come. Bud Flanagan no longer had a straight man, as Chesney Allen had died a few years earlier. So I was to take Ches's place.

THE LEGENDARY BUD

The first time we met, Bud had been told it was my first big TV show and asked if I was nervous.

He then said, "Never be nervous. This business is ten per cent talent and ninety per cent luck." He then got up to rehearse 'strolling' and every one of the forty people present cried openly – it's amazing what you can do with ten per cent talent.

Next day, Bud brought in a sketch for us to perform. I

couldn't believe it. It had been written in 1938, the year I was born, and was all about politicians messing everything up. All he did was change the names and it was ideal for a twenty-nine-year-old rerun.

My part was amazingly simple, and I never even got a copy of the script. He talked over the lines I would use, like, "You don't say? You're kidding! Nah, I don't believe it. You're having me on! Get away. Pull the other one." He explained that I could use any one of these lines, in any order I liked, just to bridge from one line to the next. Then, at a certain cue, I would repeat every line exactly. He would twist it slightly and I would repeat that. This built over about six changes until he got to the tag he was looking for and shouted, "Hoy!" to bring the sketch to an end. Did it work? You could tell that with Bud, as with Harry Secombe, failure just wasn't part of their make-up.

I was so sad when, ten months later, Bud died. But I am so proud that I was the very last person he performed a double act with on television. Luckily, just after our show, he recorded the 'Dad's Army Theme' so that, even today, his voice is known to everyone. The song was written by Dad's Army creator Jimmy Perry, who, with David Croft, had written those wonderful tales of Mainwaring and the other old codgers beating the dreaded Germans. I knew Jimmy slightly and, some years later, I met him (now retired) crossing Covent Garden during the Christmas Market.

"Hello, Jimmy, how are you?" I said.

He waved a hand at the many stalls around us and, with an incredulous look on his face, said, "They're all f—ing Germans?"

THE DOONICAN DISASTER

With the ITV Christmas Spectacular now recorded, I rang Mike Hughes and reported everything had gone well. All we had to do was wait until Christmas night and the transmission. Meanwhile, I suggested he now start work on *The Val Doonican Show*, perhaps for the first week or two into the new year.

Within a week, I was asked to pop into the BBC to see Val Doonican's producer, John Ammonds. His office was busy, so we walked to an office with desks filling most of the space. John sat on the edge of one desk, and I sat on another just three feet away. He opened the conversation.

"What would you do if you were on the *Doonican Show?*"

The office was deathly quiet, and he was waiting for me to be funny. So I began:

"I was coming here today and I put my arm out to stop a bus. But I wasn't strong enough and it wrenched my shoulder. But it stopped anyway when the back end got level with me. I said to the conductor, 'How much is it to Shepherd's Bush?'

"He said, 'What, from here? Sixpence.'

"Well, I don't carry a lot of money about with me, in a strange town, so I said, 'Do you mind if I run behind for a couple of stops?'

"He said, 'Please yourself, mate.'

"So I'm running behind the bus, thinking, *Well, I'm saving a few pence here.* Then I thought, *I'm a fool. Run behind a taxi and I'd save a couple of bob!* So I caught him up at some traffic lights. I said, 'How much is it now?'

"He said, 'To Shepherd's Bush? It's one and fourpence. We're going the other way.'"

And that was that. John smiled and nodded, saying he would see what he could do. I rushed downstairs and rang Mike Hughes from the lobby at the TV centre.

"I think he's sold. Try to get it for the first week or two in January."

Two weeks went by and then, late on Tuesday around 2nd December, Mike Hughes rang. "Someone has dropped out. You are doing *The Val Doonican Show* on Saturday!"

My heart stopped. "That's no good," I said, "I've got nothing prepared – besides, there'll be no publicity. I won't even be in the *Radio Times*."

He came back with, "You can't turn the BBC down."

"But what about Rediffusion? Their contract has a barring clause."

"I've rung them, and they've released you from it. They wish you all the best!"

"But what about rehearsals?" I asked. And now came the killer!

"I've got you out of rehearsals, so you can still do the Mersey Hotel in Manchester until Friday night, and we'll go down by train on Saturday morning."

"But he doesn't know what I'm doing?"

"No – he said pop the script in the post. Have you got a pen? It's John Ammonds, BBC…"

An hour later, I was off for my Manchester gig, so on the Wednesday, I wrote my script and put it in the post. But what a terrible day that was. I was to do my first major TV on Saturday without even meeting the rest of the cast. Nothing about it seemed right!

The Rediffusion show had worked in getting me to relax and become part of the show. I hadn't been hilarious, as almost everything I did was a very brief link, but I had handled it comfortably. I also had TV experience now with *Play School* and knew how important rehearsals were, so that you and the director were playing to the same music. Instead, I was saddled with the Mersey Hotel.

Saturday came and Mike Hughes and I got the train to London from Liverpool. He wasn't the best of companions, and the journey was purgatory. We arrived at the theatre on Shepherd's Bush Green at 2.30pm and waited to meet John Ammonds.

John finally met us in the canteen at 4pm! He looked tired and dishevelled and in his hand was my envelope, still unopened! He slit it open with a knife from the cutlery drawer and read through it. At last he spoke.

"This isn't the stuff you did for me the other day?"

I tried to explain. "That material was something I thought up at the time. There was no atmosphere in that office, so I adopted a quiet style to fit the mood. Now, this is to be my first major telly. I have to get laughs. These are all tried and tested gags."

He scanned it again and said, "I don't like this joke! The fella with the bad leg."

I jumped in, "It is not a fella with a bad leg. Look – I met this fella, and he had one leg longer than the other. No, hang on, that's wrong. He had one leg shorter than the other. He had two different legs. I remember because you know in the forces they go left, turn," (with that I executed a perfect left turn), "well, he went left turn." And this time, the right leg stopped an inch above the floor, and I fell sideways. It never failed.

John Ammonds spoke, "No. We'll get complaints from cripples."

I went straight into defensive mode. "No, you won't. Not the way I do it. I have never offended anyone, ever. Not with this joke or any other."

I turned to Mike Hughes for support. In a mouse-like voice, he said, "He's the producer, John. I think he's right."

We went downstairs and onto the empty set. The whole show was on a meal break. There was one floor manager, one camera and me. John was back at his director's desk. In the middle of the huge empty set was a tiny white cross on the floor. I was to stand on that. Everyone who has ever known me will vouch for my engaging people with energy. I asked if I could enter down the steps to get the energy going.

The response from the director's gallery, via the floor manager, was, "No."

I pleaded; could I at least have a run-up to my mark? There was another discussion. The floor manager placed a second cross, one yard behind the first. I was to start there, then move forward a yard. I started the rehearsal. Halfway through, in cutting around the left turn gag, I realised the sequence was not working smoothly and I lost my way.

It was then 4.30pm and I heard, "Sorry, rehearsal time over. Get set for the show's dress rehearsal."

What? Well, at least I'll have a run through in the dress rehearsal.

But in the dress rehearsal there was a hitch with one of the dance routines and all the time was lost up to 7pm. They hadn't even got to me and the final rehearsal was over. We were live in an hour to nineteen million viewers, yet no one knew how long my spot was and what the end was.

John Ammonds said, "It's OK. I'll have your script in front of me!"

I went through every nerve-calming routine I knew until the show started. At last, it was two thirds of the way through the hour-long show, and I was on next – was I ready? Yes!

Val Doonican – who I still had not even met – introduced me from his chair and I was on! The first line got a titter, and the next gag got a laugh. Then the camera spun away! It had lost its picture – it was broken! I was in mid-stream while frantically trying to work out what was going on. A second cameraman to the left was sitting on his camera pedestal. He got a call in his earphones and jumped up and swung his camera towards me.

In mid delivery, I realised that I was happier with this camera, as the first one blocked the audience from seeing me directly. So I moved towards it, using the energy of movement, as always in my routines. Disaster! I had been lit in a circular pool of light with the taped cross at centre. Having moved, I was now in the dark, working live to nineteen million viewers!

With the better camera angle, I ploughed on. I reached my final story, which involved me talking to a small child. As I began to portray the child, my knees buckled, and I shrank to become that child.

I asked the child why he was crying, and he was saying, "It's my birthday and I'm having a party, and there's a 'magican' coming and all my friends, and we're having jelly and trifle and blancman… wobby stuff – and it's the best party ever."

To which I asked, "Then why are you crying?"

To which he answered, "Because I'm lost!"

On the tag line, I straightened up to stare straight at the camera. But the camera man had never seen the act. So when I became the child, I ducked out of shot. He waited, not knowing when I'd come up again. As I didn't, he panned the camera down and at exactly the same time, I straightened up for the tag to the whole act – and I was looking over the camera.

It was a shambles. I came off, trembling.

After the show, we went for a drink with John Ammonds, who didn't seem at all concerned, though I do remember suggesting that a full rehearsal was the least I should have had.

Now, could it get worse? You bet!

The following week, Rediffusion lost their bid to maintain their grip on London's commercial TV. The franchise went to Thames TV from Monday to Friday and London Weekend for the rest. Rediffusion would 'cease to be' at the end of March. I got a phone call. Rediffusion, in disgust, would only play repeats till the end of their contract. Any thought of a thirteen-part series involving Johnny Ball was now dead. Sid Colin retired; the producer went to California; the director went to *Coronation Street*.

I rang to commiserate with them. They said how angry they had been by Mike Hughes ignoring the contractual baring clause. It was a slap in the face after their support for me. So they cut all my publicity, including full pages in four tabloids. The triumphal 1967 had ended in disaster. The ninety-minute Christmas night show went out, with hardly a whimper.

Perhaps 1968 would bring something better – or would it?

CHAPTER 10

1968-69 – A GRADUAL CHANGE OF DIRECTION

DOWN – BUT NOT OUT!

To say that I was a bit downcast at the start of 1968 would be an understatement. I still had a full date book, but there was a clear fracture between Mike Hughes and I, which was not going to heal easily. *The Val Doonican Show* fiasco was unforgivable and I was determined that I would be leaving him. I had conquered the clubs and enjoyed doing it – but the thought that this would be my continued existence for years to come was just horrific.

But there was no immediate alternative and, after a subdued few weeks in January, I was soon back to peak form. I also had a lot of laughs and a few rare experiences.

TONY BRUTUS

I was working the wonderful Wakefield Theatre Club with Tony Brutus, a strongman act with an enormous personality and sense of humour. His girl partner, besides tearing a large telephone directory in half each night, also broke a six-inch nail with her bare hands, which is no mean feat. Using a yellow duster, she would keep bending the nail backwards and forwards in the same place until it got hot and finally snapped.

Tony was a very popular act. He would lift the two largest people in the audience on a double swing apparatus which was slung around his neck while also fully extending behind his shoulders a massive twelve-strand chest expander, or Jimmy Clitheroe's bed. Now his greatest stunt was the suicide strangulation tug o' war.

But one particular night, the stunt went badly wrong. A group of Wakefield Trinity Rugby League players had been drinking all afternoon and were already in a state. When Tony asked for volunteers, four hulking rugby pros got up. Tony explained that he would knot a tow rope around his neck and they would stand two on each side and, by adopting a tug-of-war stance, try to strangle him. All he asked was that when he clapped his hands, they would stop pulling, "To avoid a nasty mess on the stage."

The largest of the lads was clearly unsteady on his feet, but Tony controlled them well, squeezing plenty of laughs out of them, before they started to pull. The line staggered about a bit, but Tony was used to uneven pulling and, though turning an ever darker purple, he seemed happy enough.

Eventually, as the audience started to applaud, Tony clapped his hands to stop the pull. They ignored him! He took it a few seconds longer and clapped again. They paid no attention. Tony now dropped on one knee. From the back of the club, I saw something was wrong and started to run for the stage. Tony fell onto his side and the large lad actually placed a foot on his shoulder as leverage and pulled even harder. I don't know what I would have done had I reached the stage first, but Tony's partner sprinted out of the wings and with a flash of her right hand, scratched four deep wounds down the large lad's face. It is remarkable how well the human head is designed. Without the bony structure that protects us, her quite vicious nails would surely have taken out at least one eye. He reeled away. The other lads now helped their injured mate off the stage. I had now arrived and was frantically pushing the knot back against itself on the back of Tony's neck. At last he was free, but it had been a close-run thing.

Still lying on the stage, he paused for a moment, then whispered, "Leave me!"

We backed off stage and Tony slowly stood, walked forward to the mic stand and said in his ever so gentle presentation voice, "And now, a song!"

ANOTHER AMAZING LIVERPOOL TALE

I enjoyed working with Tony and so, one night that week, I said, "OK if I stay at your place on Friday night?"

He had no idea what I was on about, but immediately said, in his strong scouse accent, "Yeh, John, that'd be great."

I explained that it was the Liverpool-Everton game on the Saturday, and I would take him to Anfield with me.

"Great, John, yeh, great!"

On the Friday, we arrived at Tony's house in Toxteth in a terraced street which sloped steeply down towards the Mersey, as in the TV series *Bread*. Tony had invited a few mates for a party. As I stood with a beer in my hand, a fella thrust a newspaper racing page at me and said, "E, yar. Have a bet, John!"

"Well," I came back, "when I was a teenager, I had a bet every day, but these days I wouldn't know one end of an 'orse from another."

"Have a bet, John," the stranger said, slapping the paper on my chest.

"Nah, I'm OK, thanks!"

"Have a f—ing bet," he said in a voice too firm for me to ignore any further.

Tony came up and nodded from behind his shoulder that I should 'have a bet'. I picked out a four-horse Yankee on the betting slip and the fella moved away. Tony arrived to explain.

"He's OK, John. It's a freebee. He manages Gus Demmy's betting shop, down the road. We all have a bet and if any come up, he slips them in, and we get paid." This was Liverpool.

I next learnt that every gas and electricity meter in the street had magnets on it which slowed it down. The utilities couldn't understand why the bills in this street were so low. But to make it work, every pensioner had been coaxed out of their houses while the local lads did the work secretly, as the law-abiding citizens would have been horrified had they known they were involved in a scam, saving a good percentage of their pensions.

We arrived at Anfield with time to spare and were soon in the main stand bar. As we started on our pints, there was a sudden loud exclamation, "Bloody hell, Tony Thomson. The only lad I know who robbed a bank and caught a bus home!"

Everyone in the room spun round, while Tony shrank back and tried to disappear. But there was no escape, and a circle of people formed around us in a flash. Brutus was his stage name and Thomson is fictitious too. But now he and the fella revealed the story, which is a cracker.

Aged around seventeen, Tony had a dodgy mate with an old banger of a car. They were cruising round Liverpool one day when Tony's mate said, "I know, let's do a job!"

Surely this is a joke, thought Tony as he asked, "What kind of a job?"

His mate slowed the car down outside a bank. "I'll wait here with the engine running. You get in there and see what you can nick."

Tony took up the story. "So I wandered in, scared as hell.

I'd never even been in a bank in my life. So this fella comes in, rushes up to the desk and puts his briefcase down and starts to fill in a form. So I grabbed the briefcase and ran out."

Tony's mate was slowly edging the car up the curb when he saw Tony run out, with the fella close behind him. So he panicked, put his foot down and drove away. But there was a double-deck bus passing, so Tony simply jumped on the bus – a mistake. The bus went twenty yards and stopped at traffic lights.

Now the chasing man arrived and saw this power-packed lad, with no neck at all. The man kept his distance. All this had been watched by a uniformed policeman!

The bus was no safe haven, so Tony jumped through the knot of agitated people and off, with the policeman giving chase. Tony turned into an alley, which he found was a dead end. The policeman arrived and Tony offered no resistance and, in handcuffs, off they trudged to Dale Street Police Station.

A week or so later, Tony was in court, but the policeman spoke up and said he was sure the lad was no criminal, and it was purely a stupid stunt. He suggested that a short probation should be enough as he felt the lad would never trouble them again – the magistrate agreed. Once again, this was Liverpool and there was nothing surprising in this outcome.

As they left the court, the copper came up and said, "You silly sod. Are you going to be OK from now on?"

Tony said, "Yes, sorry!"

The copper said, "Do you remember when I arrested you? Well, I can tell you now, that was my first solo duty, ever. When I saw the muscles on you, I made my mind up – you were going to escape. The last thing I wanted was to corner you. I was so nervous, had you run at me, I'd have jumped out of the way. Do you know what you did when you knew you were trapped? Well, you've been watching too many American movies. You just stopped in the middle of the alley, placed the briefcase at your feet and raised your hands above your head. As I cuffed you and you were facing the other way, I was bursting to laugh with sheer bloody relief that I hadn't got battered."

A great story!

When we arrived back at Tony's house, after the match, there on the settee was a very distraught girl and Tony's partner with her arm around her. Her fella was the Gus Demmy manager, and he had been arrested for passing fake betting slips. I was happy I had used a pseudonym.

BEWARE THE BLACK AND YELLOW SNAKE

Soon the call came for another forces tour, once more to Singapore. This time, an RAF jet dropped us off at Gan Island at the southernmost tip of the Maldive Islands, which at that time were yet not on the tourist map. It was a paradise. There were four hundred RAF personnel on the island and they had around twenty licensed bars. I would be awakened each morning with a large vodka tonic to kick-start the day.

I am a terrible swimmer, but in the warm crystal-clear Maldive lagoons, with flippers and a snorkel mask, I soon gained confidence. Now, we had been told of just two dangers in these waters. The first was the stone fish, which often nestled down in the sand so they were not easily seen. Its sting is not strong enough to kill, but its poisons send alarm bells to the nervous system, and you can suffer a heart attack and die. The other threat was from a venomous black and yellow sea snake but seeing one of those was highly unlikely.

I had never been able to swim underwater, but in this idyllic lagoon it was a synch, and, in snorkel mask and flippers, I ventured deeper and deeper, always doubling up to rise to the surface with still ample breath left. When the others called it a day, I stayed to become more adventurous. With every dive, I tried to push myself as deep as I could go. Then, heading really deep down, I saw, on a bare rock, a two-feet long black and yellow sea snake! Immediately, I stopped pushing downwards and doubled up. I started pumping with my legs, but each pump was pulling me down closer and closer to the snake. The nearer I got, the more I panicked. But the snake decided the issue and whisked off around the rock and away. At last I relaxed and came quickly to the surface. But I was a quivering nervous wreck.

A WIESBADEN WHIMSY AND THE ROYAL HALIBUT OIL

Back home, the Combined Services group had taken to me so much that they seemed to be on the phone every other week. I did a one-night show in Wiesbaden, with Harry, Roy Castle and Dickie Henderson. It was a great experience, with a top-brass NATO VIP audience, so it was a pity we did blot our copybooks somewhat.

The large very Germanic hall was shaped like a torpedo, with perfectly rounded ends and walls of dark, smoothly polished wood. At the centre rear of the stage, the designer had pushed a piece of smooth wall forward by two yards to form the left and right stage entrance point for the performers. Ever ensuring the best hospitality, the forces staff had set up our own backstage bar. But they had set it right behind this natural curved alcove on stage.

At one point, with Harry leading, while a singer was doing her act, we all got into a silly and rather mucky gag situation and were giggling hysterically as each one of us built on the joke. There were no ladies present, and the language was pretty rich and getting louder. Suddenly, someone came rushing round from front of house. Being in the alcove, our chatter had travelled sideways around the smooth walls and every word could clearly be heard by the audience, even at the back. As it turned out, the audience's annoyance had soon turned to laughter. When Harry laughed, there was no option – everyone laughed with him.

Each year, the Forces Benevolent Fund has a charity event at the Royal Albert Hall, which I joyfully did more than once. The first time gave me a problem though, which affected me as a comic much more than the musical performers.

The event started in the afternoon, with marching bands, motorcycle display and the RAF guard dogs demo all on the central floor. It became a normal concert show in the evening, except that the huge, round, central floor area was still left completely empty. So, the 6500-strong audience was arranged in a massive circle, which made for the most difficult comedy audience I ever experienced. My gags came fast and furious, which normally was great, as the laughter built until I let it down to give them a rest. At the 'Royal Halibut Oil', it was different. The reaction to each gag took a different time to reach me, depending on how far around the circle the laughter was coming from. Instead of a laugh which I could use to time the next joke, it came in a wave growing and then diminishing, so that I was never sure where to come in next – if you haven't done stand-up, you won't have much idea of what I am talking about, but I can tell you, it was a bugger, though not a disaster.

I was now more and more often in London, which gave me a thrill for the first dozen or so times as I thought, *This is where I am going to make it!* It really was the glimmering of a new beginning – if I could overcome 1967 and the dreadful *Doonican* memories.

FILMING FOR THE BBC AND A CHANGE OF SCENE

From 1964, Dennis Newton had been my tailor and become a wonderful friend.

In 1968, he made me a Norfolk jacket with the traditional leather-lapel buttonhole and sewn-in belt and shoulder straps.

It would have graced the cover of *Tailor and Cutter*, and I wore it as I travelled south to be part of *Play School's* very first outside broadcast. I suppose their choosing me was an indication of how comfortable they were with me by now, and vice versa.

The recording was at Marsh Lock, just above Henley on Thames on a glorious summer's day. My partner was the beautiful Italian actress and J. Arthur Rank starlet Marla Landi. The show can be found on YouTube today – it is so surprisingly slow!

Working in this idyllic setting with a lovely BBC crew was a million miles from the club scene that I was locked into. I felt this was a change for the better.

DRESSING THE PART, WITH BILL SHANKLY

Almost everyone in Liverpool who dressed well, and even Ken Dodd, went to Dennis. He was such a perfectionist. He turned down Prime Minster Harold Wilson, saying, "With your stature, you'd ruin my reputation." He also sent first class Las Vegas flight tickets back to Tom Jones, saying, "My business is in Liverpool, not the USA."

It was in Dennis's shop that I had an experience that is possibly 'unique in sporting history'. As you walked into his first-floor office, a pressure bell under the mat would bring him downstairs like a spider heading for its prey. As I walked in one day, there was a fella thumbing through the swatches of cloth. It was Bill Shankly, the revered manager of Liverpool FC. We nodded, but I didn't engage him in conversation. I am naturally shy, but I also respected his privacy. Dennis came in and introduced us. The Liverpool team knew me, but Bill was no club-goer. He had called in to pick up his suit, which Dennis had sponged and pressed ready for Saturday when Liverpool would be at Wembley to face Arsenal in the 1971 Cup Final.

"All set for a good win on Saturday, Bill?" asked Dennis.

The reply was startling and very rare. Bill said, "Aye, well, it's not all plain sailing. I've got three players, John Toshack, Steve Heighway and Alun Evans. Now, I have to play two of them, but if I had my way, I would'ne play any one of them."

This was a negative Bill Shankly and possibly a unique occurrence. Bill didn't know me from Adam, and he knew that Dennis was not a football lover, so for this brief moment, he was not talking to people who would repeat his words.

As it turned out, on the day, Steve Heighway scored in extra time, but then Arsenal scored twice, and Shankly's Liverpool side had lost. His doubts had been confirmed.

But there was another reason for Shankly's doubts on that day. He had just signed a player potentially better than them all – Kevin Keegan – and Shanks already knew what a difference he would make to Liverpool Football Club and European football.

A CHANGE FROM MUM AND DAD

In my club years, constant movement meant I could not establish a base. I kept my old room in Liverpool on retention, but every time I stayed there, I had weeks of retention money to pay, which was crazy. So from mid 1967 I had been living with my mum and dad in Cleveleys, a few miles north of Blackpool. Not ideal.

Mum and Dad were wonderful and we got on very well, but most nights I got home between two and four in the morning and slept till lunchtime. Then I'd be tearing off again around seven every evening. It just didn't fit their lifestyle and caused them stress, as kids always do.

With my totally cosmopolitan life, my Bristol burr had subsided, and I didn't really have any discernible accent at all.

In fact, I found I could adopt any accent I liked. However, in the two years with my parents, their strong Bolton accent seeped back into my character and ever since then, my Lancastrian tone is quite clear. But I'm happy with that. Comedy and Lancashire accents have always gone hand in hand.

A WEEK IN PORTSMOUTH

I found myself working for a week with Engelbert Humperdinck, which, as you may know, is an anagram for 'Knickerleg Tremblebum'.

It was the week Mick Jagger was in jail on drug charges, and I broke the news to my audiences that when Mick saw Marianne Faithfull arrive for a visit, he cried, "Marianne – my heroin!"

The week went well, and I liked Engel. But I was not keen on performing short spots on someone else's theatre tour, so I was not bothered when they didn't take me on permanently. What, in my heart, I was looking for was individuality and self-determination. It was a search that was still to take a good few years and have a lot of ups and downs, as I was slowly to realise.

In that Portsmouth week, I bought a brand-new Rover 2000. It cost £1400, which I happened to have in my wallet as cash! It was to prove the worst car I ever bought.

BUT WHAT A CHANGE

But now I was twenty-nine years old, and I recalled I had said I would marry around thirty. So, it was almost inevitable that I should meet someone who might make a permanent partner.

In Fleetwood, there was a struggling club on a caravan park called the Cala Gran – why anyone should attach a Spanish name to a club on a very dreary river in Fleetwood, next door to a power station, is beyond me. But it was within a mile from home, so I popped in one night and it was then that I met Julie Anderson, who was working there. Coming from Washington in County Durham, she and her family lived close to my home, in Fleetwood. She had been a Pontins Bluecoat that summer and had two sisters who were singers, so we seemed very well suited, and we became an item.

We arranged a holiday in Minorca and Julie arrived in London by train. At a Cromwell Road hotel, I asked for her passport so that, with the other documents, I could whisk us through Gatwick the following morning. She had no passport – it had disappeared! We sat down and went through the journey in detail. Julie took the train in Blackpool and, surprisingly, met a Pontins pal who boarded at St Annes. They were soon swapping pictures, with his taken doing his drag act, which was news to her. At Crewe, he got off to get a drink from the platform café. Suddenly, the train started to move, and she shouted, "Stop – not yet," for his sake. But there was no sign of him and the train pulled out. He also had not left a bag.

In the London hotel room, we pieced it together. He had arranged the entire thing and while sitting next to her he had stolen her passport. His idea was clearly to use it to tour European-American bases as a girl. As they say, "It takes all sorts to make a bag of Bassett's." The next day, we had to get an emergency passport from Petty France near Victoria. That required confirmation of her identity, which they accepted at last by phone from her father, who had a long police record – he had been a detective in the North East. Somehow we cleared everything, got a temporary passport and rang the travel agent. She had found an alternative 3pm flight out of Gatwick. We couldn't find the flight listed, but when we did board, the One-Eleven jet was totally empty apart from the crew, who had nothing to do but wait on the two of us for the whole trip, before picking up returning holiday makers.

A GENT MORE THAN AN AGENT

Club life continued, of necessity, but outside clubland, nothing was happening. After the *Doonican* fiasco, Mike Hughes had said we would have to be patient, but I had to break free.

Out of the blue, I was called by a chap called Norman Casey. I knew of James Casey, the son of Jimmy James who had produced BBC Radio's *The Clitheroe Kid* to enormous acclaim. Norman was an agent and knew Harry Secombe. He wondered whether we could work together.

Casey came to see me work at the Mersey Hotel in Manchester, where I had also been working prior to the *Doonican* fiasco – ho hum! Norman and his wife were clearly impressed with my act. I was not that impressed with him – he was wearing tinted glasses – but he had London connections and after another meeting, I felt he was worth a try.

I rang Mike Hughes and told him that it had all come unravelled – that I would honour all the dates booked, but that I felt I had every right to sever our contract due to the *Doonican* debacle. The deed was done and almost immediately Norman rang to say that he had secured a six-week major theatre tour of Rhodesia and South Africa and at far better money than Mike had been getting. This was more like it.

THE FLOOD STREET FLAT

Now with a new agent in London and working *Play School* every five weeks, it was clear I needed a London pad. But where? Well, in the 1960s, where else? I moved to the King's Road, Chelsea.

How could I afford it there? I picked up the greatest tip when looking for a flat in London – "Aim high!" The normal agencies were offering scruffy flats for high rents. But a BBC colleague sent me to Harrods Estate Office and they were totally different, especially when I said, with no trace of a Lancs accent, that I was in London working with (not for) the BBC.

They found me a flat in Flood Street with the King's Road at one end and the fabulous Cheyney Walk and the River Thames two hundred yards south. Mick Jagger, Hayley and John Mills were around the corner, and Flood Street would soon become even more famous as the London home of Maggie Thatcher.

My first-floor flat was owned by a retired admiral who just wanted it let and looked after, which Harrods did well. The rent hadn't risen for years.

Julie and I moved in. Really, it was a single-bed flat, but we made that work. It had a beautiful lounge, bright airy kitchen and a ghost in the bedroom – or, at least, 'a presence'. On the occasional night, we would wake and sense an atmosphere in the room. The lady upstairs had mentioned 'the haunting' as soon as we had moved in. Harrods denied all knowledge but perhaps the low rent was a giveaway.

Anyway, the presence would be there, and it would wake us up in the early hours – an eerie feel and a musty smell that wasn't unpleasant but was just different. I checked under the floorboards and we had the chimney swept but found no dead birds or anything else. But now and again, the presence would be there. Amazingly, it never followed us out of the room. After a few visits, we began to say, "Hello, Ghost! Having a nice night?" and then ignore it and go back to sleep.

THE PLEASURE AND PAIN OF SOUTH AFRICA

Julie got a job on a theatre booking phone line and in no time at all I was off to South Africa, leaving her alone in London. But already we were talking long-term.

The South African tour was to be an amazing experience. A white South African pop group, Four Jacks and a Jill, were returning home from the USA to stage a triumphal tour of their homeland. So they picked up a few English acts in London to support their homecoming. I was to compère and open the show, plus another spot and then one preceding the stars' finale. Also joining us was boy-wonder trumpeter Nigel Hopkins and a singing, guitar-playing raconteur who worked the West End hotels and was already known in South Africa.

We arrived in Salisbury, Rhodesia, which, of course, is now Harare, Zimbabwe and were whisked from the airport in a convoy of decorated beach buggies proclaiming the returning stars. Then we were on a cinema balcony, looking down at the main street, jammed with screaming fans.

That night we opened the show, and I felt totally at home with the Four Jacks and my three spots.

The next morning, we rushed for *The Salisbury Times* to see our reviews, which took the whole of the back page. The picture was of the Four Jacks and Jill, but the banner headline was mine. It simply said, *This guy out hopes Bob!* The great Bob Hope had been there a few months earlier and that was the comparison they had drawn!

Surely, we were now all set for a wonderful trip? Well, sadly, no, as I can't help the way I am! Soon it was impossible for me to ignore the quite dreadful apartheid situation.

A WHITE MAN'S HOME IS – REALLY?

The theatre manager invited us to his house for lunch and explained the servant situation. Just inside the gate there was a concrete shed, designed like a rabbit hutch, with an inner and outer room. The inner room had a small window and a door to the outer room, which had a larger window and door that would open wide to let air circulate in the hot part of the day. The whole building was about sixteen feet by eight feet and it was the home of the two male servants – we'll call them Adam and Peter – and Adam's common-law wife, who we shall call Miranda. The theatre manager explained his servants in the same way he might introduce his pet dogs. Peter, the gardener, was never allowed over the threshold into the house. He would bring deliveries to the door and Adam would take them from him. Miranda would keep their shack tidy and go off to work each day but was not paid a penny.

Their actual names were very important because at the local police station, there was a card for this address and on the card were the three names Adam (Indoor), Peter (Outdoor) and Miranda (Common Law).

In a totally matter-of-fact way, our host explained that every white home had the same arrangement. Now, if there was ever any trouble, a resident would ring the police emergency number, identify the house and call for assistance. The police would grab the card, rush to the house and approach any black person on the property and place a gun to their head and ask their name. If the reply was not Adam, Peter or Miranda, they were instantly shot dead. It was the way the story was told that set my nerves jangling. Adam was pottering about serving drinks while the system was being explained to us and heard every disgraceful word.

I asked what the servants did for leisure and was told that there were centres set up for them, a store, bars, cinema and gambling facilities. These were the only places they could attend. So the money they received was either saved or fed right back into the white community. As male servants had been brought in from villages often long distances away, they needed to send money home to support parents, wives and children. The situation left me disgusted.

Backstage on the second night, I began to notice the theatre regime. The black stage crew were all in their forties but excellent at their jobs. However, they had a white supervisor, who was about twenty-two and clearly mentally retarded. He was easily confused and panicked at practically every scene change. The experienced black stage crew ignored and worked around him. When I got talking to them, they were warm and friendly and enjoyed my act. This was day two of a six-week tour and I was already not happy.

A TOUR OF CONTRASTS

In contrast, after Salisbury and Bulawayo, with a few days off, we fixed flights to Victoria Falls, which was the experience of a lifetime. At the falls, the river is a mile wide and arrives at a fault running across its width. The gorge is only about one hundred yards wide for half its length. You stand watching the mighty river race towards you and, at the last minute, throw itself down into the deep ravine below. Meanwhile, you are absolutely drenched in warm spray and rainbows glint at you whenever you turn your back on the sun. All visitors get down to the Falls as soon as they arrive, but they then go back a few hours later and again and again. Fabulous!

Then we hit Johannesburg. With my Butlin's training, I found myself smiling at people in the street in this hot bustling city. But smiling to black people was something the white people hardly ever did. So I was getting some very strange looks in return. One day, having lunch alone, I said 'thank you' each time the waiter brought something. In a voice so quiet that I could hardly hear him, which was the idea, with white people a few tables away, he asked if I was from England. When he delivered the bill, he put something in my hand, took the money and moved away. Outside, I opened the note. It read, *Please tell the world about us. Please!*

Cape Town was very special, with parties thrown for the Four Jacks and a Jill, so we often slept late. One afternoon, I awoke to find I was tight on time for the show. I grabbed my dress suit, worn the night before, and a taxi and headed for the theatre. Then we hit a traffic jam. Soon it looked like I was going to miss the opening. So, while folks on the pavement looked on in astonishment as I ripped off my clothes and changed in the back of the cab. At exactly show time, I jumped out of the taxi, ran the last hundred yards, in through the door, threw my other clothes down, ran up the stairs and straight on stage without a pause – hitting the mic precisely as my music cue ended – phew.

THE REALLY WILD SOUTH AFRICA

The saving grace of the tour was an extension that took us from Johannesburg to the smaller towns getting ever closer to our goal. On Good Friday, we entered Kruger National Park just after dawn, aiming for an exit gate some hundred miles north by the end of the day. We saw more game than I could ever have imagined, and some very close up indeed.

We were in a zebra-painted van and several of us had a turn at driving. Nigel Hopkins's dad, in his fifties, was at the wheel when we came across a bull elephant. It was quietly minding its own business, destroying a tree as we approached. We were about fifty yards away when the elephant stopped work on the tree and looked around at us. The van edged closer, but at about thirty yards, the bull arched its trunk and puffed out its ears to show its full size. Then, as though in slow motion, it began to move towards us, and we saw the dust puffing up around its feet as it gained speed. We were in trouble.

One of the Four Jacks yelled and dragged old man Hopkins out of the driving seat, jumped in and grabbed the gear lever. He slammed it into reverse and screamed backwards – the elephant was now no more than a dozen yards away. The van turned in a half arc and now the bull was heading to hit us side-on. The van lurched forward in first gear and curved away, then into second and then third and at last the elephant was receding and we were safe. Phew!

We were lucky. Just a few weeks earlier, a rogue elephant had taken a dislike to an Austin 1100 – who wouldn't? – and trampled it into the hard road surface until the highest point was about nine inches above the level of the road, and that was the engine block.

The only creatures we hadn't seen as the sun began to sink in the west were lions and now there was no time, as we had to get to a gate still thirty miles away by sundown. So we picked up speed and rounded a corner and slammed on the brakes. There was a full pride of lions lying on the road and completely ignoring us. We could see them looking to the right and, after a minute or two, we heard a scuffle and warthogs stampeded out of the bush.

A lioness had made a kill and eventually the other lions slowly got up and walked off for their dinner and we could continue. There were no mobile phones in those days and when we got out an hour late, the gate staff played hell with us.

We then had a 150-mile drive to our hotel. On the way, on a straight road, we saw a long way in front a vehicle stopped and people around. Some waved at us, but our driver, who was one of the group, just jammed his foot harder down on the accelerator. We then saw something lying in the road. There was a loud *thuddud thuddud*, but we drove on.

I shouted, "God, you've hit someone."

We never slowed down, and no one spoke a word for many miles. We had most definitely hit a black human being and for me that was the last straw in apartheid-tainted South Africa.

Back in Johannesburg, I picked up the wholesale diamond I had chosen ten days earlier, helped by the Four Jacks' manager. It was an emerald cut at just over a carat and was now set beautifully in a cross-claw gold ring. I had paid about twenty per cent the UK price.

MARRY IN HASTE?

Meanwhile, Julie had been desperately lonely in London while I had been away, although Kerry Jewel, the son of Jimmy Jewel and old Pontins friend, had shown her show business from the inside, including meeting his dad, Thames TV people and Spike Milligan.

Julie loved the ring, and we started to plan a summer wedding. The whole thing had been rather thrust upon her and that was all my doing. I was ready for marriage but, in retrospect, I'm not sure Julie was. She was only twenty years old.

Business-wise, I arrived back to good news. Norman had fixed me a summer season at the Central Pier Blackpool, which meant us saying goodbye to the Flood Street flat. I would be playing 'second top of the bill' to Andy Stewart and an otherwise all Scottish cast. When I was eighteen, I had seen Morecambe and Wise second top there with Ken Dodd third, and just three years earlier, Bob Monkhouse had starred with Mike Yarwood second top.

I was thrilled, but we both agreed it seemed sensible to get married before the Central Pier season started, so everything became quite rushed. We were married in a free church in Fleetwood. Lancashire comic Tommy Trafford, at his Hotel in Preesall, owned by Jimmy Clitheroe, produced a great wedding spread and my best man Peter Millington got some very good laughs.

However, after the meal, Freddie Davies came up to me, put his hands on my shoulders and said, "What are you playing at, John?" So it would seem they could see glaring clues that all would not go well. I was totally oblivious to all this.

For a wedding gag, Tommy and the staff painted my maroon Rover in six-inch wide orange chevron stripes, which was a great laugh. It also took the shine off the paint and a week later I had to get the whole car resprayed.

We had a few days in a beautiful hotel in Keswick and then moved into a furnished flat a few hundred yards from Blackpool Pleasure Beach. It was massively over-decorated by the lovely Jewish owners, but very fitting for a newly married couple.

CHAPTER 11

BLACKPOOL/LONDON/ BLACKPOOL - UP AND DOWN IN MORE WAYS THAN ONE

MY FIRST SUMMER SEASON

I arrived for rehearsals for *The Andy Stewart Show* and got a surprise. For a second top, I would have expected the first half closing slot, but no – Andy had that, as well as an opening slot and a character sketch slot, being on three times in the first half. The second half opened with a music act and then me, with a short music interlude before Andy for his fourth and closing spot. The next shock was that instead of at least fifteen minutes, I was to have just twelve!

The music came from Jimmy Blue and his accordion band, and the other acts were fine, but the whole thing was more Scottish than haggis. As a result, when I at last appeared, I found that the audience had been lulled into immobility. I had to spend the first few gags just warming them up. The theatre is at the far end of the Central Pier, over the sea, and you could hear the waves hitting the steel supports below.

So my opening gag was: "Hello, are you enjoying the voyage?

Didn't you know? The pier came loose just after we started. We're halfway to the Isle of Man by now."

Looking back at my material, it was so simple and very seaside, but as each night went by, I got it tighter and tighter. But even on the first night, I was clearly taking the 'who's best' at the end.

A TALE WORTH TELLING

The morning after opening night, I met my agent and his wife for breakfast at the Imperial Hotel. The Open Golf Championship was at Lytham St Annes that year and the dining room was a who's who of famous faces, with Jack Nicklaus, Lee Trevino and Gary Player along with David Coleman and several more of the BBC TV crew. Norman and his wife had a two-seat table by a pillar. So I grabbed a chair from an adjacent table, only to here a shout.

"Oy, not one of mine. Take one from one of her tables."

This was a remarkably surly waiter who snatched the chair off me and replaced it. I got another and the waitress arrived.

"Don't mind him. Crabby old sod. What can I get you?"

We ordered and grabbed our fruit from the buffet. On arrival, both drinks and food were wrong in several ways.

The waitress said, "Oh sorry – is that alright then?" and left things as they were.

We finished eating and started a business chat. Then, while Norman was in mid-sentence, we heard the waitress again.

"Enjoying your stay, are you?"

We looked round. She was leaning on a pillar, apparently totting up something on her pad.

Norman said, "What?"

She repeated, "You enjoying your stay, are you?"

Norman replied, "I'll tell you what, I will never stay in this hotel again, as long as I live!"

Without a pause, she came back, "You're right. It's gone right down the bleedin' nick!"

BACKSTAGE BLUES

After the opening night's success, nothing changed much other than my spot got more and more successful and Andy Stewart stopped even speaking to me. Our dressing room doors were next to each other, and I got the feeling he actually avoided making contact with me, as every night he would leave without looking through my open dressing-room door.

At his last night curtain speech, he did say he thought I had great potential and a great future before me, which got a huge response from the audience. Then, catching me at his dressing-room door, he said, "Would you like a drink, John?"

I said, "Yes," and he poured me a neat scotch. He did not pour one for himself and just sat there while I drank it. I asked where he was going next and got a mumble about Scotland. I never met anyone in the business quite so bloody awful.

But I had clearly been in the wrong show. Agents and bookers would come up from London to catch the bigger Blackpool shows. But no one ever bothered to come to see the all-Scottish *Andy Stewart Show*. I was second top in Blackpool, in the theatre where I had seen Morecambe and Wise second top and Ken Dodd third top.

But things had changed, and I was the hit of the show – but totally invisible.

WRONG ABOUT THE MAN. RIGHT ABOUT THE WRITING

At the end of the season, the news from Norman wasn't good, either. On my name alone, he had formed a relationship with the Richard Stone Office, where he had clinched in quick time the South Africa tour and summer season. But he had not managed to attract any other promising acts. The result was, he no longer warranted his office space, and he was out. He was a trained accountant, and he had straightened my books out for me, which was perhaps the only consolation. But in club terms, I was far better connected than he was. In fact, the other northern agents were pleased to have me available direct, as there was no love lost between them and Mike Hughes. They ensured I had enough club work, but I really was now on my own.

As the season ended, we took a two-bedroom unfurnished flat in St Annes, which halved our rent, and I enjoyed furnishing and decorating it. A close friend now had a carpet business and said he could get me a really good discount. So we carpeted the hall, stairs, landing and large living room, with top-quality carpet. He got me the discount – 2.5 per cent!?

But career-wise, I was now determined that I had to change direction. I had to write myself a career and I wanted to start that right now. And I did have a very strong TV idea.

SEEING TRIPLE!

On a forces tour I met The Karlins, a Scottish identical triplet act or, as they called themselves, three twins. They were great fun and had achieved a few good TV appearances. One night at their flat in Chiswick, they talked about needing a TV series built around them and I immediately said I would try to write it.

So, in St Annes, I set about it. My premise was that I would be their road manager and apart from getting them onstage, I would also have to sort out perpetual advances from lads, some welcome and some they wished to avoid. As they were clearly difficult to recognise apart, the comedy would come from me, the viewers and the girls being the only ones actually knowing which was which. To make this work on TV, each would be colour co-ordinated so that the audience were kept in the picture.

Over a few weeks, I wrote the first draft of episode one and their senior BBC Light Entertainment producer friend in Glasgow loved it. On the phone, he said, "If their new LP gets in the charts, BBC Scotland will certainly give this a series. It's great!"

A few weeks later, their first album was released and surprise, surprise, it never created a ripple and the girls were soon back in Scotland. I never saw them again.

Meanwhile, Dad came down and improved the kitchen in our flat, but he could clearly see that after less than six months, our marriage was not working well. We went through the motions of being happy with our friends and had a super fancy-dress party for Julie's twenty-first birthday. Tommy Trafford drove from Southport in full panto dame drag and donned wig and make-up in the car, before taking his teeth out, for his final grand entrance.

NEW AGREEMENT? A NEW LIFE?

In London, I met up again with Harry Secombe and his manager, Jimmy Grafton, who said they would be happy to manage me from now on, via Jimmy. Harry was starting an autumn season in Coventry, and they would recommend me to his producer, Albert J. Knight. This was definitely the best option in sight, so I said OK.

I was working at the Hunter's Moon, a theatre pub in Birmingham where I always scored a great success. Each night, the manager kept an empty table in an otherwise packed house, and I took to the stage and looked for the sign of my agent arriving as promised. Every night I stormed them, but Albert J. Knight's table was always empty.

Jimmy apologised but said Albert had now 'set' the Coventry show and could see me the following week. Could I make Caesar's Palace, Luton on the Monday at around 7pm? At last!

I arrived and found that the club didn't open until 8pm, but they had arranged for the lights to be on. Albert expected me to work to just the two of them – in the totally empty club. What? With nothing and no one to bounce off, other than two humourless fellas, I died an unmerciful death. Without reaction, there was nothing for me to build on. Once again, an agency-arranged opportunity had become a humiliation.

Caesar's was to feature again a few years hence and this time the result would be totally different, and it would also form another major milestone in my career.

However, this agency idea was always a non-starter. Over the entire year, Jimmy Grafton got me three days' work – in Northern Ireland with Harry for HM Forces, a job I would certainly have got myself. Other than that, he never came near.

A PREGNANT PAUSE

Meanwhile, it was in April 1970 that Julie announced that she was pregnant. The shock hit hard, and it was clear that I was counting weeks.

"Yes," she assured me, "it was that night!" – the only night we had made love around that time.

I don't remember Julie having pregnancy sickness, but my hair started to fall out. On 23rd November 1970, precisely while I was reading a *Play School* story at BBC Television Centre in London, Julie produced our daughter at Blackpool General Hospital Maternity Unit. I was desperately sad not to be there, but when we got the news, Cynthia Felgate and I took the *Play*

School team to the BBC Club and we cracked a few bottles of champers in celebration. I rushed to Blackpool after the recording the next day. We decided on the name – Zoe Louise Ball.

THE GODFATHER!

Zoe was christened at the Fleetwood Church where we had been married. As main godparent, we chose Tony Febland, who was my closest friend in those days – though Jewish! Tony was an exceptional character. His parents were very successful dealers in porcelain and the country's principal importers of Capo di Monte, supplying Harrods and other major retailers around the country. They were a delightful couple. Julie and I were invited to their daughter's wedding, where their warm and generous welcome was overwhelming.

Being Jewish, Tony asked what his duties were as a godparent to Zoe. I explained that they were simply an acknowledgement of friendship and a casual agreement that if ever needed through unfortunate circumstances, they would 'look out for the child', but that none of those commitments were either contractual or binding.

Tony honoured that pledge in spades. In over fifty years, he never missed Zoe's birthday. Her first birthday present was a full-sized stuffed sheep, which had pride of place in our living room. We even sprinkled raisins under its back legs to make it even more lifelike. Although we never cut the wool, it was a sheer delight – ouch.

Years later, when the tabloids were crowing at how much money Zoe's husband Fat Boy Slim was making, Tony sent 'To the girl who has everything!' a 2/– postal order pinned to a card (long after we had gone metric).

A UNIQUE COMEDY OPPORTUNITY

I was still very well-known and respected in Northern club circles, as was proved one day when I got an unusual request. A world-renowned star had been talked into working Batley Variety Club. This was something of a coup as he had never worked a club before and would never do it again. This did not mean he did not enjoy the week, as he thought it was wonderful. The sell-out audiences thought he was wonderful too and why wouldn't they? It was Roy Orbison.

I was invited specifically and had the thrill and pleasure of working for forty minutes as his warm-up act and the week went like a dream. I recall meeting him, but any conversation was momentary. However, I did add the experience to my own act for a while after.

I built a very short piece where I recreated Roy's choreography. It wasn't difficult but was funny in its simplicity. Roy would enter wearing his usual stag costume, guitar and dark glasses. He would wave as he walked but not look round. He arrived at the mic and faced the front. There was a short lull in audience reaction, but he went straight into his first number and, on recognition, the applause rang out. But now he was away and soon everyone settled down to listen.

When the number ended, leaving his left foot exactly where it was, he spun ninety degrees back to look sideways. He then stayed there until the applause passed its peak. Then he swung his right foot back, so he was at the mic once more, and went straight into song number two. That was repeated exactly between every song until his false exit when he waved but only looked ahead till he disappeared at side stage. Then he would come back and repeat the simple moves exactly as he had for the previous numbers. This limited-movement routine did not add or detract from his performance one iota. He was a truly brilliant megastar with a musical programme of continuous, ingeniously constructed solid hits.

OF CABBAGES AND KINGS

There was no doubt now that I was trying to make the most of my BBC contacts. I got the idea of writing a comedy history sketch series for kids and we were given a pilot. The show was to be called *Cabbages and Kings*.

Derek Griffiths had recently joined *Play School* after being seen in *The Black Mikado* in the West End, where he stole the show. He was an obvious casting and Julie Stevens, a stalwart of the early *Play School* years, made up the trio.

For me, this was the start of a new career. My history knowledge was quite skimpy, but the fascination experienced in reading my encyclopaedias as a youngster had sewn the seed and I was happy researching. I was determined the historic detail had to be as correct as we could make it. There would be no Queen Elizabeth and Walter Raleigh on the telephone jokes. I spent hours reading complex and unnecessary detail before I sat down and started writing sketches. Churchill's *A History of the English Speaking Peoples* taught me one of his secrets. Always make sure the first sentence and the last are absolutely memorable. That rang bells with my stand-up comedy, where the same rules applied. Above all, my new show had to be structured like an adult show with all the ingredients as well as music. The pilot went well and the following year we were given just three shows, as with the cost of costumes and sets, the budget was twice the normal half-hour costs.

I also decided each show should have music. So, for the first show, *The Romans In Britain*, we ended with the Romans leaving Great Britain around 400AD, with roman soldier Derek wandering off into the distance, singing to the tune of 'Goodbye' from *The White Horse Inn*. However, almost all the words were lost as Derek disappeared over the horizon. But we also had the musical trio finish which wound up every show.

It was great fun, and the BBC was where my chances lay, so my base had to be in London!

THE MOVE TO WHEATLANDS

I started house-hunting in Chiswick, where several mates lived, but the prices were out of my range. Then I saw a house in Heston, which sounded a bargain. Now, Heston was seven miles west, between Hounslow and Southall – a far cry from Chiswick, but for me it was perfect. It was a town house priced at £8000 and owned by Roger Cook of Cook & Greenaway, who had just made a fortune writing, 'I'd Like to Teach the World to Sing (In Perfect Harmony)'. That was success enough, but when Coca Cola made it their trademark theme, Roger was in clover and moving to a house today worth millions but which then cost the astronomic £40k.

I quickly secured a loan of £7000 with no complex insurance strings and we moved to number 55 Wheatlands on an estate built on the site of ancient wheat fields that stretched down from Harrow on the Hill to the Thames near Richmond. It was here that Henry VIII hunted while Anne Boleyn's life was suddenly and severely shortened.

The terraced town house had an integral garage and large garden room at the back that would become my office. The first floor had a big living room and kitchen diner, while up one more we had three tight bedrooms and a bathroom.

The estate was designed around a show house which became the inspiration for the set of *Boeing Boeing*. While it was being built, they also filmed *A Home of Your Own*, a British *Carry On*-style comedy, which closed with a stone being engraved with the legend, 'This Stone was paid for by 'pubic' subscription.'

The place was so friendly and peopled by others like us who needed to relocate to near London for work. Soon we were having drinks parties every Friday evening in one house or another.

ADJUSTMENTS ARE NECESSARY

However, soon work was not going that well. I still had regular *Play School* weeks but, having moved south and become particular about which northern clubs I still wanted to work, some club bookers were starting to neglect me.

Now, 'stand-up comedy' is never a simple task and any weaknesses quickly rise to the surface. I had conquered the club scene magnificently first time around, but having to do it all over again, to ever more noisy audiences and reduced discipline, was much less fun.

I remember a conversation I had with a neighbour, when I made a statement and was shaken rigid by my own words. I said, "In my current position, it might be that no one will ever employ me again." Being totally freelance and having no agent, I had clearly reached a very low point in letting such a statement come out of my mouth. But the reason for my depression was most certainly our marriage.

Everyone at Wheatlands knew Johnny and Julie as a great couple and never suspected (as far as I knew) that there was anything wrong – but on occasion when we were alone, in sheer frustration at the difference in our attitudes, I would explode. At the Ideal Home Exhibition, we chose a beautiful but expensive circular teak drum table with six chairs which fitted our square dining area perfectly. Within three weeks, the table had an iron burn on it!

I was getting close to rock bottom. But still, on occasion, a job that I relished would appear as a ray of sunshine.

A NAVY LARK WITH PAN'S PEOPLE

In early December, I got an urgent call. The navy had asked Jimmy Saville to 'fix it' for them to have a visit from Pan's People, as they were far from home and lonely. What? Lonely in Mombasa – a beach paradise in equatorial Kenya? Who was kidding who?

'Jim fixed it' but then couldn't 'fix it' due to BBC *Top of the Pops* commitments. So they called me and within two days I joined a gathering party for Pan's People, the other acts on the show and a full BBC film crew, as the opportunity for 'Pan's People with the troops for Christmas' concept was a very strong magnet. As the girls only did short dancing spots, with a change of costume after each, they needed someone to hold their show together and that was my job. However, the entertainment needed to be richer and so there was a normal show coming along as well, and I was to compère that too. So I would be busy and need a lot of material – all fine.

We landed in Mombasa! A warm and sultry paradise far away from the cold British winter. I have often wondered if the trip wasn't the BBC's idea all along.

The shows went brilliantly, and the navy were great hosts. It was amazing to see the lads gather around Pan's People whenever they could – but they were always on their best behaviour and careful not to touch or be seen to be too forward. The girls felt flattered by their behaviour.

The BBC got loads of great material in the can as we performed in the open air on the deck of *HMS Belfast*, which has since been retired and sits on the Thames near Tower Bridge.

A newish comedian was on the tour along with his pal, Nookie Bear. It was Roger de Courcey's first forces tour, and he just couldn't settle to it. It made no difference, because back home he went from strength to strength and soon made the *Royal Variety Performance*. But he never forgot that trip and would graciously say whenever he met me again, "Johnny Ball, funnier than I'll ever be." Cheers, Roger!

Too soon the tour was over and we boarded the plane to come home. Mombasa Airport is tricky for pilots. Because of the humidity, planes can suffer from lack of lift and the runway is pretty short. It can't be any longer, as, at one end, a sheer cliff falls away. We hurtled along gaining speed, but just when we felt lift off had to happen, the pilot jammed on all the brakes, and we just managed to stop about thirty yards from the fence and cliff edge. The pilot tried several times, and even had the passengers taken off the plane for one last try. Then he decided the RAF aircraft was not fit for purpose, and we were taken back to our hotel.

On forces tours, everyone gets a pay book with cheques already made out for the amounts you had previously agreed to draw. So, like the rest of the forces staff, you got paid on Thursday as the correctly dated cheque was cashed. But when you were stranded, the system collapsed. We were told we would be three to four days before our plane could be replaced. As had happened on forces tours before, Derek Agutter would then rush round the tour personnel and borrow any spare money they had, giving them an IOU. Then he could lend money to anyone short, as required, and sort it all out back in the UK. But I was an old hand at forces tours now and knew what would happen. In five minutes, I had got round the entire tour with the mischievous instruction, "When Derek asks if you have any money – all of you claim you have less than a fiver."

Derek came to see me an hour later. "I don't understand it. The buggers haven't got a penny between them? I've got to call the UK."

An hour or so later, he called us all together to say, "I've been on to London and said we are stranded without money. So they have opted for the only alternative. For the few days stuck here in this hotel, you can all just sign for your drinks."

So for three consecutive nights, we would be in the pool with Pan's People and the other girl acts on the bill. In this sultry climate, the best time of the day was around three in the morning, in the outdoor pool, when each fella would have a Pan's People girl on their shoulders as we frolicked, till the early hours, while the row of glasses and bottles of all different shapes and sizes stretched in a line from one end of the pool to the other. Yes, I'm still smiling!

We got home on 18th December, a week late, but in nice time for Christmas. Pan's People had asked me formally if I would consider touring with them as their official compère, but when we explored it, I felt it just wouldn't work, as my own career had to take precedence.

I BECOME LEGITIMATE

In early 1973, a call came through. Derek Griffiths asked if I would do a favour for a friend of his, David Wood, soon to be known as the National Children's Playwright. David was looking to produce *The Owl and the Pussycat Went to See* for the first time in London and he needed someone with a TV name that would draw very young audiences – would I play Owl?

This was my first offer as an extension of my *Play School* work and at David's house, I agreed to do the show for a three-week run in March at the tiny Jeanetta Cochrane Theatre in London, with a two-week rehearsal. It was only when we got into rehearsals that I asked the fee. David told me it was £32 a week. I thought it was a great joke but found he was serious. There was a bigger shock to come. The rehearsal money was £18 a week. I was all for pulling out, but by now, David had issued the publicity with my name as the star. As luck would have it, I had some cabaret work in Reading at around £50 a night, which I could still do as the performances were during the day. So I stayed on.

Apparently I was the highest-paid performer but still at the lowest money I had ever received in my career. But I was enjoying my first venture into 'legitimate' theatre. To play the wise young Owl, I wore extra-large glasses with pale make-up behind them, and a kipper school tie. But to be bird-like, for the whole time I was nervously attentive, hopping on the balls of my feet.

During rehearsal, I had been asked why they couldn't find me listed at Equity. I explained that my real name was Graham Ball. They were back the next day saying they couldn't find that listed either.

"Not surprising," I said, "I'm not a member." The rehearsal was stopped two minutes later.

David explained that they said they could not work with a non-Equity person. There was furious debate, completely ignoring me.

At last I stepped in and said, "Throughout all this, no one has asked if I am willing to join Equity?" They hadn't thought of that, but when they asked, I said, "Yes!" and paid the money there and then, which I think was about £10.

I had now worked for the BBC for six years, with never a question asked regarding Equity. I had also worked for nine years in clubs. I had once paid to become a member, but the Equity deputy in Birkenhead pocketed my money and neglected to send a membership form. Now I was an accepted Equity member and the dress rehearsal on the theatre stage could go ahead. Being a solo artist, rehearsing was new to me and so I played it quite low-key. But in the dress rehearsal I gave it a fullish performance for the first time and realised that all the others had been giving it everything all along and had nothing more to give. Very strange.

Next day, I arrived early for the opening show to find David looking desperately worried. The Equity deputy had pointed out that some actors were wearing costume that hid their face, or pushed stage furniture while performing, each of which warranted at extra £1 a week. David said that he was already going to lose on this exploratory run and just did not have the extra money to offer. That was when I arrived to find them all gathered on stage.

After listening to the argument, I explained, "You all agreed, as I did, to do this show for the money offered. We all had the opportunity to say no – we all accepted. You cannot now hold David to ransom."

No one budged. I then heard kids filing in to their seats for the show.

I spoke again, "Are you telling me that you will refuse to work to an audience of children that has already paid and are taking their seats? Is this how professional you all are?"

They agreed to work, at last, and David thanked me. However, the cast then sent me to Coventry! How can people behave in such an unjust and frankly juvenile fashion? If this was legitimate theatre, they could stuff it.

The curtain went up, and I gave my first full performance. I did not encroach upon anyone's space or lines, but I was several notches up on the dress rehearsal and very strong, which swamped the Pussycat, who I sadly disliked anyway. She was totally humourless.

On the second day, an even greater problem occurred. The ceiling fell in, sadly not on the cast, but on the kids in the first five rows. The idiot actors tried to continue, but I immediately came out of character, stopped the show and cleared the stage while I jumped down and helped staff and parents get the kids to safety. It was only thin ceiling framework and plasterboard that fell, but if covered about five rows of kids from four to eight years old and scared them to death. There were a few cuts and bruises, and a lot of tears, but no one was badly injured.

A few days later, we had moved to the Bloomsbury Theatre, and a two-year-old Zoe Ball chose a quiet and scary moment in the show to shout at the Plum Pudding Flea, "Don't you eat my daddy." It was, I think, Zoe's first taste of show business.

AN EXOTIC OFFER

Around March/April, out of the blue, I got a call. Would I be interested in playing the lead in a West End show? To this day, I don't know how he got my name, but I said I'd consider it. But first of all, this chap needed to see me work.

I was playing a nice club in Stoke-on-Trent the following week, sharing the bill with Vince Hill. Now, I dressed well in those days, but this West End impresario outshone Vince and I, arriving in his white suit in his white Rolls Royce. After our spots, he came backstage to see us. He was none other than Paul Raymond, the Porn King, who turned out to be both a great fella and great company. He was knocked out with my show and asked if I would audition with his leading lady, Miss Fiona Richmond.

The show I had been offered was *Pyjama Tops* at the Whitehall Theatre. I went to see the show a few days later and took Rick Jones, another *Play School* presenter, with me, who, apart from doing *Fingerbobs* on TV, had links to London theatre. I needed advice.

Pyjama Tops had quite a unique set. The front wall of the raised stage was the glass wall of a swimming pool. As the lights went down, to music, three totally nude girls dived into the pool, swam around and played ball games for about four minutes. Then they got out, giggling wildly, grabbed towels and made their way offstage. Then in came an extremely sexily clad Fiona Richmond who cavorted across the patio to answer the door to the comic lead, which was to be me, should I take the job.

From the moment he was on stage, the comedian was in charge. The audience had already seen complete nudity and following that with more nudity has surprisingly little impact. Fiona would appear in more and more outrageous costumes throughout the show and was always good value as she got into all kinds of sexually tight corners as the farce developed, but it was the comedian who controlled everything. If he got laughs, the audience loved it. If he failed, then the show was worthless. The other thing was, the comedian had to play it gay. He was never the one who got entangled with Fiona – quite the opposite; he would always save the day with camp jokes and misdirection.

I actually liked the show a lot. Oh, it was 'just acceptable pornography' with an eighty per cent male audience, but apart from the nudity, it was a Whitehall farce, all be it a very sexy one. Almost all the comic's lines were near the knuckle, but it was far milder than the *Stag Show* material I had witnessed in the northern clubs. There were definitely no four-letter words, as sadly would be the case today. It was totally acceptable West End material.

But could I take this part on with my background in children's TV? Rick, in the pub afterwards, felt that there should be no problem. So, next day, I rang Cynthia Felgate, my *Play School* boss, and talked it over with her, describing the show. It needed little in the way of describing once I had mentioned Paul Raymond and Fiona Richmond.

Perhaps surprisingly, she said immediately, "Of course you must do it. With your comedy training, you'll be perfect. I'm a bit worried about you playing camp – that definitely isn't you. But apart from that, OK. There is no obvious link between this show and *Play School* any more than in doing Shakespeare and then pantomime."

So I agreed to the audition. Fiona was wonderful fun and sent herself up all the time. Raymond was also warm and generous, and they liked what I was doing. I had a good memory for the opening gag sequence with all the usual gags, like eyeing her low-cut top and saying, "If you are going to drown those pups, I'll have the one with the pink nose."

They were clearly very happy and felt I would work in the part fine. Paul mentioned the fee at £200 a week and asked who my agent was. I wavered a moment and explained that, having recently moved to London, I had dropped my northern agent. Could I get the new one to ring him? He was happy with that, as was I, because I didn't think that fee was necessarily the best offer available for the West End.

AN AGENT – BUT NO GENT

That night, I thought about agents. The decision I made was majestically wrong and, as it would turn out, the greatest and most perfect mistake I would ever make. It would change irrevocably the rest of my life – but in ways no one could have possibly predicted.

I rang Dave Forrester. Why, I shall never know, except that he was the only London agent that I knew having worked the Central Pier Season with Andy Stewart for him. But what I knew of him should have warned me off from the start.

One famous story tells of when he accompanied the main speaker to a dinner at the Midland Hotel Manchester. The comedian went down brilliantly, and afterwards a chap came across, gushing with praise and handing the star a brown envelope. In an act near to panic, Dave quickly grabbed the envelope, opened it, counted it, and then pocketed well over half, after which he finally gave what was left to the totally embarrassed star of the night as his cut!

So, Dave was not a complete stranger. I explained the Paul Raymond situation and that £200 might not be the top fee.

He came back, "Leave it to me. I'll get the best deal for you. Don't you worry about that!"

I suppose, in retrospect, I should have worried.

He also asked what other work I had and was quick to point out that, as with all his artistes, he required a contract and ten per cent of everything, though he was bound to improve all my earnings, which would easily take that into account. Like a fool, I accepted.

A couple of weeks went by with no word, so I rang Dave again. The news was quite a shock.

"He's gone off you!" I asked why and he said, "I've no idea. But he's gone off you! But," he continued, "you're in luck. I've been working on it for you, and I think I can get you into the Blackpool South Pier for the season with The Grumbleweeds."

Now, I had never been sure that I wanted the Paul Raymond nude show in the first place, but to have lost it seemed incredible, as he and Fiona had loved me. But worse still, he was offering me another season in Blackpool? I had hardly a date in the book and knew I would not be able to refuse.

So I said, "Oh, thank heavens for that!"

To which he replied, "Yes, you're in, but it's been quite a squeeze so I can only offer you £100 a week."

What? That was the fee I had been on four years earlier. It was dreadful. But I had no option, as I had to be working to pay the mortgage. Over the next few days, I felt very low.

But worse was to come. Julie said she did not want to come to Blackpool for the season, even though her folks lived a few miles away. I accepted that and even said that perhaps the short split might help our relationship somewhat. I don't think even I believed what I had said.

So, I travelled up to Blackpool for the 1973 season, found the cheapest room I could, so I could send the biggest portion of my fee home to pay the bills. Then, when I got to the South Pier, another shock hit me. The agent had expressed his regrets that 'he had only just managed to get me into the show'. Really? There on the marquee and hoardings around town was my name just slightly smaller than The Grumbleweeds. The clear second top of the bill was Johnny Ball. Some squeezing me in.

With my marriage dead in the water and now having been duped by Dave Forrester to be alone in Blackpool for four months, I was clearly not in the right frame of mind when the show started. From the opening night, my performance was a shadow of what it had been four years earlier.

After a couple of weeks, Peter Webster said to me, "Here, John, are you a bloody comic or what?"

The Grumbleweeds tried to help, but I would not be moved. I was extremely down and as low as I have ever been in my entire life.

CHAPTER 12

COMING BACK TO LIFE

The Blackpool summer season seemed to just stagger on, and I was desperately lonely in my St Annes rented flat. The only friend I made was the butcher who sold me wonderful steaks and Cumberland sausages, which I cooked for myself, to eat alone. My performance in the show was down and stayed down. I couldn't 'die' with a holiday audience, but I certainly wasn't bringing the roof in. I was missing my BBC friends and especially my young daughter Zoe. I could see nothing but dark clouds on the horizon.

A TOTAL CHANGE OF FORTUNE

Now, I have never believed in fortune telling, but one evening, I was approached by the pier's resident gypsy fortune teller, Madam Petralengo. Would I come onto the pier one morning and have my picture taken with her, for display outside her booth along with the other stars?

So, the following Wednesday and for the only time in the whole season, I arrived around 11am, in a smart jacket and tie, and a local photographer captured the scene. I wasn't then to know that, forty years later, the picture would resurface.

With the picture in the can, Madam Petralengo offered me a free reading, as a thank you. I said no, as I really don't believe in this kind of thing, but she insisted. So we went into her tiny consulting room, where she explored my left hand for a few minutes and then looked up and said, in her professional tone, "You have two women in your life."

I was puzzled and said, "My wife and daughter?"

She repeated, "You have two women in your life!"

I looked more puzzled. "My wife and my mother?"

A look of impatience came over her face. Her next statement lost all theatricality.

"I don't make this up, John! You have two women in your life."

I shook my head.

She continued, "Look. This is one of the best hands I have ever seen. You have a career that goes on and on and on. It's an incredible hand. But look – there, you are at a crossroads, and you have a choice between two women. Make the right decision now and your future will be incredible. But it's all down to what happens now!"

I didn't know what she was talking about. I told her so and left.

Having never been on the pier in daytime, I walked around talking to the stallholders who like to make contact with people in the show. They must have all known that my performance was a bit of a letdown.

After perhaps ten minutes, I headed towards our theatre at the far end of the pier, to check if I had any mail. In front of the main doors, there was a circular area with a small stage where Peter Webster, our boss, would run his long-standing kiddies talent show, offering sticks of rock and other small prizes for kids who would perform for the deckchaired audience. His assistant was a bright girl in a stage assistant's brief skirt and tight top but with a personality that hit me fully thirty yards away. Who she was, I had no idea.

As they finished their show, I knew she would pop backstage to change in our dressing rooms, so I gave her a few minutes and then popped back myself, catching her in the corridor.

"I liked the show," I said, "you were great with the kids. Do you fancy having lunch?"

That surprised me more than her, as I had never asked a girl to lunch ever before. In fact, with my marriage a non event, I had not looked at any girl, at all – I was sexless and lifeless.

"Oh, I'd love to," she said, "but there are three fellas in our show all away from their wives and they're not looking after themselves, so I'm cooking them lunch. But you're coming to our party Thursday night, aren't you – the Central Pier?"

So, she was working the Central Pier. Well, since *The Andy Stewart Show*, they had turned to *Old Time Music Hall* and were a little out of date compared with the other shows, which was why we mostly ignored it.

"Yes, of course I'm coming," I said – and was amazed to discover that I meant it.

That Thursday, after our show I trotted along to the Central Pier and met the girl again. She was called Di. I also met her mother, dad, silver-haired gran and younger brother Paul as well as Snuffles, her white Pekinese. The family were up from Swindon for the week, but soon they disappeared. The party eventually got very silly. In a group picture, I had a stick of celery stuck in one ear. However, I had made sure I was right behind Di. The next night, Friday, we went for a meal and knew that something really powerful had happened.

On the Saturday, at around 11pm, I got in the car for the 240-mile drive back to London, as I did every second weekend, providing I had no Sunday concert. I arrived home at around 3am. On the hall shelf, at least four red bills stood unopened. I was furious, as I had been sending almost all my money home and was living on very little. In the bedroom, as I undressed in the dark, I realised Julie was awake.

"What are all these red bills?" I asked as I drew the duvet back and lowered my bum into bed.

She came back, "You've got more to worry about than red bills. I'm leaving you!"

The effect was as dramatic as any moment in my entire life. As I landed on my back, an orchestral brass section played *da, da, dada da-tta!* and the ceiling flew away. A blanket of grey clouds parted, and I swear, in the dark with my eyes closed, a brilliant and perfectly round sun shone down on me! I had been living through a broken marriage, but I neither had the nouse nor drive to admit that it was futile. Was it male pride? I suppose so. Now Julie had made the first move, and it was clearly the best move to make.

First thing next morning, I rushed to see neighbours Basil and Daphne Peters and told them we were splitting up. Basil thought it was some kind of joke. I had been too proud to admit the marriage was a wreck and none of our neighbours had any idea – or so they said. I asked if they would be referees for us. I would seek a solicitor in Blackpool and Julie one locally. If either of us thought things weren't fair, then we could bring in Basil and Daphne to help. After trying to make me reverse the decision, they finally agreed. Back home, I spent an hour working out how much in the red we were as we moved around each other.

I drove back to Blackpool on the Monday morning and, on arrival, rushed to Di's flat. She wasn't in. I drove around the streets trying to find her. Why? I hardly knew the girl. I'd made no secret of the fact that I was in a loveless marriage, but what had it got to do with her?

That night, after our shows, I spent the whole time telling Di what a relief it all was. There was no mention of our becoming a permanent fixture. But it was clear that the incredible weight of my failed relationship had now been lifted.

Now, I have never believed in fortune tellers, but I mentioned backstage what the gypsy had said. Our hairy drummer, left over from the flower-power age, piped up, "Oh John. I do the tarot. Let me have a go?"

Sometime later, he shuffled a normal pack of cards and got me to cut. He laid down the top card and said, "Right, that's you." He then dealt a card to the left – it was the Queen of Diamonds. The one he dealt to the right was the Queen of Hearts! He looked up and with a gaping jaw, said, "You've got two women in your life, John."

But I don't believe in this sort of thing.

A TURN FOR THE BETTER

Meanwhile, the biggest change in that week was my performance. By the Wednesday, my act was so strong I was clearly getting the best response at the walk down, although, of course, The Grumbleweeds had been applauded for their hilarious spot just prior to the finale.

The main thing was, the unbearable weight had now been lifted. A week later, I had a Sunday night spot at Batley Variety Club, where I was already a firm favourite – including in 1969, where I had been specially invited to be the support act for the fabulous Roy Orbison. It was to be the only time Roy would ever play a British club date and it was a huge event. This Batley trip gave Di her first chance to see me work. On the way in the car I told her how Ken Dodd's fiancé of some fifteen years always took notes and scored each joke as he worked.

Now back to my club stamping ground with a thirty-minute slot, I stood them on their heads. I then cheekily asked Di what she thought of my performance.

She said, "It was great! Do you want your notes now or later?" Without a word, Di had taken the Doddy story as a cue. I was suddenly experiencing true happiness again. I was no longer alone!

FIRE IN MY LIFE AGAIN?

Each night, Di and I were separated by a mile of promenade and sandy beach between our two piers. One night, the South Pier crew got some extra entertainment, when the front end of the Central Pier caught fire. We were in a perfect place to watch the catastrophe unfurl. With the famous Blackpool breeze whipping it up, the fire was soon raging. So the question was, would the theatre at the far end, with its audience and cast including Di, be able to escape or would they all be lost at sea?

The fire was soon under control, but the show had been stopped and the audience lead to safety. After our show, I raced up there to find that Di was still missing. In fact, the girls sharing Di's dressing room didn't know when the alarm went off whether they were safe and were quite anxious! Then three firemen arrived to convince them there was no need to panic. So they didn't and the six girls and three hunky fellas finished off four bottles of wine in quick time. Only then were the girls heroically 'saved'!

Di and I would call each other from our respective backstage phone booths each night and Di needed ammunition to keep our chats cheerful. She started to ask Jim Coulton for a joke she could tell me down the phone. Here is one, as near as I can get it, as she told it to me:

"There was this plumber who had just fixed the gents' at a posh golf club. Before leaving, he said he'd love a game sometime. He didn't have a handicap, so he realised he would have to play off scratch. He also knew that in a posh club like this, they all probably played for about £50, which he didn't mind; he just wanted a game. The brigadier, who was a four-handicapper, heard this and offered him a game the next morning. Not wanting to be seen playing with a plumber, he suggested teeing off at 8am. 'OK,' said the plumber, 'but I might be a little bit late. I won't be a lot late. But I might be a little bit late.'

"When the brigadier arrived next morning, there was the plumber on the tee ready to go. The brigadier made a beautiful drive, but the plumber hit one fifty yards past him. To cut it short, the plumber won four holes up, with only three to play.

"The brigadier asked for a chance to get his money back next day. 'But let's not start too early. Would nine o'clock suit you?'

"The plumber said, 'Yes, but I might be a little bit late. I won't be a lot late, but I might be a little bit late.'

"At nine next morning there is the plumber on the tee, but with left-hand clubs? This time he won by an even greater margin. The brigadier said, 'You're a fantastic golfer, but yesterday you played with right-handed clubs and today with left-hand clubs. Why the change?'

"The plumber said, 'Ah, well. When I wake up in the morning, if the wife is lying on her right side, I play with the right-handed clubs. If she's on her left side, I use the left-handed clubs.'

"The brigadier said, 'Well what happens if she's lying on her back?'

"The plumber said, 'I'll be a little bit late!'"

You may like the joke or hate it. But when Di told it to me over the phone, I slid slowly down the phone-booth wall in uncontrollable hysterics.

THE BIG BREAK

Soon, our South Pier season was at an end. Di's *Old Time Music Hall* would continue for another two months right through the

Blackpool illuminations. But for me, it was time to get home to sort out the mess of a failed marriage.

As there was a last-night party and nothing to rush home for, I arrived around noon on the Monday. Julie and I had agreed that she and two-and-a-half-year-old Zoe would be out of the house when I came back and so they were. The house was cold and desolate. There were more red bills and one that rang alarm bells. I checked my Barclaycard account. It had been overdrawn to the limit of £3000 – but I never went into the red? Some months earlier, Julie had suggested we have a Mastercard as well, for some convenience reason. I agreed under protest but had never even seen it. I found the papers and rang the number. It had been overdrawn to the limit of £6000. The cash I had would pay the outstanding red bills but nothing more. Except for a *Play School* some weeks ahead, I had no work that would pay immediately.

As I crunched some cornflakes – the only food in the house – the back door rattled. No one had ever approached our house by the back door. There was a neighbour from a house behind ours. I let her in, and she burst into tears. I asked if she knew we had split up and she said yes, and the tears flowed more freely.

As soon as she had gone, there was a knock at the front door. Another lady from three doors away said she knew we had split and was worried about Zoe. Five minutes later, a much closer friend, Elspeth, rang and asked if she could come round. I popped the kettle on.

Elspeth had a story. Her daughter Karen, aged thirteen, had been asked to babysit on a Friday evening a few weeks previous. At 11pm, she rang her mother, who took over. Eventually, at 1am, Elspeth left a message and took Zoe back to her house. They were worried about Julie but had no phone number to make contact. Julie eventually rang to say she was coming home on the Sunday afternoon! There had been no warning that she would not be back on Friday night!

I knew that Zoe was in a day nursery and so, around 2pm, I went round to see her. As I walked in, Zoe saw me and screamed, "Daddy," in the most anguished way imaginable. She ran to me, and I could see four grey tear lines down her face, which was very messy with nasal waste that had not been cleaned up. Her clothes were a mess, incredibly drab and dirty. I picked her up and took her into the infants' cloak room and kept hugging her as she cried. I remember the low coat hooks digging into my lower back. One of the staff came in and told me that I could not take Zoe away. The look on my face ended that conversation! I asked what time Julie would pick her up and was told 6pm. I said I was taking Zoe now and to tell Julie that I would be at her house at 6.15pm with Zoe. She told me the address and I knew the road. I also told the lady that Zoe would not be coming back to the school – I was told the fee for the month had been paid in advance. I didn't ask for a refund.

I took Zoe home and realised that there was no food in the house? We went to the local shop and afterwards I found some toys and we played until it was time to take her to her mum.

At 6.15pm, I knocked, and Julie let me in. She had left me for Jim, also from a split marriage. He was a quiet guy whose job was changing the films in jumbo jets at Heathrow Airport. As we came in, Jim was sitting in front of the telly. I nodded hello but started to tackle the problem right away. I told Julie that Zoe was not going to that awful nursery again. I had no work for a few weeks, so I would pick her up fifteen minutes before they left in the morning and have her back fifteen minutes after they arrived home in the evening. That was agreed and I calmly gave Zoe a kiss. As I was on the way out, Jim spoke.

"I don't want to take your place, John!"

I looked him straight in the eye and said, "Well, somebody has to!"

The next morning, I arrived. Julie let me in and said, "We've talked it over and decided it would probably be best if you had Zoe for the time being!"

It was the last thing I had expected. Julie handed me a tiny case, which I had never seen before. It was about 40cm x 25cm x 12cm. There was nothing else. It was all Zoe's clothes! No toys, no dolls. That was it!

As I drove Zoe home, I recalled that Julie's sister June had left her first husband with twin girls and then changed partners a third time and hitched up with Tom, who could play the guitar to back her when she sang in local clubs. As the saying goes, 'Love is blind, and marriage is an institution – for the blind!' But now I was a solo parent.

I remember, the next day, getting Zoe to eat lasagne by pretending it was elephant's ears. It seemed to work. Four or five female neighbours buzzed around. I was grateful for their concern, but managed OK, though in a sort of daze.

When happy, a child's intelligence is something to marvel at. We had around a dozen EP records of nursery rhymes and we played them together. But still far too young to read, when I asked for any of the tunes, Zoe immediately picked up the relevant record and passed it to me right side up. She was never wrong. She must have somehow learnt not just the colour of the label but also the pattern of the wording on each one.

On the second day, a lady health visitor arrived. How she knew what was happening, I had no idea. She was very nice, but very concerned. She said that it would be very unusual for a father to keep a child. She asked if there could be any reconciliation. I said not a chance. I told her she was welcome anytime and that I would comply with anything asked of me and that I would certainly be able to cope with Zoe.

She left and in minutes, as planned, Zoe and I were in the car, heading for Blackpool and my parent's home. They repeated that they never thought it would work, but I didn't want to listen to all that – it was now in the past.

I found Di and told her that I could not ask her to join me and take on my daughter as well – I just couldn't ask. She said instantly that she wanted to come to us as soon as her season had finished, some seven weeks away.

So I next took Zoe and Di to see Julie's folks. Her mum was in hospital and her dad was with Julie's older sister June. I told them it had not been right for some time, and it was over, but that they would always have access to Zoe any time. They thanked me and we left.

I don't recall them ever asking to see Zoe, at any time, ever again!

Back in Heston, we agreed that Julie would have Zoe over the weekends, and I would pick her up again on Monday morning. We also sorted out books, records and other things we had collected along the way, which didn't take too long. We agreed that our only asset was the increased value of the property since we bought it. The carpets and furniture would stay with the house and almost all our bedroom and lounge furniture I had made myself, including a range of elegant drawers and cupboards in white with rosewood beading. I am always a happy man with sawdust in the air.

We split the credit cards, with Julie taking the new one, but all the debt on both. What she had done with the £9000, I never understood. I was happy to maintain the mortgage. Selling the house was not on the cards immediately, but she could, of course, borrow on her half of the increased value over the £7000 mortgage, which we estimated would be £10,000 each maximum.

Her solicitors tried to create trouble, even after we both submitted our agreement to them. Eventually, we wrote a combined letter, and at last they accepted that the arrangement was fair and nothing needed contesting. The decree soon came through.

A COMPLETELY NEW START

Just before my Blackpool season came to an end, the BBC had come up to see me and ask for more sketches for *Play Away*, which had started just over a year before, but, more importantly, a new season of *Cabbages and Kings*. They would want to start filming in the new year, so I had to start writing right away. Yippee!

Meanwhile, some bloke offered to service Di's Morris Minor car. After several weeks, she contacted him again and he said the car had 'gone missing'. I encouraged her to get the police to check and the car was found, in an awful state, as the bloke had been living in it! It would still go, and so, from London, I told her to get my dad involved. The two of them then drove it to Swindon, as Dad was required to hold the passenger door on, all the way. When her dad saw it, the dear old car went for scrap.

There was also a little trouble in Swindon when Di announced that, at the end of the season, she was coming to Heston to live with me, even before going home. Her mum hit the roof – after all, I might be a nice fella, but I was a married man?

Di arrived at Heston and the following weekend we headed to Swindon. Di's mum and dad were celebrating a wedding anniversary at a local hotel, and we arrived mid party. Everyone gathered round and made me feel totally at home. We had a truly wonderful evening.

It was only a few weeks later that Christmas was upon us, and Di's family were, under protest from Di's mum, Rene, coming to us for the holiday. They arrived and as Di's mum walked in, there was enough frost in the air to decorate the Christmas tree.

I had decided to make a Christmas Eve punch and asked Rene if she would help. So we mixed and sampled and, finding that not quite right, we mixed again, sampled, added a little sugar, sampled, tried another mix and sampled that – and suddenly it was perfect. Everyone gathered round to try it, and they all agreed. However, by this time, Rene and I were both pleasantly drunk and our friendship was cemented for ever.

Christmas Day was glorious with all the clothes and presents they had brought for Zoe. But it also revealed something about Di's little ways. I found a long thin rod with a weight on the end, which, when I unwrapped it, was a golf putter. I thanked Di with a kiss, and then another rod-shaped item suddenly appeared to be lying around. It turned out to be a Lee Trevino driver. All day long, another long package was suddenly lying around until, all in all, I had five woods, ten irons and a putter, or four clubs more than you are allowed in your golf bag at any one time. It was a clear indication of Di's supportive nature. It also showed that some callous salesman had really taken advantage of a girl who knew nothing about golf.

There is a tag to this story, which I will feature at the begging of the next chapter.

AGENTS – AGENTS!

After the Blackpool season, I still had a contract with Dave Forrester but was getting nothing from it. Worse than that, he was still getting a percentage on my *Play School* work. So I wrote and told him our partnership was at an end. He wrote back, demanding future commission on all my BBC work, secured long before I joined him. I rang him and asked if he still reckoned himself to be the best agent in the business. He agreed that he was.

So I said, "Yet, big as you are, you are still trying to hang on to business you had no part in attaining? That doesn't strike me as the actions of 'the biggest agent in the country'."

I had hit the very nasty man where it hurts – and the contract was at an end.

WRITING AWAY AND *PLAY AWAY*

From first moving close to London, I was offering sketch ideas to BBC Light Entertainment, with some success, having the odd sketch accepted by the Dave Allen and Les Dawson shows. The BBC paid £35 a minute and I always set my sketches at around four minutes. But everyone suffered the same fate as script editors cut them to a maximum of two and a half minutes.

At that time, the Oxbridge crowd who would eventually make up The Goodies and Monty Python teams were also submitting sketches and suffering the same fate of being paid £87.50 max. It was impossible to achieve £100 in a week. Also, the way the editors hacked at your work was painful, especially when you had suspicions that missing jokes might well appear a few weeks later in other sketches. I told a major producer I was not sure the script editors were particularly good at understanding how comedy works.

He replied, "Why do you think they're script editors?"

Then came *Play Away!* After my first *Cabbages* success, the BBC children's department had set this show up for Brian Cant to host on Saturday afternoons. The idea was for a slightly older *Play School*, played to a young children's audience – but although Brian was great, the material was terribly middle class.

But worst of all was the joke-telling, where Brian or Floella would say, "Why did the chicken cross the road, softly?" And then deliver the punchline, "Because it couldn't walk, hardly!"

And then destroy the whole idea by shouting at the audience, "Do you get it?"

So when I joined the show, I immediately began to ignore age and just write clean and acceptable material for kids that their parents wouldn't find too excruciating. I had realised long ago that Walt Disney did not make films for children at all. He made films for their adult parents to accept on their behalf.

The ploy worked and I was soon writing for most of the shows. So producer Ann Reay suggested we put it all on a business footing and asked how much I would want. Explaining that, as the adults paid £35 per minute, perhaps £30 a minute? Anne agreed, and in the first week I clocked up sixteen minutes! Suddenly, I was earning far more than I could achieve sketch-writing for adults. I also had my second *Cabbages* series round the corner. So my fate to stay with children's TV was sealed.

CABBAGES AND KINGS, AND KNIGHTS AND MONKS AND REDCOATS AND YANKEES!

By the new year, 1974, I was busy writing the new *Cabbages* series, though we were only given four shows, as doing history on TV is so expensive. For the first series, we breached the entire costume budget on the first day when our make-up girl arrived with a taxi full of wigs!

Now I had a much clearer idea of what I wanted to do, and my sketch ideas were becoming more ambitious. I was also at last in the right frame of mind again. So, in April, just before the summer season started, we arrived for ten days' filming in the Isle of Man. Di and Zoe came as well, but, sadly, filming is so very slow and boring to watch, and ten days of often wintery weather was not easy for any of us.

Peter Ridsdale-Scott had chosen the Isle of Man when he saw an intended Viking sketch. The locals had built a full-sized replica of a Viking longboat and were happy to crew it for us, just for beer money. So they rowed it round to Peel and moored it in the lee of the castle for the night. However, that night there was a terrible storm and next morning all that remained was the mooring rope with a single lump of wood still attached to it. It was heartbreaking for the boatmen, but also for me, as now I had to write loads of non-boating Viking gags.

However, Peel Castle was a perfect location for an ambitious 'The Knights of the Round Table' sketch. We had made a quarter of a Round Table, so we could film the sketch in four sections with three characters in each, all played by Derek, Julie and myself. For instance, the Black Knight (Derek) was flanked by an apparently nude Sir Rubber Duck of the Bath (me) in a bath, splashing soap suds, until the Black Knight pushed him under. Sir Plumtuous (Julie) got fatter with rage, until she suddenly burst. Sir Ravenous (me again) ate ferociously and threw bones to howling dogs – which dragged me over my chair back and finished me off. Soon, ten characters had met their deaths. The Black and White knights spun the table to gain the crown. Food flew everywhere, then cutlery speared them to death. Twelve people dead in five minutes. An ideal sketch for children's TV? It worked like a dream!

For 'The American War of Independence, the Battle of Bunker Hill' sketch, I recalled my school prefect's ladder with spy, glass and hill signs on it. I used that idea around a grassy mound some ten feet high. The three British troops were watched by three Americans, and they all moved around Bunker Hill without ever finding each other!

By the time we finished filming, the budget was blown, and we still had the studios to come. So, on the back of an envelope I moved sketches around, as all had played longer than intended. With a few short links, four shows became five and saved our budgetary bacon. Monica Sims (Head of BBC Children's TV) saw the rough edited sketches and, pleased as punch, eased our budget a little more for us to complete the series.

Our most ambitious studio sketch was 'The Grand Opening of the Crystal Palace Exhibition in 1851', which was attended by 2500 people. Why not? There were three of us. In contemporary drawings of the occasion, amongst the dignitaries was a Chinese man in full costume. The true story goes that everyone thought he was a Chinese ambassador, when in fact he ran a restaurant on a Chinese junk on the Thames and had conned his way in.

So, Queen Victoria, with Prince Albert (Derek) with strong German accent, opened the exhibition surrounded by glass, with suitable sound echo, and:

Queen – Albert, dearest – there are so many people?

Prince – Jawohl – 2,500 people have paid £5 each to be here for the opening. But there are 250,000 outside.

Queen – And have they paid too?

Prince – Nein – they have not paid ein penny.

Queen – Well they're all looking in through the windows. Look. Do something, Albert. Breathe on the glass.

Prince – (AFTER A COUPLE OF BREATHS) I zink we should proceed mit the opening, meine Liebchen.

Queen – Oh, very well. Ahem. I name this ship—

Prince – Nein, nein, nein.

Queen – Oh, er – I name this – er – shed? Aston Villa.

Prince – Nein, nein, nein. Crystal Palace.

Queen – Oh, Crystal Palace. May God Bless her – and all who pay to come in.

With that, she spies the 'Chinaman'.

Queen – Albert – whom is this oriental person?

Prince – I presume, an ambassador, meine Pumpernickel? Make him welcome!

Queen – Oh very well. How do you do – you come here – junk?

Chinese – No – me no come junk. Me never junk. Me no jink jink. Me always sober. Me come, pekin.

Queen – Ah! You come from Pekin?

Chinese – No no. Me not come from Pekin. Me come to peek in. Me come to peek in flew glass.

Queen – Ah, I see.

Chinese – Ah, you see – but me no see – 'cos he bleath on glass.

Etc.

Today, this would probably be classed as racist. But my intention was never to upset, but to merely have fun with a historic situation that actually happened.

SLIGHT OVERCHARGING

At last, the studio work was done. But we needed one more day's filming for a sketch which perhaps was the most ambitious of all, with the budget now long gone.

So, I became a 'do it yourself' television prop maker. Over a week, with the help of Brian Morgan, a BBC drama production assistant, we built, in my garage, three horses – luckily they did not require legs as they were the pantomime variety, where the rider fitted through a hole in the middle, manipulating the beast with reigns, while braces over the shoulders stopped it falling to the ground. The frame was cane and sculpted papier-mâché, and paint finished the job, with hair for main and tail. Then off went the whole lot to the moors outside Manchester. We also took along two 8ft x 6ft plastic sheet mirrors. Why? I edited Tennyson's 'Charge of the Light Brigade' poem down to about a third, and the mirrors made the three of us look like six hundred, or at least more than three. But what a filming day! I wrote a film gag for every line as cannon balls, ram rods and sabres flew around, and the gallant six hundred became 450, then 297, then

84, and finally one. Then costume and even moustache were shot off, till the last man was naked apart from the horse.

To achieve this, we actually completed 127 film camera set-ups in one day. I have never met anyone who experienced that many in one pre-digital filming day. Towards the end, Julie Stevens collapsed with exhaustion and was wrapped in blankets and fed brandy. We kept shooting until the light was gone.

Years after, when I went up to BBC Manchester, the crew would remark on how they often showed the sketches from *Cabbages and Kings*, partly because they were funny, but more because we had achieved on a tiny budget some quite remarkable television.

FINDING WORK – AS A WRITER

The success of *Cabbages and Kings* enhanced one career immediately, but not mine – the brilliant Derek Griffiths was called by Yorkshire Television to front a show called *Don't Ask Me* with Magnus Pyke, Miriam Stoppard and David Bellamy.

Derek immediately asked for his own writer and my phone rang. The producer, Duncan Dallas, asked if I would write Derek's lines for the show, which answered viewer's questions about anything scientific. I said yes! Totally unbeknown to me at the time, that was the very moment my factual information career began.

Duncan would ring me the day before programme recording and list the planned items, asking me to come up with any jokes that might help Derek keep it jollying along. I would write a huge selection of gags and lines over the next twenty minutes. But, five hours later, I would phone and dictate the best gags to Duncan, so the time lag justified my fee.

Derek loved my jokes but hated the show and insisted it was right up my street. He left after one series, but they ignored my requests and got Bernard Cribbins in for a special. I found Bernard to be the consummate TV studio professional, keeping crew and audience giggling all day and delivering my lines and his own ad libs brilliantly.

Next came MP Austin Mitchell and, a year later, Brian Glover, the loveable plug-ugly ex-wrestler who said, "This is money for old rope, John!" and asked, as I was writing the gags, why they hadn't chosen me.

LEARNING FOR THE FUTURE

I stayed with *Don't Ask Me* for five years because it was easy money and I was learning about TV production all the time. Soon, when I attended recordings, besides writing the jokes, I would quietly reconstruct items so that a presenter was happier and the information was expressed more clearly. As an example, a university department had designed a bicycle with an adjustable front wheel, to show 'why, scientifically, we can ride a bike'. In essence, for a bike to be stable, the front fork needs to be along a pivotal line that bisects the line between the centre wheel hub and the ground contact point. Push the wheel further forward, as with laid-back motorcycles, and you can ride as though sitting in an easy chair, but steering is more sluggish. Push the wheel back, so the fork line is ahead of the wheel hub, and as soon as you turn it, the wheel disappears under the bike and you fall off.

The script given to Magnus was cluttered, unclear and jokeless. Quietly, I blocked the piece as I would have done for *Play School*, revealing each point in a clear progression. To add suspense, I delayed his mounting the bike until the under-steer part, when he fell off. It worked a treat. Magnus was over the moon! The idle producers, on the other hand, seemed oblivious to what I had done.

Magnus became a good friend and many of my jokes made their way into his lectures and after-dinner speeches.

One week he had to explain the science of snooker balls. But he had never watched snooker in his life. So when, on hitting another ball, the white ball spun backwards, he grabbed it and was looking for magnets. He just couldn't conceive my explanation that if you cue through the ball very low, it imparts back spin, which only takes effect on hitting another ball. Then the spin grips the cloth and the ball runs backwards.

Magnus, as a celebrated nutritionist, published a new book almost every year. He showed me that scientists, though great in their own field, can often be scientifically quite ignorant on many other subjects. But he opened my mind to this fact! 'Knowledge is power!'

COULD DO BETTER?

My occasional visits to the show recordings showed me that some producers could be very dodgy. I remember a dolphin being driven from Cornwall in a water-filled canvas hammock in the back of a dormer van in a terrible state of health. Transferring it to the plastic pool in the studio was a nightmare. David Bellamy was very concerned, but the producers got their shots. Whether the creature ever made it back to Cornwall, I don't know, but I doubt it.

For one show, they had a large friendly lion on a lead, which suddenly got unfriendly and jumped on the owner's back and grabbed his neck in its jaws. The fella fell to the ground in real distress, while insisting no one do anything until the lion herself decided to let go. After some fifteen minutes, it at last did. Its grip had been strong enough to prevent any escape, but on release, the teeth hadn't even broken the skin. The lion had made its point!

On another occasion, a police escort came from Manchester University along the M62 at 30mph, escorting a 3500-year-old Egyptian mummy and a very delicate mummified doll. After a break, the lady curator came into the studio, stopped dead in her tracks and started shaking visibly. Magnus had passed the mummified doll to the audience and people were shaking it to see if it rattled and picking at the bindings.

She got it back and was just calming down when the producer took her to one side and said, "This week's programme is a little cramped. Could you bring it all back again next week and we'll film it then?"

Everyone heard her swear loudly that she would never again work with Yorkshire Television!

It was, of course, totally incompetent producing. They could have recorded the piece that day and slotted it into another programme at a later date. Slowly it dawned on me that I need not be daunted by writing and producing my own TV shows. I certainly couldn't do much worse.

FIESTA TIME

I still had connections in the club industry, and I got a call from Keith and Jim Lipthorpe who ran the Fiesta Club, Stockton-on-Tees, which I had worked a good few times. The brothers had just built a sister club, the Fiesta Sheffield, which was then the biggest club in Europe. So they arranged a special gala opening week. For this, they managed to persuade the Bee Gees to perform one week of cabaret, which in itself was unique.

Shortly after that was agreed, they rang to ask if I would be happy as the support act. I was highly honoured, as they could have chosen absolutely anyone. It was quite a week as the opening night just happened to be my birthday.

A ROUND OF BOXING

It was not long after Di joined me in London that we attended a Variety Club dinner in honour of Muhammad Ali in Park Lane. We arrived late and were directed down a corridor as the main entrance to the banqueting room was awaiting the top table.

As I opened a pair of gilt doors, an identical pair further down the corridor opened and through it walked Muhammad and the top-table entourage. Di and I stood to one side, but the great man headed straight for Di, saying loudly, "Who's this lady?"

Di's mum had made her a stunning dress and she looked fabulous.

Ali now held her hands and said, "You're a very lucky man!"

I agreed that was true and they passed on.

The dinner was fabulous, and the speeches were very funny, especially from the champ. But as it was a boxing occasion, there was a pro boxer on every table, and ours, Terry Spinks, was seated next to Di, with me on her other side. As the dinner came to a close, I saw Terry writing his phone number on a card and handing it to Di.

I stood up and moved around the back of Di, picked up the card and tore it into pieces, saying, "I'm sorry, but Di is with me!"

He stood up. He was actually shorter than I was, but he was a pro boxer.

"Wow, you're a chancer, aren't you?" he said, and I smiled. He took my hand and shook it. End of story!

IF AT FIRST YOU DON'T SUCCEED?

Now Di and I were together, she was always trying to help with my career in any way she could. When I explained that in the Mike

Hughes days I would often have no more than a dozen nights off a year, she wanted to know why I couldn't go back to him – so one day I rang him for a chat. He agreed that we could work together again, immediately booking me into a few clubs, and I was soon back in the swing and putting in some great performances.

Knowing of my writing ambition, Mike suggested that most great shows were written by writing partnerships – Galton and Simpson, Muir and Norden, etc. He suggested I form a partnership with the comedian Mike Goddard who I had seen in *The Danny La Rue Show*.

Mike took me to Thames Teddington TV Studios to meet Jack Smethurst, famous as the racially abusive white man in *Love Thy Neighbour*. It was odd having lunch with Jack, as he demanded a fine bottle of red wine and smoked a huge Havana cigar, but in the studio canteen? Mike had brought a gift of five more cigars and Jack introduced us as his new writers.

He was to join Cannon and Ball in panto at Bradford Alhambra, but his part as King was really very small. He asked us to write some material, and we took a copy of the script. For each King entrance, we listed perhaps a dozen lines, some simply variations on the previous line. Mike suggested nothing but standard club jokes. In alarm, I explained that club gags don't suit pantomime. Mike sent the stuff we wrote to Jack, who said it was perfect.

We went up to Bradford to see the show when Jack told Mike he was not getting on well with the rest of the cast and had to stand his ground. When he came on, we understood why. Jack delivered the material we had written word for word, even though some jokes were just a different version of the same joke all over again. It was just terrible.

Mike tried to explain to Jack after the show while I went straight to Cannon and Ball, who I knew well, to apologise and repair the damage.

NO HOLDS BARRED

In 1960/61, while working in the shipping office in Liverpool, I had had an idea for a TV series on dockers. I mentioned it to Mike Goddard, but it was soon clear that he could only think in terms of club gag material, none of which was even original let alone suitable for TV situation comedy. The 'partnership' was a complete waste of time.

Soon, on my own, I had completed the first show and mapped out the first series of six. As most plots involved dockers steeling cargo, I called it *No Holds Barred*. It could be set in Liverpool or London, but I had already decided to predate it to the 1950s Teddy Boy era, which I had personally experienced as a teenager. Modern day dockers all wear issue overalls in identical colours, whereas in the 1950s everyone came to work dressed as they pleased; the older ones with jackets, muffler scarves and flat caps, while the younger fellas would turn up in Teddy Boy gear with haircuts which needed constant attention. There was far more scope for character.

I had researched the Dockers Union disputes and disruption over many years. Strikes had the effect of slimming London Docks to a shadow of its former glory. New container traffic all went to new port installations, not in the grip of Dock Unions. The union antics were amazingly disruptive and packed with comic situations. One leading union docker had terrible lungs, suffered dizzy spells and was half blind. But management dare not sack him! Now, dock warehouses have trap doors and openings on every floor, so are very dangerous. So, and this is a totally true story, this docker was only allowed to work if he sat down all day and only moved under escort!

With Jack as the ringleader, surrounded by half a dozen very funny support characters, I had the makings of a show to rival *Dad's Army*. My first draft, along with five others sketched out, was ready in two weeks, during which time I had had no contact with Mike Goddard.

I sent it straight to Jack Smethurst and he loved it. But he then talked to Mike Goddard, who then rang Mike Hughes, who rang me to say that both my idea and script was partly his property as my agent, and that I could not sell it unless Mike Goddard got fifty per cent, even though he had not written one single word! My only comment was, "See you in court!"

Then a shock hit me! Just a few years earlier, Thames TV had planned a docker's series for Reg Varney of *On the Buses* fame. When they began planning, the Dock Unions issued an ultimatum. If Thames TV ever tried doing *On the Buses* with dockers, they would close the Port of London and all the other UK ports as well!

So, my so strong TV series idea, getting raves from all who read it, was dead in the water!

DOMESTIC BLISS

Di and I had settled quickly into life at Wheatlands, with just a few mishaps! We installed a chest freezer in the garage, and once I had plugged it in, Di insisted on cleaning every corner before putting any food in it. I turned and was halfway up the stairs when I heard a scream. I rushed back to find that Di, in reaching for a far corner, had fallen into the freezer and the lid had slammed shut. It wasn't locked and she quickly kicked the lid open, and I helped her out. Di didn't think it was funny, but I did enough laughing for both of us.

But the next catastrophe was all mine! I was repainting the inside of our upstairs window frames. With only a foot of windowsill remaining, I ran out of paint. So, only needing perhaps five more brushes' worth, I opened a new can and carried it upstairs. Oh no! Halfway up the stairs, I tripped! The large can of white gloss paint landed on its side, three steps from the top, on the expensive carpet I had transferred from St Annes when we moved. An involuntary banshee wail uttered from my lips. I was scooping paint back into the tin with my hands. For an hour, we worked to get the paint off the carpet and back into the tin. Then the whole length of stair carpet went into the bath, with the cold water tap full on. Luckily, the carpet was high-quality wool, but it took two weeks of constant cold water sluicing before it went back on the stairs again, looking remarkably clean!

NEIGHBOURLY ASSISTANCE

I loved our neighbours at Wheatlands, but one neighbour was to have a huge impact on my future and that process had already started. Basil Peters and his wife Daphne were Jewish with two bright sons, David and Stephen, who were at a private day school.

It was in the early days of my arriving at Wheatlands that Basil mentioned the lads seemed to be losing interest in maths. So I said I might fire up their interest. Soon I was showing them maths tricks and puzzles from my collection of maths books. Within weeks, they were back on the 'maths is wonderful' track. In fact, David eventually went to Cambridge and became Wrangler, a title given to the university's number one maths student. They thought more of him than he did of them, because shortly after that, he decamped to Tel Aviv to finish his studies in Israel.

One day, Basil asked if I would speak at the Ladies' Night dinner for a society of which he was secretary called 'The Research and Development Society'. It was only when I had said yes that I discovered they met at The Royal Society.

So, one night, with our ladies well decked-out and in our black-tie evening dress, we arrived. Now, there are many Royal

Societies – of architecture, civil and mechanical engineering, and so on – but there is only one 'Royal Society', founded by Charles II in 1660, which encompasses all the sciences. On this occasion for the R&D Society, I would talk on 'Humour – My Research and My Development'. As we gathered in the foyer, seeing the illustrious historic scientists gazing down from the walls, I was so nervous my coffee cup and saucer wouldn't stop rattling.

My talk went well and after dinner I answered questions for another half an hour or so and really enjoyed the experience. But it was the next move that was to change things!

Basil and I frequently chatted about science and technology subjects that might be in the news, and seeing I had a surprisingly wide knowledge through my early factory work, my forces experience, and my general inquisitiveness, he invited me to R&D meetings.

I enjoyed these visits tremendously. They spent a lot of time talking finance, rather than the technology, but I always seemed to find a question to ask, as they say in the USA, 'out of left field'! The meeting would then take off.

When Basil suggested I should join the society, I laughed, but a few weeks later I received my membership papers and a letter of welcome which stated: *Welcome to our Society which is essentially for the Captains of Industry!* I was a stand-up comedian and TV comedy writer who never entered sixth form, let alone university?

It was when we laughingly discussed this that Basil said, "But I've been thinking for ages, you shouldn't be doing comedy, funny though you are! You should be doing maths and science on TV. That is clearly what would suit you most."

I didn't really note the significance of that statement at the time. This suggestion was so far away from what I had been doing. Or was it?

"WAIT!" BY ROYAL COMMAND

Meanwhile, life went on. One morning, in early 1976, I was painting our front bedroom, as Di was keen to stamp her personality on her new home, when Freddie Davies rang. There was a charity opening of a new theatre in London. Roy Hudd was booked to appear but had been called to do a Quick Brew Tea ad and had cried off. Could I do a spot?

I said yes and asked when.

"You need to be here by 4pm latest – and bring your music; there's a twelve-piece band. Oh and royalty will be on hand."

The event was at Guy's Hospital where they had built not an operating theatre but a true theatre with stalls, balcony and huge backstage facilities.

I arrived to find that Frankie Vaughan was on the bill along with *Ipi Tombi*, the top West End show at the time. Meanwhile, I was trying to get the paint off my hands and sort out a few suitable gags. Then a gift dropped into my lap.

The major news story of the day was that an English lad in his twenties had got a job selling porcelain. He met with the caterers at the Palace of Westminster, and they had agreed to buy, at enormous expense, a completely new set of porcelain for the restaurants and dining rooms for both the House of Commons and the Lords. Only when the contract had been completed did anyone realise that it was all 'Made in Germany'. The story hit the papers that day!

Eventually, the Royal Rolls Royce arrived, and it was show time. The reception party met and greeted the Duchess of Gloucester and as they passed through the foyer, the band got the cue and started the national anthem.

"No, no, no!" screamed the duchess. "I need the loo first!" And off she trotted with her lady's maid. Someone waved at the conductor and the national anthem ground to a shuddering halt. Backstage, whispers put us in the picture. Then, all was ready and once more the national anthem began, and the duchess took her seat.

Very early in the show, I walk on with, "Welcome. What a wonderful theatre. It's all absolutely state of the art. Even the porcelain is British – don't worry, it's been checked."

The instant laugh from the duchess and everyone was very strong. After ten minutes of my tried and tested gags, I left the stage to be declared one of the hits of the show.

Backstage, a well-dressed fella rushed up and grabbed my hand. "Where the hell have you been? Who's your agent?" I told him Mike Hughes and he said, "I know Mike. Where's he been hiding you? Get him to ring me. I can see you going places. Amazing!" And with that, Leslie Grade, the cousin of Lew Grade and Bernard Delfont and a partner in the UK's most powerful showbiz agency, walked away!

The next day, I called Mike, but he was not available. I asked for him to ring back. It was ten days later that I finally told him the story.

All he said was, "Well he's a bloody crook anyway!" And that was the end of that!

Shortly after that, I was working Caesar's Palace, Luton for the week, where I had suffered so badly playing to Jimmy Grafton and a theatre producer when the club was totally empty. The top of the bill was one of the musical groups and I got a call at home on the Wednesday to say that their lead singer had gone sick, and they couldn't work that night. So the boss asked if I could find another twenty minutes' material and top the bill. No problem. That evening, with Di on hand, my longer spot went very solidly indeed.

The boss declared, "You can top for the rest of the week!" And we agreed a reasonable extra fee. For the next three nights, I ended to a standing ovation, which got stronger each time.

I rang and told Mike. He booked me back, still as second top – at £50 more for the entire week. This slap in the face was the last straw! After a few days, in agreement with Di, I decided not only to say goodbye once again to Mike Hughes but something far more life changing. I decided right then to retire from stand-up comedy – for ever!

CHAPTER 13

NEW CAREER, NEW ATTITUDE, NEW EVERYTHING

LET'S START WITH SOMETHING THAT ENDED

As I mentioned before, for our first Christmas together, Di bought me new golf clubs. Well, around Easter, after announcing I was giving up stand-up comedy, I also announced that I was now giving up mid-week golf. My decision was that, from that day, I would write myself a new and successful career. So I sat down at my desk around 9am and didn't leave my desk until 5pm, every single day.

I had no way of knowing that this ploy would work.

LOVE ON A ONE WHEEL BIKE

Derek Griffiths was chosen for a new LE show, which tried new faces each year. They wanted three boys and three girls for what was provisionally to be called *The Battle of the Sexes*. I was asked to write for it, which I agreed to immediately, as final casting had not been agreed.

I suggested *Love on a One Wheel Bike!* as a better title, but that was rejected. But in an effort to charm the producer and get the last remaining male slot, I wrote a couple of sketches for already-selected Julia McKenzie and Derek. One was a 'Tarzan, Jane and the Chimp' sketch, where Tarzan and the Chimp were in a complete bromance which drove 'Jane' up the wall. The young males swung from one spot to another, crashing into their tree-house home, shaking everything off the walls. The other was an adult version of the Jack and Jill rhyme after seven years of marriage. Here are a few snatches:

Jill – "Well what about you and Miss Muffet? Eh? Let's have it on the level. It wasn't the spider who sat down beside her – it was you, you randy old devil."

Jack – "Well what about you and the Duke of York? The story's all around town. You came home with your drawers like his 10,000 men. They were neither up nor down!"

Till, finally – narr – so, one day Jack climbed up the hill with a very troubled mind. At last he arrived at the wishing well and started to unwind. But Jill came racing after him, her mind on evil bent. But she suddenly slipped and hit the wall and over the edge she went. Jack waited till he heard the splash. Then his face took on a smirk.

Jack – "It's a funny thing about wishing wells! I didn't think they worked?"

They loved the sketches, but the producer gave the final cast spot to a chap of, to my mind, very limited talent – perhaps so the favourites, Derek and Julia, might shine?

A couple of years later, I met Julia in a BBC lift, where I told her that, as I didn't get a part, I never wrote for BBC Light Entertainment ever again.

"But," she said, "those were the best scripts I ever got at the BBC! Honestly! What a terrible waste."

MY MOST SUCCESSFUL ACHIEVEMENT OF ALL

On 14th June 1975, I married my darling Di at the Methodist Church in Old Swindon. It was a fabulous day, full of love and happiness, laughs and surprises.

I drove from Wheatlands and picked up Di's brother, Paul, as my best man, but arrived behind time. As we parked in sight of the church steps, I could see the vicar frantically calling for us to hurry. He explained that Di's car was on its second 'time-wasting' lap around the neighbourhood so that I got to the church first.

No problem, as Jonathan Cohen, the *Play School* and *Play Away* pianist, was playing the organ for us. On realising things were running late, he began playing TV signature tunes and BBC children's TV themes, and the whole congregation joined in. Fabulous!

The service was so very moving for me, as I was now sure everything about it was right. But, as Di and I turned to leave the church, I met the problem Di's dad had on the way in. At the end of every other pew there was an umbrella bracket and copper dish at the bottom, which stuck out into the aisle by a few inches. But that was enough, as Di's wonderful dress, made so proudly by her mum (and the best wedding-dress maker Swindon ever produced) forced me to walk very close to the pew ends. As a result, for every other step, I had to lift my right foot over the umbrella stand cup in a very silly Monty Python walk.

A mass of photographs were taken, including of the four bridesmaids, one of which was four-year-old Zoe, who took pride of place. We took the first car to the reception at The Goddard's Hotel, some half a mile away. Then bridesmaids and Paul followed and my mum and dad and Di's dad and main guests. In all this, Di's mum took it upon herself to usher people forward into the next awaiting car. It didn't take long for the return trip, and it all went smoothly. Then, as the last car drove away, Di's mum looked to see she was the only person left!

So poor Rene, mother of the bride, set off to walk the half mile to The Goddard's Hotel, all alone, as the boiling sun streamed down.

Di and I, and Di's dad and Paul and my folks, welcomed everyone into the reception, wondering where Rene had got to. Finally, when everyone was in the hall, Rene appeared, rushing up the stairs, looking very hot and flustered, like Hyacinth Bucket from *Keeping Up Appearances*. Poor soul!

OUR WEDDING NIGHT

After the wedding breakfast, where Paul shone with his speech, Di's folks welcomed more casual friends to the evening dance, which was so wonderful Di and I didn't want to leave. So I made a call to our hotel, telling them we would be slightly late but we only required two grilled steaks and a bottle of wine for supper.

We eventually left at around 9.30pm for the short trip to Castle Combe, the prettiest village in England. Instead of the top hotel, I had chosen the small old inn with a room that looked down the old main street, past the pump, towards the river and bridge that formed such a wonderful setting for the *Doctor Dolittle* film. Surely it would be perfect?

Well, I parked the car outside and got the bags in. I came straight out again to find I had a parking ticket on my windscreen – at ten o'clock at night?

Inside, a young girl informed us we were too late for food. I said I had rung ahead.

"No," she said, "service stops at nine-thirty."

After another round of that, I smilingly took her by both shoulders and said quietly into her face, "No, dear – it's arranged. Go and get your boss!"

Then I attempted to get the bags up the stairs, which went so steeply up in a spiral I had to lift the case above my head and push it up, while holding on to the rope banister.

The boss and the steaks arrived and soon it was time for bed.

Sadly, the old inn didn't have a straight wall or floor. So our room, including the double bed, tilted to the left. To make things worse, to the right was a huge chest of drawers, which looked like, at any minute, it might topple onto the bed and us.

Suffice it to say that whatever we did on our honeymoon night, we did it very carefully.

The next morning, on the advice of the landlord, I knocked on a cottage door down the street and the now sober traffic warden apologised that he had 'been in the pub' and ripped up my parking ticket.

THE ROOM WITH A VIEW?

For the next couple of days, Di and I motored around my old childhood haunts near Bristol, after which we were on the plane for our Malta honeymoon.

Now, although I had decided to give up stand-up comedy, two things prevented a totally clean break. I still needed cabaret income while other branches of my earnings developed some momentum. An agent friend had fixed a week in Malta for two, provided I did one cabaret spot on the last night. They would also throw in £50 spending money. Perfect!

So, we arrived at the high-rise Preluna Hotel. As we entered the room, something seemed odd. The light wasn't quite right and the windowsill seemed high. The reason was soon clear. The square hotel had been built with a square tube down the middle. But they had then popped a cabaret room on the very top, so the tube was devoid of natural light. So under each windowsill they had rigged a fluorescent light, which they would switch off at night.

So – for our honeymoon – we had a room with absolutely no view. In minutes I was in reception, correcting the error. When I explained I was on honeymoon, they of course snapped into action.

But then the clerk said, "I can't find you on the guest list?"

"But I'm your cabaret for Thursday night!" I cried.

"Ah!" he said. "So you're staff?"

My heart sank as I realised that being on the payroll meant I had no clout whatsoever, when even paying customers had similar dark and dismal rooms.

So, after copious tears (Di's, not mine), we had a meal and a good few drinks and I explored how to compensate. Across the road was a Hilton Hotel with lovely gardens and swimming pool. So, next morning, we strolled in. I immediately ordered drinks, paid cash and tipped well. We soon had great sun beds in a prime spot. All day with every drink or a snack, I tipped. It worked and for the rest of the week, the staff welcomed us as though we were actually staying at their hotel.

We had a wonderful week, though two particular days weren't quite perfect!

TWO THINGS ONE SHOULD NOT LOSE ON HONEYMOON

Our hotel room was so dark we could have developed our holiday snaps in it, but we made the most of our holiday by hiring an Austin 1100. On the Sunday, we motored to Gozo and took up residence on a beach.

Now, Di had summered in Blackpool for four years and had become an expert sun bunny. So, as she lay face-down on the Gozo beach, I poured sun oil and as it ran down her spine, I swear it sizzled. Meanwhile, I sat cross-legged like a Buddha in the shade under a canopy held up by four canes.

With walks and dips and games, we had a wonderful day, until we made our way off the beach. The car was oven-hot, so we put our gear on the roof while we spread our towels on the roasting seats. As we did this, someone passing shouted, "It's Johnny Ball off the telly!" and I turned and waved. Then we got into the car, and I drove away.

As we headed for the local small town, I asked Di if she was putting her jeans on, as the devout Maltese in those days didn't like too much flesh in and around their churches.

Di said, "Yes! Are you putting your slacks on?"

I immediately knew that my slacks were not in the car. I had left them on the roof, while draping the seat. While still driving, with my hand through the open window, I felt on the roof for my trousers. They had gone!

I turned the car around and halfway back we passed four or five local lads on scooters. We couldn't find my slacks or the few quid inside them and came to the conclusion that the lads had probably taken the money and the trousers. So I was now on my honeymoon, trouserless! I might not have looked so vulnerable had my legs not been so marble white. Oh dear.

So, after some discussion, I squeezed into Di's jeans – just – and she pulled her shirt down as far as she could, to cover her lower end for the rest of the day, including the ferry crossing, till we got back to the hotel.

How embarrassing, but nothing compared to the next day at St Peter's Pool, the old Roman dock, I knew from a previous forces tour. This small dock area had been levelled and paved. Surrounded by cliffs, it was a perfect sun-trap, holding perhaps 150 sunbathers. The water was around eighteen inches lower than the paved area but with no shelved slope to the cool water, it was instantly some ten feet deep – and I do not swim. But I had snorkelled and so we borrowed a mask and flippers from some RAF lads nearby.

So, in my too small mask and flippers, I sat on the edge of the dock, looking like Jonah Jinks, ready to lower myself into the water. Di was already in, ready to help my safe passage.

I dropped off the edge, submerged, and as the water hit my ears, I panicked. As I thrashed about, I could see Di calmly pushing me back to the edge of the dock. I hauled myself out and sat on the dock edge, very deflated.

Di said, "Stay there while I get the camera!"

While she was gone, perhaps thirty seconds, I felt the ring finger of my left hand. There was no wedding ring!

Di came back, lined up the picture and asked me to, "At least smile!" She snapped and then I said, in a plaintive voice, "Di! I've lost my wedding ring!"

Di was struck dumb but only for a second, as, in total anguish, her mouth opened and out came a stifled 'scream' with the words, "Some – times – you – make – me – so – sad!"

The words rang around the cliff walls and 150 people instantly sat up and said, "What?"

In minutes, half a dozen RAF lads and a couple of Maltese gigolos were in the water, diving down time and again in search of the ring. I tried to direct them that it couldn't be over there and had to be down here somewhere. After perhaps ten minutes thrashing around, one by one they gave up and got out of the water. It was a lost cause!

Standing on the edge, I just couldn't leave the scene. As the water settled, a glint hit my eye. Just a foot or so below the water line, right under where I had been sitting, was the ring, hanging on a reed on the wall of the dock. On my knees, I reached down and, "Got it!" As the word went around, there were a good few cheers!

The following week, I worked a large caravan park in Cornwall, and this time, with Zoe along as well, we had a blissful extended honeymoon, even with some swimming.

ANOTHER ENDING AND A HUGE NEW BEGINNING

It was now a long time since I had seen Harry Secombe, but one day his manager, Jimmy Grafton, rang to see how I was getting on. I found it odd, as he had done nothing for my career since the Caesar's Palace debacle! I quickly filled him in with my writing for BBC Children's department and the strong bond I had formed with Cynthia Felgate, Head of Under-Fives; Peter Ridsdale-Scott, my *Cabbages* producer; and Ann Reay, Head of *Play Away*. I told him I had packed up stand-up except for the necessity of earning and was now determined to write factual information shows following my Yorkshire experiences and incorporating my love of maths.

I could hardly believe my ears when he rang back an hour later and said he had arranged a West End restaurant lunch with these three TV executives. This seemed so odd, as I could have walked into their offices any day of the week and told them of my ideas.

So, the day arrived, and the four friends had lunch with an almost perfect stranger, who added nothing to the conversation. They opened, saying they were considering a new concept for me after my *Cabbages* and *Play Away* efforts.

I said I wished to try a, "Factual info show, based on maths."

Their three jaws dropped!

As an example, I mentioned the grains of rice on a chessboard story. This historic tale talks of the inventor of chess, who explained the game to a king. He loved the idea that everyone could be killed except the king, who could only be cornered. In gratitude, he offered the game's inventor anything he desired. So the inventor asked for a grain of rice on the first square of the chessboard, two on the second, then four on the third and so on, doubling up each time. The king immediately granted the wish, thinking he had a bargain. However, by doubling up the grains over sixty-four squares, the total amount of rice needed would exceed 200 billion tons – far larger than the world's annual output of rice even today.

They loved the idea and lunch, which I paid for. I never ever saw Jimmy Grafton again.

TAKE YOUR PARTNERS

For the pilot show, which was still some months ahead but needed forward planning, Cynthia offered as my director Peter Charlton, who was a great friend and music hall exponent in his own right. However, when we met up, my factual info ideas and his seemed immediately at cross purposes and I could see it would not work.

But they suddenly gave Peter a new series called *Star Turn*, based on his own idea of a chairman with two teams of three celebs competing in silly games. Peter loved the idea of employing comedy stars from cabaret, theatre and even film.

Peter got me on board as a writer, as each show required a comedy sketch for seven characters, in which 'Ivor Notion had a notion!' He named the criminal, but not before the viewers and studio audience had been asked to spot three silly mistakes.

First Graeme Garden played host, followed by Bernard Cribbins, while Myles Rudge, who wrote 'Hole in the Ground' for Bernard and me, would take turns writing the Ivor Notion sketches. It was to prove an arduous but totally enjoyable task, as the brief was to write a story, give seven characters roughly equal lines and a part that would suit them, include three deliberate mistakes and arrive at a final solution, all in seven minutes.

In all, over four years, Myles and I each wrote thirty sketches for sixty shows. I loved it and some of my best efforts featured in *Plays for Laughs*, which, along with several of my *Play Away* sketches, I published with Puffin Books in 1983.

As an example of the material, Graeme Garden, as a circus ringmaster, had the opening line, "Right, the circus is underway, but we're very short-staffed. I've got a trapeze artist scared of heights, a fire-eater with heartburn, a sword-swallower with hiccups – and the India Rubber Man has just gone to jail for a long stretch!" Writing this silly stuff was an utter joy.

One sketch involved the *Carry On* team, with Kenneth Williams as Detective Ivor Nosefrit and Barbara Windsor as his assistant Sheila Restum in a bikini on a lilo which is suddenly punctured by a stolen diamond thrown from a balcony. "What a letdown?"

Meanwhile, for my own new series I was paired off with Albert Barber; a partnership made in heaven, as we would make thirteen wonderful series of award-winning *Think* shows together.

JOLLY BOATING WEATHER

As with today, I like a couple of pints in a pub. I have always kept it to two pints since, one day, Di asserted that she knew whether I had had two, two and a half or even three pints.

She explained, "With two pints you are perfect. But after two and a half pints you come home and you argue with the television."

I asked about three pints.

She said, without a pause, "Oh, with three pints, you come home and *stand up* to argue with the television!"

My favourite pub in our Wheatlands days had a largish canal cruiser on wooden supports in the car park. One day, the landlord announced that the boat was at last going into the water at Teddington. A week later, in midsummer 1976, heavily pregnant

Di and I, Zoe, plus the Swindon Four – Di's mum, dad, gran and Paul – set the motors running and headed up the Thames.

At first on a river boat, the slowness is difficult to handle, but on the second day we all settled into the new relaxed pace, and it was fabulous. I was soon in a call box ringing the pub.

"Can we have her for two weeks instead of one?"

Yes, we could! Fabulous!

But the trip was not without mishaps. One day, we spied an actual sandy beach on the left side of the Thames, as the sun streamed down. So we stopped a few yards further on, against a bank, so we could place a plank for Gran, Rene, Di's dad Vyner ('call me Fred'), Paul, Di, Zoe and I to skip across with the two Pekinese, Snuffles, who now lived in Swindon with the family, and Teddy, who I had bought as a present for Di.

As we made our way onto the beautiful beach, Paul (who, as a teenager, once swam for England) dived in and was soon across the river. He turned to look back while treading water and saw an identical beach just one hundred yards further upstream. But on this beach there was around two dozen huge pigs!

Paul shouted, "Oh my god, pigs, lots of them!"

And that is when the smell first hit us. Our 'sandy beach' was actually pig guano – or, as Gran immediately said, "Oh no. It's all pig shit!"

Di and Zoe were already filling a bucket with sand. Stinking to high heaven, we all waddled back to the boat, hosed each other down, including the dogs, then quickly sailed to leave the smell behind us.

THERE IS A LOT OF HANGING ABOUT IN CANAL LOCKS

One day, on our return and downward river trip, we arrived at a lock and by now everyone was happy to help with ropes and bollards and such. But then came the 'oops' moment. As our boat descended, so Rene's hand was suddenly caught between the edge of the dock wall and the rope she was holding. Rene was suddenly on tip toe, trying to remove her trapped hand. Then she was hanging on the side of the lock. Paul and Fred rushed to help but couldn't lift her for laughing. Just in time, her hand came free. Just as well! You can't just leave mothers-in-law hanging on dock walls, can you?

GETTING IN, TO GET OUT, TO GET IN AGAIN

Di was now within a couple of weeks of having our first child, but that didn't stop us seeking a great day out. Low and behold, Liverpool were playing Everton in the Charity Shield at Wembley, and heavily pregnant Di was still up for coming with me.

I had left it till the last minute to ask Ken Addison at Liverpool for tickets. It was too late to put them in the post, as around match time, ticket post from Liverpool FC can seem to get lost. So Ken was bringing the tickets with him on the coach with the players' wives, it being his job to chaperone them.

The coach would be the only vehicle allowed in an area right in front of the old Wembley Stadium, but when Di and I arrived, there was no coach. We wandered through the happy crowds to return perhaps five minutes later, where we saw the coach had now arrived. But it was already empty.

I rushed down to the coach and the driver told me they had all gone in through Gate E but had not left any tickets with him. So our tickets were now in the ground and somehow I had to get in, to come out again, to then go in. But it was already about fifteen minutes before kick-off.

The old Wembley had a staircase with white awning over it, which went up to a balcony area between the Twin Towers. So I parked Di at the bottom, in her pleated white expanding skirt, scarlet jacket, white blouse and Liverpool hat, while I went up to try to get in. But as I was about to set off, three Liverpool supporters happened to be passing, and these are the exact words they uttered on that day. I'll never forget them!

On seeing heavily pregnant Di, supporter no. 1: "Hey, lads! We're one up already!"

Supporter 2: "Yes. Look, love, when we score, don't jump up and down!"

Supporter 3: "You go on and jump, love! If it's a boy, we'll put him on at half time."

Still laughing, I ignored the *Strictly No Admittance* sign and climbed the steps for the balcony. At the top, some eight yards away, a commissionaire opened a glass door just to tell me I could not come in. I walked towards him, trying to explain, but he was very stroppy. Then he looked past me to see Di arrive breathless at the top of the stairs. Seeing her condition, he immediately let us in.

I explained that our tickets were with the Liverpool wives, and I needed to locate them. He ushered us into an oak-panelled room with antique oak furniture and a chest of drawers with glasses on a silver tray. It was the waiting room directly below the Royal Box. Most surprising of all, it had an eight-panelled Georgian window looking out onto the playing pitch!

The commissionaire arrived with the Liverpool chairman, who was happy to help but had no idea where the players' wives might be.

Through the window, both sides were lined up on the pitch for the presentation, and we could actually see the Liverpool lads all waving at their wives.

"Look," I said, "the team are waving at them. They're up there!" I pointed at an angle, up through the ceiling above us.

Quickly, the commissionaire and I found our way to the wives and Ken Addison. I tapped him on the shoulder.

"Bloody hell, John!" he said. "How the hell have you got here?"

I explained; he gave me our tickets; I collected Di; we left the ground by the VIP entrance and rushed a hundred yards to our gate. We got to our seats just as the match started. Talk about 'in, out, shake it all about'.

Just ten days later – 19th August 1976 – with me by her side at Queen Charlotte's Maternity Hospital, Chiswick, Di gave birth to our son, Nicholas Alexander Ball.

She must have found it pleasurable, as she was back fifteen months later to deliver son Daniel James, born 9th December 1977. Now, with Zoe, we were a family of five. Wonderful.

EARLY FAMILY DAYS

Nick, at a very early age, was to show an amazingly artistic trait. Di would take toddling Nick to the shops, with younger Dan in the pram or pushchair. But for every trip, Nick insisted on stopping down the narrow lanes to pick strands of grass. When they got home, Nick would toddle straight into my office and present me at my desk with around eight or nine strands of grass, in a tiny bunch, but every one was chosen as being uniquely different from all the others. His artistic mind was already at work.

THE START OF THE *THINK* SHOW YEARS

At long last, time was allotted in early 1977 for me to make a pilot programme on maths. Albert Barber was to prove an ideal partner through the coming *Think* show years.

Trained as a graphic designer, Albert started in presentation, thinking up all kinds of tenuous visual linking ideas. So, for each of our shows, on hearing my ideas, he would immediately sketch how each scene would look on TV. From this, every member of our team had a clear idea of what we were aiming at. It was to be a partnership made in heaven.

As soon as we got together, I started to put forward ideas for a pilot show. We decided to call it *Think of a Number*, implying that just doing that as a start could lead you anywhere! We had three months to create the pilot, which is just as well, as deciding what to include and what to leave out proved a terrible nightmare. For one thing, the chessboard story was far too long, and we needed much shorter, snappier ideas. But slowly it came together and on one memorable day, we invited a dozen or so friends along with the technical crew to a BBC rehearsal room in Acton and set ourselves up for our first technical rehearsal.

We started the clock, and I began, delivering the script as though it were a comedy spot with jokes sprinkled between the facts. With a toilet roll for a phone and metal posts for doorframes, I walked from scene to scene, talking continuously until, after twenty-four minutes, I seamlessly came to the pay-off gag and said goodbye!

It was as though all my comedy years had been leading up to this moment. Everyone in the room just stood, grinning and applauding wildly. *Think of a Number* was born! We recorded the show a few days later and everyone loved it. But then we were told to wait a year before our first series could begin.

THE FOUNDATIONS OF FEAR

I needed ideas in order to create a TV series of some kind. *No Holds Barred* had definitely been good enough but had floundered.

One day, Kerry Jewel suggested I come to see a friend who

had a cellar museum full of torture instruments and items linked to witchcraft. He showed me pictures, but I realised that the collection was very limited and would be dwarfed by the stuff in national museums.

But I had an idea and began to write *The Foundations of Fear!* which would be a TV series that traced horrors both true and with literary origins. I set it in an old house being battered by storms. Below ground, an old door was being lashed by rain. As the camera approached, and the title music came to a crescendo, the large knocker raised itself to knock. The host, dressed in black, would welcome viewers and bid them follow. As they progressed down a long hall, a stuffed alligator winked one eye.

The first episode I wrote was on the subject of premature burial, and I soon had some amazingly dark yet true stories, like a woman in Guildford who was buried alive – twice. She was addicted to laudanum and had been presumed dead. Her husband, away on business, sent instruction for her to be buried. Shortly afterwards, schoolboys heard graveyard screams. The grave was opened and the coffin lid removed. The lady had been alive. Her nails were broken but she now appeared to be dead. As a coroner had to witness the event, she was left in the coffin, in the church yard with two men to watch over her till morning. When it started to rain, they popped the lid on and put her back in the grave while they went to the pub. The next morning, the coroner arrived and found that she had been buried alive a second time and in anguish had forced her own fist into her mouth. She was now definitely dead. When the dreadful story was revealed, the Government punished Guildford for their negligence by putting a shilling on the rates for a year. True!

I had soon finished the script, though writing it had given me the heebie-jeebies. I sent it to Thames Television and next day, Peter Rogers, the producer of the *Carry On* films, rang me. He thought the script was wonderful and a sure winner. Then he said, "Leave it with me. You are going to make a lot of money, John, if you are not too greedy!"

That seemed like a warning to me, and I already knew of the extraordinarily low wages Rogers paid to the *Carry On* team!

Someone suggested I ring agent Roger Hancock, and we soon met up where I remembered meeting him with the Black family in Blackpool when his brother Tony was suffering so badly. He was now an agent for The Goodies and several of the Monty Python team.

He met Peter Rogers and then rang me to say, "Don't go near him with this idea." The last three *Carry On* films had lost money and he had no money to pay for the rights to my script.

So Roger sent it to a BBC producer. He never told me the chap's name but said he had gone to California and would get the script in the right BBC hands on his return. The script and original TV idea never again saw the light of day!

But now I had the *Think* series in hand. I told Roger and introduced him to Albert Barber. I then signed away ten per cent of my *Think* programmes, before the first series was made.

Soon, Di and I were having dinner in an old school building that was his house. It was huge and very pleasant, but through the single-glazed windows we could see the tailplanes of jumbo jets as they turned at the north-west end of the runway at Heathrow, 150 yards away. As they revved up to take off, conversation stopped until the truly almighty din had subsided, to be followed by another, just two minutes later. I asked why he had not fitted double-glazing.

Roger replied, "What's the point?"

The walls had copious pictures of clowns inherited from brother Tony, and Di and I, as we left, said we couldn't imagine anything more sad and depressing.

THINK OF A NUMBER, SERIES 1

But at last I was happy, though under pressure, writing *Think of a Number*. Looking back, the sheer amount of material I got into the first six shows was quite amazing. I needed research sources and once again Basil Peters' help was vital.

He had been given the job of editing the entire field of mathematics into double-page spreads for a major encyclopaedia published in sections from 1976, entitled *The Mitchell Beazley Joy of Knowledge*. The structure was far better than *Britannica* or any other I knew and was to prove invaluable to me. Along with Jacob Bronowski's *Ascent of Man* as a sounding board, the two underpinned all my programmes and covered almost all branches of science and technology.

But now I began writing more rounded scripts than anything at Yorkshire TV or the BBC's Tomorrow's World, where they simply picked six totally unconnected topics for each show. For all my themes, I produced a complete appraisal of the subject, with intro; jokes; tangential ideas; sketches as illustration and large or small props from museums or specialists to enrich the presentation. Our brilliant set had secret doors and cupboards, so every new prop was revealed in a surprising way. We also had an audience, so through them, our TV audience would feel involved.

Each show had a seven-part structure (as had my comedy routines), which ensured in-depth concepts along with jokes and ways of looking at the subject from odd or oblique angles. It was all to be written by a lad who got two O Levels and left school at sixteen a total failure!

Every show ended with a trick and an invite to write in, and we would send the solution free of charge. This ensured feedback, which we felt essential. After a few series, Paul Daniels was heard to complain that, "Johnny Ball keeps giving our magic secrets away."

Someone immediately chipped in with, "The trouble with you, Paul, is you think it's bloody magic!"

In truth, I only ever gave away the 'mathematical secrets' which made the tricks work. Paul was, in any case, a friend who had always called me 'Johnny Ball – the Shy Comedian'!

CHOOSING THE SUBJECTS

I began programme one with 'Stored Energy' and a joke Stone Age calculator with holes, so my fingers poked through, to count on. Then the stored energy in a bow was used to light early fires, as well as a weapon. We explored elastic-band exploding models, the Van de Graaff stored energy device and, finally, Hero's Aeolipile, or first steam engine, of two thousand years ago.

One programme in each series was dedicated to the human body, starting with the brain, how we can calculate quickly, and great achievers in this field. Other senses like smell and balance and optical illusions followed.

Each show always involved maths, so for 'Materials', we looked at tree growth and Fibonacci maths, things Da Vinci designed in wood, possibilities using paper and how thin plastic films were materials that would change our future.

For 'Water', we saw an impossible Victorian drinking cup, the amount of water in the atmosphere (often ignored by climate alarmists) and how freshwater icebergs could be used. We explored the weather, the geometry of soap bubbles and water under pressure.

For 'Money', I touched on gambling and how people are easily fooled. I later covered money in *Think Again* and featured the Dick Whittington story. Benny Green in *Punch* called it 'the TV highlight of the week, explained with such clarity that even the Chancellor of the Exchequer would have had little difficulty following it.'

Finally we arrived at programme six. But by now the reaction to the programmes was apparent, with kids writing in to say they wanted to become scientists because of me. These letters made my hair stand on end. I was actually affecting thousands of young minds.

Little did I know that, over forty years later, people would still be telling me I affected their own self-belief and career choices with my shows.

But back then, suddenly the sheer weight of responsibility became an immediate weight on my own mind. Now, whatever I did, it had to be right, it had to be sensible, and, outside the intended jokes, and it had to be true. As a result of the pressure, my last script on time got to the office so late they all called it 'Not Before Time' as they scrambled to get it all ready for the recording day.

On the actual day, after the dress rehearsal, we realised we had to cut a couple of minutes. Our producer was dear Ann Reay, who was a stalwart of under-fives television. But she had no idea of science at all, as we saw when she said, in all seriousness, "Don't cut the bit with the sun moving through the sky. I'm beginning to see how a sundial works."

A month or two later, after transmission, Albert Barber rang to say we had won a BAFTA for Best Children's Factual Show.

I said, "Great! What's a BAFTA?"

At the star-studded BAFTA Awards, at last the announcement came, "In the category of Children's Factual Programs, the award goes to the BBC's Ann Reay and *Think of a Number*." Ann received the award, and we were soon celebrating the Harlequin Award, sponsored by Rediffusion Television, for the very last time. The following year and beyond, the award became the famous BAFTA Mask that we all know so well.

Then someone mentioned that the award would have to be

taken back to the BBC next day and we would get photographs of it. Albert and the rest of the team looked sympathetically at my crestfallen face. However, minutes later, the gold award completely disappeared. We looked everywhere but it was never found that night.

In truth, the award somehow followed me home. It was tucked down the back waistband of my dress-suit trousers. It got back to the BBC a week or so later and was locked up for ever.

MEMORIES OF THINGS THAT MIGHT HAVE BEEN

Some six or seven years into my TV writing career, I was in Windsor and met the old manager of Caesar's Palace, where I had taken the top spot and stood them on their heads. He asked why I was in Windsor and when I told him I lived seven miles away, he cried, "Then why have you never played Blazers for me? I've been the manager here all that time."

I then told him I had quit stand-up almost immediately after working for him. He looked shocked as he said, "But, Johnny, you were the best. The very best. What a bloody waste."

A BIT OF A WIND-UP

From that period, little did Di and I know what the future might hold in store for us. We definitely had no conception that my professional achievements would dwarf everything that had gone before.

My comedy experience was to stay with me for the rest of my life, as in everything I do, it is the comedy angle that is essential in creating and holding interest in factual information and that was to underpin all my writing through twenty series of one-man TV shows and so many other writing projects that were to fill my life for the next forty years. So, when I began writing the *Think of a Number* shows, it was as though I had come home!

From now on, for me and my young family, the only way was up. I became friends with the presidents of the Royal Society and The Royal Institution, who both recommended me to present the institution's TV Christmas lectures, only to be told by the BBC producers that as I did not have a degree, I did not qualify.

I opened the first 'Hands On!' exhibit at the Science Museum and helped them set up James Watt's workroom, salvaged from his home in Birmingham, explaining what so many items were – they wondered if I had known him personally.

I was thrilled to work for education departments of political parties of both persuasions. I opened several major Government maths promotions, one with the Duke of Edinburgh as my willing assistant.

In the 1980s alone, I worked for around a hundred corporate organisations, mixing my newfound style in explaining all things scientific with my hard-learnt comedy skills. I wrote and presented videos on nuclear power, on the gas industry, four video hours on materials technology, and spent seven years explaining for National Grid how they keep all our lights on.

Perhaps most pleasurable, I wrote, created and starred in several stage musicals which played to theatre numbers every bit as large as Ken Dodd's audiences at their height.

But all that, I think, I'll keep under my hat ready for part two of my autobiography.

I do hope you have enjoyed coming with me on this journey and that you'll come along for the ride in part two, which I am provisionally calling *Johnny Ball – Stories That Must Be Told!*

Till then, my thanks for coming with me and very best wishes,

Johnny Ball – March 2025.

BOOK 2, *STORIES THAT MUST BE TOLD* WILL FOLLOW SHORTLY.

ABOUT THE AUTHOR

Johnny Ball is best known for his twenty-year television career with the BBC, where he made a name for himself writing and presenting educational shows. Starting as a stand-up comedian, he joined BBC's *Playschool* in 1967, later creating hit series like *Think of a Number*, which won a BAFTA. His expertise in explaining science and math led to successful corporate work with major organisations. At eighty-six, Johnny continues to captivate audiences with lectures and stage shows about mathematics and his life in comedy.